Austrian History

A Captivating Guide to the History of Austria and the Habsburg Empire

Table of Contents

Part 1: History of Austria

A Captivating Guide to Austrian History

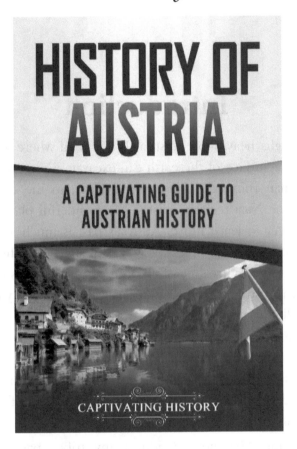

Introduction

History weighs heavily on Austria. It is a land where any scratch made on the surface of the earth can excavate a piece of the past. From Roman ruins, the Habsburg dynasty, to the most recent victims of the Nazi regime, Austria is a wonderful playground for scholars eager to learn more. Austria's past is much greater than the small territory it occupies today, and it spills over the modern-day borders into the realms of all of its neighbors. It is often hard for modern Austrians to come to terms with their history because it is one filled with oppression, war, mistreatment of various ethnicities, and war atrocities. But as much as Austria is to blame for its past, it is also its victim. From its earliest point in history, the territory was a place of strife. Its geographic position in central Europe means Austria's destiny was to be the point of conflict—if not militarily, then ideologically.

During the Migration Period, many tribes passed through central Europe, and many of them fought each other for the right to settle in the fertile Danube Valley. During the Roman period, the Austrian territories were a border region, better known as the European Limes. A defensive system of fortresses was erected to protect the Roman Empire from the German tribes to the north. But when the Frankish tribe to the east rose to fame and started its

Carolingian dynasty, the territory of what is Austria today was turned into the Eastern March. Yet another conflict came with the arrival of the Magyars, and under their pressure, the Eastern March collapsed.

With the rise of the Holy Roman Empire, Austria was finally able to take a break from war. But another conflict started, this time ideological. The Catholic Church, the backbone of the Holy Roman Empire, became a money-grabbing, corrupt institution where nepotism ruled. Many rose against such ideals and started preaching the old, more humble, and conservative Christianity. The ideological war, known as the Reformation and the Counter-Reformation, occurred between the Protestants and the Catholics. However, history proved that many ideological conflicts are followed by violence, oppression, and extermination. The Reformation was not an exception. The Habsburg rulers warred against the Lutherans and Calvinists in their territories. The Reformation also sparked an even bigger conflict, known as the Thirty Years' War, one of the bloodiest military conflicts in Europe, with over seven million deaths. But the war wasn't solely religious, as it set the scene for an everlasting battle for European supremacy between the Habsburgs of Austria and the Bourbons of France.

The Age of Enlightenment was a period of European history that promised a new kind of rule, a constitutional monarchy. For Austria, it meant only more trouble as none of the rulers of the Enlightenment were capable of grasping the importance of a constitution. Set in their old ways and driven by their motto of "A.E.I.O.U.," as well as by their divine right to rule, the Habsburgs were unable to see how the world now demanded change. But even when one among them proved to be ready to bring forth changes, he found it an impossible task. So many ethnicities lived under the Habsburg umbrella, each demanding its own set of rights and self-determination. The Habsburgs faced the possibility of the dispersion of their empire. Desperate to preserve the integrity of

Austria and later Austria-Hungary, the monarchs of the Habsburg dynasty indulged in even more conflicts.

Finally, the multi-ethnic Austria erupted into World War I with the assassination of Archduke Franz Ferdinand. But the assassination itself was only an excuse to start the war, which would, as the Habsburg emperor hoped, return the dynasty's old glory, allowing Austria to take its old place as a great European power. But that didn't come to pass. Instead, Austria and its allies were defeated and thrown into economic poverty, humiliation, and despair. The Habsburgs were no more, and the remaining Austrians struggled to find their own identity among the many nations of central Europe. For so long, they had been a part of something great, and they had trouble settling for the small territory they inherited from the once vast Habsburg Empire. Instead, Austria chose to indulge in its German identity. Unfortunately, this also meant accepting the Nazism that was on the rise, which included its antisemitism and the ideology of the great Aryan race.

World War II found Austria as a willing participant as a part of Germany. No longer was Austrian history Austrian. Only with the utter defeat of the Nazi regime did Austria get a new opportunity to separate itself and become an independent nation state. The Austrians were finally given a chance to build their own national identity. They finally realized that this identity didn't have to be of one ethnicity but rather of the Habsburg heritage. With this realization and smart financial politics, Austria quickly rose to be one of the richest and most prosperous countries in Europe.

In modern times, Austria resents conflict and strives to keep its military neutral. As such, it is the peacekeeper of Europe, a country that welcomes various immigrants fleeing wars or in search of a better life. Austria continues to be a multi-ethnic mash-up that rose above petty conflicts and became a truly cosmopolitan society.

Chapter 1: The Eastern March

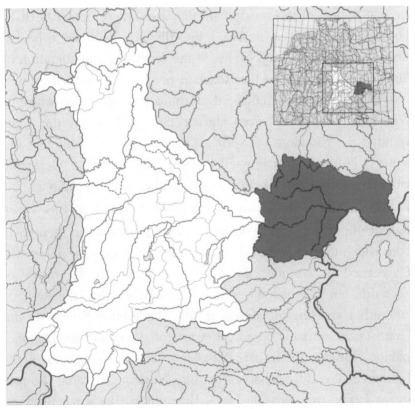

Margraviate of Austria circa 1000 CE

Alphathon /ˈælfə.θɒn/, CC BY-SA 4.0 <https://creativecommons.org/licenses/by-sa/4.0>, via Wikimedia Commons https://commons.wikimedia.org/wiki/File:Austria_locator_map_(1000).svg

Early History

The first written evidence of Austria dates from 996 CE when it is mentioned as "the Eastern Land" or, in local German, *Ostarrichi*. This area was the Eastern March of the Duchy of Bavaria; thus, it was a part of the German Kingdom. Austria started its history as a military district on the southeastern frontier of Germany. However, human activity in this area started thousands of years before its first mention in written texts.

The area is mountainous, which means that there were very few settlements. Because of its geographical position and being unapproachable, Austrian territory saw the Iron Age culture known as Hallstatt very late, approximately 800 BCE. The Illyrians were the first settlers of this region, and they lived there until 400 BCE. The Celtic migration displaced the Illyrians, and the tribes of Norici and Taurisci then occupied the region. A confederation of Alpine tribes, known as the Rhaetian people, was formed around 500 BCE, and they remained dominant in the mountains of Vorarlberg and Tyrol even during 200 BCE when the Celts founded the Kingdom of Noricum in the east. At the turn of the century, Noricum was pressed from the north by the Germanic tribes. By 15BCE, it had become part of the Roman Empire.

Roman rule of the region that is today Austria lasted for more than five hundred years. The Romans used Noricum as their base, from which they launched the occupation of Pannonia to the east. They tried to conquer the Germanic tribes to the north of Noricum, but they weren't as lucky. In 9 BCE, when the Romans suffered a catastrophic defeat in the Teutoburg Forest by the Cherusci, a Germanic people, they retreated south of the Danube, making Noricum the imperial border area. The Celtic settlements that were already established within Noricum became Roman towns: Lentia (modern-day Linz), Brigantium (Bregenz), Juvavum (Salzburg), and Vindobona (Vienna). The capital of Pannonia Superior was Carnuntum, and at its peak, the city had approximately fifty thousand inhabitants. Today, the remnants of this city are located in Lower Austria, but in 50 BCE, Carnuntum was the main fortress of the European Limes, the Roman Empire's border defense. The Romans built an extensive road network to connect the region with the rest of the empire, and they introduced viticulture in what is today Austria. The civilization flourished during Roman rule.

Roman rule over the region was relatively peaceful until the rule of Marcus Aurelius (r. 161–180). He came into the region in 172 to defend it from a Germanic invasion. Tribes such as the Marcomanni, Quadi, and Naristi, north of the Limes, threatened the Roman Empire. This was the first time that Vienna claimed fame, as Roman historian Aurelius Victor claimed Marcus Aurelius died there. But ancient Vindobona was merely a part of the Roman province of Pannonia, in which the emperor died, but his death actually occurred in another Roman city, Sirmium. The conflict with the Germanic tribes continued even after Aurelius's death.

When the Huns arrived in Europe around 370, the Romans allowed some of the Germanic tribes to settle within Pannonia, on the other side of the Limes. The fleeing tribes even agreed to enter into the Roman army and defend the region. By 433, the Romans had evacuated Pannonia, as they could no longer fend off Attila the Hun and his armies. But when Attila died in 453, the whole region was settled by the Goths. Noricum was occupied by the Germanic Rugii tribe, who ordered the Christianized and Romanized population to leave. The region of Raetia, which lay west of Noricum, was taken over by the Alemanni confederation of Germanic tribes. In 493, the Roman rule of what is modern-day Austria was over. The Eastern Alps was part of the Ostrogothic Empire of Theodoric the Great.

But the migration of the tribes from the north and the west wasn't over. Their goal was the valley of the Danube River, and the Lombards appeared in the region at around 500. They came from the north and east, but by 567, they had been expelled by the Avars and Slavs. The Lombards then settled in northern Italy. Another Germanic tribe, the Bavarians (*Bajuwaren*), came from the north and west. They were the vassals of the Franks, who had also entered the region. The contest of the Avars and Slavs on one side and the Bavarians on the other began. They fought for control over the region that would one day become Austria.

The Avars were the predominant tribe, and by the beginning of the 7th century, they controlled a vast area from the Baltic coast deep into the Balkan Peninsula. At that point, the Slavs were the Avars' vassals, and they were employed to contest with the Bavarians over the Eastern Alps. But the Slavs turned against the Avars when they attempted and failed to take over Constantinople in 626. The Northern Slavs took a Frankish king, Samo, as their ruler, while the Slavs who inhabited the region of the Alps known as the Carantanians took a Bavarian king, Odilo. The Avars eventually managed to conquer Samo's kingdom, but the Carantanians remained under Bavarian rule. The Bavarians took the whole region of the Danube Valley from the Slavs and Avars. In the second half of the 7th century, the Slavs started retreating under the pressure of the Bavarians and ended up behind the Enns River.

The Bavarians became the dominant power in the region, and during the 7th century, they were left pretty much to their own devices, although they were officially Frankish vassals. They continued to push to the east and south, and eventually, they took control over Carantania. But in the 8th century, the Frankish kings remembered the Bavarians and reaffirmed their dominion over their vassals. Charlemagne led his Frankish army, joined by the Bavarians, against the Avars in 791. They managed to drive the Avars back to the Fischa and Leitha Rivers, tributaries of the Danube. This opened much of the region for settlement. From the Danube to the Adriatic Sea, the Franks set up a system of marches, creating a buffer zone. The area was still under various attacks, whether they were internal rivalries or invasion attempts by the Bulgars and Great Moravian Empire. But the worst came in the 9th century with the onslaught of the Magyars, also known as the Hungarians.

The Magyars started appearing in the region in 862 as they were fleeing the Eastern European steppes that were overrun by more powerful tribes. In 896, the Magyars came in greater masses and settled in what was to be known as the Hungarian Plain. Although the Hungarians started serving as mercenaries in the Frankish army, they started fighting each other. The horse-based Hungarian army was superior in the early years of the conflict, and they had no trouble raiding the lands that surrounded them. They defeated the Moravians in 906, and in 907, they destroyed the Bavarian army at Pressburg. The marches founded by the Carolingian dynasty collapsed under Hungarian pressure, and the Bavarian frontier was moved back to the Enns River. The Hungarians terrorized the region for the next fifty years, but in 955, King Otto I and the German confederation defeated the Hungarians, who were joined by the Bavarian rebels.

Otto's victory brought him prestige and power, which he used to proclaim himself Holy Roman emperor in 962. One of his first acts as emperor was to regain the land east of the Enns, and once he did, he founded a new march with the pre-Hungarian society that still lived in the region. In 976, the march was headed by Leopold I, who became the first margrave of the Babenberg dynasty. But the Bavarians were not satisfied, and they continued to push the march's border farther to the east along the Danube, and in 1002, they reached the area around today's Vienna. Earlier, in 976, Carantania became a separate dukedom, and it was renamed Carinthia. There, marches were also established, as well as in Carniola and Styria.

When the *Ostarrichi* region was mentioned by its name in 996, that wasn't the definitive start of Austrian history. The region already had a very complex heritage, with various tribes and peoples inhabiting the area. None of the groups who previously lived in what is modern-day Austria really disappeared, and they all left their distinctive mark on the territory. The Bavarians were the most numerous, and they were the bulk of Austrian society. But the Alemanni turned out to be the most numerous in the western regions, toward Lake Constance. All the deportations, evacuations, and slaughters that occurred in the region were incomplete. Thus, the modern Austrian demography reflects its history with many Germanic, Slavic, Hungarian, Celtic, and even Roman traces still lingering in its social makeup.

The Babenbergs

Hungary converted to Christianity in 1000 during the reign of King Stephen I. The Bavarians were still pushing their eastern border, but now they had a Christian enemy to deal with, which set new limits on their actions. Although the German-Hungarian conflict didn't end at that point, the Danubian area became relatively stable. This stability allowed the development of the regional power blocs. One of them was the Austrian bloc under the leadership of the Babenbergs. To the north and east, Austria met the non-Germanic but Christian kingdoms of Bohemia, Hungary, and Poland. The margrave of Austria seemed a petty political player when compared to these great kingdoms. He was, after all, a subordinate to the duke of Bavaria, at least until 1156.

The first Babenberg margraves controlled only a small portion of what is today Austria. Salzburg was part of Bavaria and was developing into a clerical territory with its archbishop. Small lordships remained in place in Tyrol until the 12th century, when its counts won control over the whole area. Vorarlberg remained a feudal region under Alemannic influence. Carinthia and Styria to the south and southwest were developing independently. In 976, Carinthia became a dutchy, and it remained a waning power for the duration of its existence. It was often torn by internal conflicts, and after the Eastern March broke apart, Carinthia lost much of its territory. Some of the regions lost were Carniola, Istria, Verona, and Fruili. Styria was initially populated mostly by Slavs, but it would soon be under the control of the Traungauer family. They ruled from their fortress in Steyr, which gave the name to the whole region, Styria.

The second family that rose to power in the area was Otakar, and in 1180, Ottokar IV gained the status of a duke, which means Styria was no longer subordinate to Bavaria. But the independence didn't last for long. Ottokar failed to produce an heir, and in 1186, the Georgenberg Pact was signed. With it, the gravely ill Ottokar IV agreed to leave Styria to Duke Leopold V of Austria and his son, Frederick, who were both of the Babenberg dynasty. The Babenbergs took over control over Styria in 1192 after the death of Ottokar IV.

The Babenberg march was only one of many in the region. And even within it, the dynasty didn't have full control. Much of the territory was controlled by clerical authorities, such as the archdioceses of Salzburg and Passau. The rest of the territory was under the feudal system; therefore, it was controlled by noble families. The Babenbergs had only their own feudal territory under their full control. However, they started increasing their direct holdings through marriage, inheritance, and by forfeit and purchase. Nevertheless, other noble families remained powerful, and the whole Austrian region was under a constant power struggle. The Babenbergs sought to pacify the region through agreements with other families or military conflicts. They introduced *ministeriales*, the individuals raised from serfdom and put in positions of power. One such was the Kuenring family. They were indentured servants to the Babenbergs but were given large administrative and military responsibilities because they proved they were loyal to the family. Over time, the *ministeriales* became a new nobility, and they remained in service to the Babenbergs. They were a potential source of power to be used against the ducal power of other noble families. But the Babenbergs couldn't simply get rid of its rival noble families. They were in mutual dependence and had to work together to defend their march against its very powerful neighbors. However, by the 13th century, the Babenbergs managed to rise in power. They gained control over both Austria and Styria by using their entrepreneurial and diplomatic skills. They also managed to ally themselves with the Holy Roman Empire's ruling family, the Hohenstaufen dynasty, through marriage.

The Babenberg dukes were risk-takers, and they had to be. The success of medieval dynasties was a lottery only the bravest could play. The best-laid plans could be easily foiled by sudden death in battle or disease. The unpredictability was also increased by the constant imperial battles against papal power. This crisis started in 1076 with the Investiture Controversy. The church and the state fought over the ability to appoint bishops and abbots. The result was a fifty-year-long war in Germany. During this conflict, the Babenbergs often changed sides or even served both sides at once, depending on what was beneficial to them. Two of the Babenberg margraves proved to be exceptional players in the imperial-papal conflict. Leopold III (1073-1136) became the margrave after his father, Leopold II, was temporarily deposed by Holy Roman Emperor Henry IV due to his opposition to the imperial power. He supported the rebellion of Henry V, Henry IV's son, and for his accomplishments, he was declared a saint. But he was also dear to the emperor, and he won the hand of Henry V's sister, Agnes of Waiblingen. This marriage greatly increased the Babenbergs' prestige, but it also put a strain on the family's involvement in the conflict. After the marriage, Leopold III had to distance himself from imperial politics, but he still worked on pacifying the Austrian nobility.

Leopold VI (1176-1230) followed a similar pattern of politics as his ancestor, Leopold III. He supported his relatives, the ruling Hohenstaufens, but he also remained a patron of the church and founded various monasteries across Austria. In addition, he joined the crusades in the Middle East and western Europe (against the Muslims in Spain). He also married his daughter to the son of Emperor Frederick II, Henry VII. In 1230, before his death, Leopold VI mediated a settlement to the imperial-papal conflict. Austria was already a duchy at the time, and Leopold VI increased his control over it by buying off several towns, such as Linz, Freistadt, and Wels.

Other Babenbergs didn't achieve as much, although there was Henry II, the first Austrian duke. On September 17th, 1156, Holy Roman Emperor Frederick Barbarossa (Frederick I) issued the *Privilegium Minus*, a deed that elevated the Austrian march to the status of a duchy. Austria also became a hereditary territory, belonging to the House of Babenberg. However, Henry II received this deed only as a consolation prize, as he had to give up the Duchy of Bavaria, which had come under Babenberg control in 1139 when Leopold IV received it from King Conrad III of Germany.

Henry II's successor, Leopold V, was perhaps the greatest risk-taker of the Babenberg family. He was the one who negotiated the Georgenberg Pact with the Stryians. He also imprisoned Richard I of England, which resulted in his excommunication because it was against papal laws to imprison a crusader. However, Leopold V was ready to risk his soul in exchange for the ransom money he received from England. He used this money to connect Vienna to Styria by roads, built walls around some of the cities, and issued new coins in Austria. The imprisonment of Richard I was a result of a quarrel the two had during the Siege of Acre in 1189. Both Richard I and Leopold V were there, but while Richard was a king, Leopold was only a duke. When they took the city of Acre, Leopold's cousin raised the flags of the Duchy of Austria and the Kingdom of England side by side. This angered Richard, who considered Leopold less worthy, and he lowered the Austrian flag. Leopold, in turn, complained to Holy Roman Emperor Henry VI.

Henry already suspected Richard of the murder of the new king of Jerusalem, Leopold's cousin, Marquis Conrad of Montferrat. Thus, the emperor permitted Leopold to imprison Richard.

Vienna started as a Roman military camp, but its position on the Danube allowed it to develop into a trade center. The commercial advantages of the city only further grew once the Babenbergs moved their residence to Vienna in 1150. Leopold V spent half of the money he got for Richard I's ransom on building Vienna and improving its infrastructure and walls. But it was Leopold VI who made Vienna a true urban center of the Duchy of Austria. In 1221, he gave the staple to the city's merchants. The staple right was a medieval privilege given only to some ports, by which the merchant ships had to unload their goods and try to sell them in that port for several days. This gave Vienna's merchants control over the Danube trade route. Due to the acquisition of Styria, Vienna's importance grew since contact with Venice was established. Erzberg, one of Europe's largest iron mines, brought significant revenue to Vienna, helping it grow into a commercial urban center. The prosperity Vienna gained was reflected in the lavish rebuilding of the city. In 1147, the building of Saint Stephen's Cathedral started, but its rebuilding in 1230 is what gave it the look it still has. The fast-developing city also attracted many artists, especially writers and musicians.

The Babenbergs' good fortune in Austria didn't last for long. When Leopold VI died in 1230, he was succeeded by his son, Frederick II (r. 1230-1246), who didn't have his father's diplomatic skills. He proved unable to administer the duchy, its institutions, church, and the new noble *ministerial* social class. He also proved to be unsuccessful in negotiating with his neighbors and Holy Roman Emperor Frederick II (r. 1220-1250). The first years of Frederick's dukedom saw rebellions of nobles, which led to the Holy Roman emperor outlawing Duke Ferdinand II. But once the emperor was distracted by events in Italy, Frederick regained control over Austria again. He was lucky, for the renewed imperial-papal conflict occupied the emperor's mind, who often utilized Frederick's help. The Mongol invasion of eastern Europe in 1240 confirmed that Austria needed a stable ruler.

Once the duke confirmed his control over Austria, he started managing his territory. He divided Austria into two administrative units: Austria above the Enns (Upper Austria) and Austria below the Enns (Lower Austria). In 1244, he granted a Patent of Protection for Jews in Austria, intending to regulate the financial services offered by Jews. Everything looked as if the second half of Frederick's rule would be much better, but in 1246, the duke was killed in the Battle of the Leitha River, which was fought against the Hungarians. Frederick left no male heir, and the *Privilegium minus* was unclear if it allowed the succession on the female line. What followed was a decade of warfare before the crisis could be stopped and the new line could take the place of the Babenberg dynasty.

Chapter 2: The Habsburgs Enter the Scene

Habsburg coat of arms

The Battle on the Marchfeld was a decisive one for the history of Austria. It happened on August 26th, 1278, in the north of the Vienna Basin. There, Rudolf I of Habsburg (1218-1291), King of Germany, defeated the armies of Ottokar II (1233-1278), King of Bohemia. With this victory, the German house of Habsburg became the ruling dynasty of Austria. From this point until 1918, Austrian history would be tightly bound to the destiny of this dynasty. The Habsburgs would raise their position and become the imperial rulers of the Holy Roman Empire, but they intended to rule the whole world. Austria was only a small element, a starting point for a dynasty that would propel itself into the ruling world of Europe. The entry of the Habsburgs, who originally came from Switzerland, on the political scene forever changed what it meant and still means to be an Austrian.

The Battle on the Marchfeld was the result of the end of the Babenberg dynasty. The succession crisis after Frederick II's death lasted for three decades. Some of the nobles grouped together and invited Ottokar, King of Bohemia, to take over the rule of Austria in 1251. But they didn't do it on a whim. Ottokar was married to one of the female heirs of the Babenberg dynasty, and he seemed as if he would be a legitimate ruler. Ottokar came to Austria, subdued the nobles who resisted him, and established an effective rule over Austria, Styria, Carinthia, Carniola, Friuli, and Aquileia. But during this process, Ottokar divorced his Babenberg wife so he could form an alliance with Hungary through marriage. He had much bigger aspirations than to rule Austria. With his own Kingdom of Bohemia to the north and through further conquests, Ottokar almost established an empire that spread from the Baltic to the Adriatic Seas. But he was only able to do so because the Holy Roman Empire descended into chaos after the death of Emperor Frederick II. Ottokar was one of the candidates for the imperial throne, but the German prince-electors voted for Rudolf of Habsburg, who became the emperor in 1273.

Rudolf was the first king of Germany after the long interregnum that followed the death of Holy Roman Emperor Frederick II. Kings of Germany were given a special title, "King of the Romans," as their power was equal to the Holy Roman emperor. The latter title could only be granted by the pope, though, as only the pope could bestow imperial power to a ruler.

With Rudolf's election in 1273, the Habsburgs became the kings of Germany; they were also known as count-kings, a term coined by historians to differentiate the rulers who reigned until 1438, which was when the Habsburg dynasty finally obtained the imperial title. As the King of the Romans, Rudolf worked on returning the imperial rights that had been lost since 1250. His power and influence were ever-growing, and Ottokar finally had to submit to him in 1276. But when Rudolf placed Austria in the hands of his own family, he started losing the support of the nobles and the Austrian people. To Ottokar, it seemed that the Habsburg king was losing his power, and he thought that the time was right to attack. Rudolf's victory on the Marchfeld in 1278 only proved how wrong the Bohemian king was. The Habsburgs claimed Austria, Styria, and Carniola, and Rudolf divided these territories between his two sons, Albert (Albrecht) I and Rudolf II. Due to a mutual agreement in 1283, Albert became the sole heir of the Habsburg lands.

Rudolf was elected king only because of his relative weakness as the count of Upper Alsace and Aargau in what is today Switzerland. The prince-electors believed he could be more easily controlled than the king of Bohemia. However, with the acquisition of Austria, the Habsburgs' prestige was greatly enhanced. Rudolf also expanded his control to include the northern approaches to the St. Gotthard Pass in the Alps, one of the most important medieval European trade routes that connected northern and southern Switzerland. With this much power, the Habsburgs became a real threat to the German princes. But they didn't dare to remove Rudolf from his position as the king of the

Romans. After he died, his son Albert didn't manage to win the votes of the prince-electors, and his cousin, Adolf, Count of Nassau, became the new king of the Romans. But Adolf was quickly deposed from the position because of his policies that affected the prince-electors' plans.

Once again, Albert entered the electoral race, and this time, he was chosen as the next king in 1298. But he ruled for a very short time as he died in 1308. He was murdered by his nephew, John "the Parricide," since Albert had deprived him of his inheritance of the Bohemian throne. Again, the prince-electors chose another dynasty to be the successor to the German throne; this time, it was Henry VII of Luxembourg. Yet, again, this proved to be a misjudgment on the prince-electors' part, as Henry's imperial ambitions were great.

Albert's sons, Frederick the Fair and Leopold, showed themselves as good candidates for Henry's replacement. However, the Habsburg brothers sided with Henry, who proved to be powerful enough to take Bohemia for his son John and who planned an imperial coronation in Rome for himself. Henry was crowned as the Holy Roman emperor on June 29th, 1312, but not in Rome as he had planned. Nevertheless, his rule as emperor was short as he died in August 1313.

The Habsburgs tried to regain the imperial mantle, but their right to rule Germany was contested by Louis IV, Duke of Bavaria. The prince-electors thought Louis had a better claim than Frederick the Fair, so conflict ensued. It lasted until 1325 when the Treaty of Munich was signed, and the Habsburgs gained the right to rule as joint rulers. Louis and Frederick were both the kings of Germany, but the Habsburg was a king only by name. He didn't really have any executive power. Frederick died in 1330, and his younger brothers proved to be less ambitious. They were ready to trade Habsburg imperial ambitions for more local gains.

The imperial power struggle in Germany weakened the Habsburgs and undermined their interests in their power base in Switzerland. In 1291, the Everlasting League was formed to contest the Habsburg claims. This league was the nucleus of the future Swiss Confederation. The Swiss nobles thought the Habsburgs were a danger to them because they recognized feudal rights. Swiss society never followed feudal norms and resisted bowing to them. In 1313, the Everlasting League's forces raided the Abbey of Einsiedeln, and they defeated the army of Leopold of Habsburg in 1315. This was a turning point not only for Swiss history but also for the Habsburg dynasty. The power of the league grew, and in 1315, it turned to become a confederation. By the 15th century, the Habsburgs were excluded and ejected from their home base in Switzerland, and the Confederation took over the rule.

It was during the reign of Frederick the Fair that the Habsburgs started styling themselves as "of Austria," or *dominum Austriae*—the rulers of Austria. Frederick's successors then concentrated on their power base in Austria at the expense of their Swiss and imperial interests. His brothers, Albert II and Otto, made a deal with Holy Roman Emperor Louis IV. They gave up their rights to rule in return for the acquisition of Carinthia and Carniola in 1336. When his brother died in 1339, Albert became the sole ruler of Austria, Styria, Carniola, and Carinthia. He avoided meddling in imperial issues, instead concentrating on the consolidation of his power in the lands he ruled. But he ignored the Swiss problem, and during his rule, Zurich and Lucerne were lost to the Swiss Confederation. Nevertheless, Albert II led strong fiscal politics, which meant he was able to respond to the disaster of the Black Death, which ensued in 1348.

Albert's successor was his eldest son, Rudolf IV (r. 1358-1365). Rudolf continued his father's policies of strengthening Austria, and he reformed the administration and taxation of his lands. He also founded the University of Vienna in 1365 and rebuilt the nave of the Saint Stephen's Cathedral. For this, he was named "the

Founder," although his aspirations were motivated by the relative weakness of the Habsburg dynasty. The University of Vienna was established only as a response to the foundation of the University of Prague in 1348 by Holy Roman Emperor Charles IV of the House of Luxembourg. The Luxembourgs, a rich German family, had overshadowed the Habsburgs, and Rudolf would have none of that.

Duke Rudolf IV married Charles IV's daughter in 1353, despite the resentment he felt for the emperor. In 1356, when Charles issued the Golden Bull, which diminished the role of Austria and Bavaria in the Holy Roman Empire, Rudolf responded with one of the greatest frauds committed in medieval Europe. He commissioned the *Privilegium maius*, a document he claimed was granted to the Babenberg dukes by Emperor Frederick Barbarossa. Rudolf "found" this document, which would greatly enhance Austria's status, in 1359. The *Privilegium maius* supposedly granted the Austrian dukes the status of archdukes, claimed the inseparability of Austrian territory, set the rules of inheritance to the firstborn, and gave the archduke permission to display symbols of his rule. Holy Roman Emperor Charles IV rejected some of the rights the *Privilegium maius* allegedly gave to Austria, and he also refused to confirm the validity of the document. It was actually a famous Italian poet and scholar named Francesco Petrarca (also spelled as Petrarch), the king's advisor, who recognized the *Privilegium maius* was a forgery. Nevertheless, to appease his son-in-law, Charles accepted the inheritance and inseparability acts, but he forbade Rudolf to call himself archduke or display his ruling insignia. A century later, when Frederick III became the Habsburg emperor, he proclaimed the *Privilegium maius* to be a valid document.

In 1363, Rudolf became much more cooperative because Charles IV supported the Habsburgs' acquisition of Tyrol. The next year, Charles approved the inheritance treaty between the Habsburgs and the Luxembourgs, by which the two dynasties could succeed each other. At the same time, Rudolf planned to create a new alliance across the Alps through marriage. But before his plans could come true, Rudolf died; he was only twenty-five years old. His brothers, Albert III and Leopold III, succeeded him, and they ruled jointly, continuing the progress Austria had been making under Rudolf's rule. They managed to keep Tyrol, and they even expanded their territories to Istria and Gorizia. They linked the Austrian possessions with Swabia by acquiring Freiburg im Breisgau and some territory in Vorarlberg. But they were unable to continue ruling together due to constant quarrels. In 1379, the Habsburg lands were divided. Albert III gained the heartlands of Upper and Lower Austria, while Leopold took everything else. For another century, the lands of Habsburgs would remain divided.

All the lands that the Habsburgs ruled were referred to as *Domus Austria*, the "House of Austria." The territories were under the same roof, even though they were divided between the different branches of the family. The Habsburgs' territory split again in 1396, and some adjustments were made during the 1400s. Two lines sprouted: the Leopoldian and the Albertian. But the brothers and cousins continued quarreling about the territories that they inherited, splitting the House of Austria into three parts: Lower Austria (which is today Lower and Upper Austria), Inner Austria (the Adriatic territories, Carniola, Carinthia, and Styria), and Upper Austria (Habsburg possessions in Swabia and Alsace, as well as Tyrol). But this division didn't mean a Habsburg triumvirate was in place. The situation was much more complicated than that. The whole dynasty of the late 14th century was enveloped in internal drama, much like today's soap operas. The Habsburgs continued dividing their territories, and brothers and cousins would often exchange parts of their lands.

A much more important conflict for the history of Europe occurred in the imperial House of Luxembourg. The conflict occurred between the sons of Charles IV: Wenceslaus IV, King of Bohemia, and Sigismund, King of Hungary. The Habsburgs played a major role during this conflict, for Sigismund imprisoned Wenceslaus and delivered him to Vienna to be kept as a prisoner of William the Courteous, Duke of Austria, who was a head of the Leopoldian line. Sigismund took the throne of Germany in 1411 and became the king of Bohemia in 1419.

Even though the Habsburgs sided with Sigismund, Frederick IV, William's younger brother, decided to help Antipope John XXIII escape from the Council of Constance in 1415, for the council had decided that a new pope should be elected. Sigismund was infuriated, and he had them both captured and imprisoned. Frederick was also placed under the imperial ban, which was the Holy Roman Empire's way of outlawing a person. This also meant he was legally dead, and all his possessions were immediately passed to his successor or were confiscated. If someone was to kill a person under the imperial ban, he would face no consequences as the person was already regarded as dead. The Swiss Confederation took the opportunity of Frederick's legal absence to gain control over the remaining Habsburg territories in Switzerland.

Frederick's brothers continued to argue over the Leopoldian inheritance. Albert V of the Albertinian line was still a minor when he succeeded the throne of Lower Austria. His older cousins of the Leopoldian line argued about his guardianship. The result was a civil war in 1404, which shook the Austrian lands to their core. Austria saw an influx of foreign mercenaries, as well as bands of Hungarian and Moravian soldiers who were hired by Austrian nobles. The situation was finally resolved in 1411 when the Lower Austrian estates finally kidnapped Albert V (with his permission) and installed him as their duke. Due to the effective rule of young Albert V, order was restored. Nevertheless, he managed to involve Austria in the Hussite Wars since he was married to Sigismund's daughter and owed allegiance to the Holy Roman emperor.

In 1421, the duke of Austria took the opportunity of the Hussite Wars to proclaim the Jews in Vienna as Hussite allies. The horrendous persecution of the Jews thus started, with 212 of them being burned at the stake. But the real result behind the persecution of the Jews was their wealth. Albert V needed money to finance his expeditions against the Hussites, and he started imposing extra taxes on the Jews. Finally, he decided to simply confiscate all their possessions, accusing them of collaborating and trading with the enemy.

Albert was a junior partner of the Luxembourg family through his marriage with Elisabeth, the daughter of Holy Roman Emperor Sigismund. But Albert played the game of politics well, and upon the death of his father-in-law in 1437, he was crowned the king of Hungary and Bohemia. But most importantly, he was elected as the king of the Romans, ruling as Albert II. Unfortunately, Albert died two years later of dysentery while fighting the Ottoman Turks. Albert's wife was pregnant when the emperor died, and she later gave birth to a son. He came to be known as Ladislaus the Posthumous, and he was Albert II's successor. However, only Austria accepted Ladislaus as their ruler, even though it was Albert's last will for his son to inherit all of the lands he controlled. Since Ladislaus was a minor, he became the ward of his uncle, Frederick V of Styria, together with Sigismund, the son of Frederick IV. Thus, the Styrian duke held all the powerful cards of the Habsburg dynastic play in his hand.

Albert II's fight against the Ottoman Turks was not a coincidence. This was a moment in European history that proved decisive. Alongside the Hussite Wars, the Ottoman invasion of eastern Europe was of great significance for the future of the whole continent. The Habsburg response to these events would shape the political scene of the region for the next three centuries.

Chapter 3: A.E.I.O.U.

King Frederick's records with A.E.I.O.U. inscription (1446)

Frederick V of the House of Habsburg (1415-1493) was the undisputed head of the dynasty since he was the duke of Styria, Carinthia, and Carniola; he was also the regent of the Albertinian lands, with Ladislaus the Posthumous as his ward. As a cousin of Albert II, he became a candidate for the German kingship. In 1440, a unanimous vote of the prince-electors made him the king of the Romans. He ruled as Frederick III, and in 1451, he started his journey to Rome, where he would be crowned as the Holy Roman emperor. Tradition called for the emperor to be crowned in Rome, but Frederick III would be the last to do so. He was also the first of the Habsburg emperors to be crowned by the pope in Rome. He started the Habsburg monopoly on the imperial office, which lasted until 1806, although there was a brief interruption between 1740 and 1745. But while Frederick was undertaking his journey, back in Austria, unrest brewed. The people demanded the return of their rightful duke, Ladislaus, who Frederick had taken to Rome.

Frederick III's dynastic politics played an important role in shaping the monarchical rule of his successors. The Habsburgs thought of themselves as holding the divine right to rule, and they sought this right for three centuries: from Frederick III until the reign of Maria Theresa (1717-1780). But the Habsburgs were no longer satisfied by ruling their own dynastic lands. They wanted to rule the whole Christian world as God's chosen dynasty. It was Rudolf I (1218-1291) who first started the idea of the dynasty's divine right to rule, but Frederick III gave it its final shape in the motto "A.E.I.O.U." The acronym was created by Frederick before he was crowned the king of the Romans. He started signing documents with this acronym as early as 1435, and he even explained it in his personal journal. "A.E.I.O.U." stands for the German phrase *Alles Erdreich ist Österreich untertan* and for the Latin phrase *Austriae Est Imperare Orbi Universo*. The German and Latin phrases have the same meaning, and it translates into English as "It is for Austria to rule the world." Nevertheless, there are some scholarly doubts about the authenticity of Frederick's explanation, as it is the only entry in his journal that was written with different handwriting. The Habsburgs almost realized this rule of the whole Christian world a couple of times. Through marriages and alliances, they threatened to achieve hegemony in Europe. And as Holy Roman emperors, the Habsburgs certainly had superiority over Western Christendom.

Even though Frederick III had a very high opinion of the Habsburg dynasty and had an exalted view of the office of the Holy Roman emperor, he was a weak ruler. His rule was long (he was the Holy Roman emperor from 1452 until he died in 1493), but he was overshadowed by other significant political figures. For the first twenty years of his rule, his brother, Albert VI, and Hungarian military general John Hunyadi, as well as the Bohemian leader George Podiebrad, eclipsed Frederick's power. In this period, Frederick's main source of power was his grip on young Ladislaus, Duke of Austria and King of Bohemia. Frederick refused to release Ladislaus even when the young duke turned twelve, which was the legal age to rule in Austria. Frederick also neglected his Austrian lands, which led to the formation of the League of Mailberg in 1451. The goal of this league was the liberation of Ladislaus and the establishment of a legitimate government in Austria. By 1452, the league included Hunyadi and Podiebrad, and by September, Frederick felt pressured enough and agreed to release Ladislaus.

The remainder of Frederick's rule was a period of inaction and impotence. When Byzantium fell in 1453 and the Ottomans marched toward Hungary, the emperor did very little to help defend the borders of his empire and Christendom. John Hunyadi had to work alone to defend Belgrade from Turkish attacks. The heroism of Hunyadi led the Hungarians to elect his son, Matthias Corvinus, as their king after the death of Ladislaus the Posthumous. In Bohemia, it was a similar situation. George Podiebrad was favored as a king instead of another Habsburg ruler.

In 1461, Frederick III's brother, Albert VI, challenged his rule by invading Lower Austria. The masses there welcomed him as a savior who would free them from the oppressive emperor. But in 1463, Albert died, and both Upper and Lower Austria came under Frederick's control.

After these events, Frederick started ruling Austria with more competence. He gained bishoprics for Vienna, Laibach, and Wiener Neustadt. He also bought the Port of Fiume (today's Rijeka, Croatia), but he never managed to repair his relations with the Austrian nobility. As for the Ottoman attacks on the southeastern border of Hungary, Frederick did almost nothing. However, he did establish the Order of Saint George in 1469, whose mission was to advocate for Christianity; however, Frederick's original intention for this military order was to use it to defend Inner Austria if the Ottomans ever approached. The order was never sent to defend the Hungarian border, though. Emperor Frederick III also never sent resources to the front, which forced local nobles and peasants to organize the defense. The untrained army of farmers never stood a chance against the mighty force that was the Ottoman Empire, and they were defeated in 1478.

Frederick was occupied by another threat to his rule, one that he found more dangerous than the Ottoman invasion: Matthias Corvinus. The Hungarian king was angered by the emperor's passiveness toward the Turks, and he declared war on Frederick in 1482. Corvinus had help from the archbishop of Salzburg, who recruited people to the cause. Matthias Corvinus's army swept through Austria and conquered Vienna in 1485, as well as Wiener Neustadt in 1487. Frederick had to abandon his favorite residence and flee to Linz. The war ended in 1488 with an armistice, and Matthias Corvinus died of a stroke two years later. His unexpected death allowed Frederick to regain all the parts of Austria he had lost, but he failed to force the Habsburg succession of the Hungarian kingship.

There was one aspect of ruling in which Frederick III was more successful. His dynastic policy brought the Habsburgs a marriage alliance with the House of Burgundy. Burgundy lands were scattered in both French and German territory. Among their territories were some of the most prosperous areas of Europe. Because of this, the House of Burgundy was one of the leading powers of medieval Europe, but it never gained a status of a kingdom or any other form of independent governance. The Burgundy family was also one of the richest in the world, so, of course, they had their own political ambitions. For instance, Charles the Bold (1433-1477), Duke of Burgundy, wanted a kingdom. Sigismund of Tyrol wanted an alliance with Burgundy, and he convinced his cousin, Frederick III, to marry his son, Maximilian, to Charles the Bold's daughter, Mary. In 1473, Frederick approached Charles, asking for his daughter's hand for his son. But further negotiations were stalled when Sigismund joined the Swiss side in the conflict against the Habsburg claim on the territory. This ended the Habsburg dynasty's interests in Switzerland for good. The marriage negotiations continued in 1476, and in May, an agreement was confirmed. But the next year, Charles died, and Maximilian had to rush to Burgundy to secure his engagement to Mary. The couple got married on August 19th, 1477, setting a new path for the Habsburg dynasty.

Maximilian had to stay in Burgundy and defend his wife's estates against other Burgundy nobles and, most importantly, King Louis XI of France. Unfortunately, Mary died in 1482, and to secure peace, Maximilian had to cede a large part of Burgundy to the French king. Still, the majority of the territory remained under his control, which brought him great prestige and wealth. In 1486, during the irregular election, Maximilian was elected as the king of the Romans. But his father, Frederick III, gave none of the governmental powers to him. He was afraid his young son was too inexperienced to rule. But Maximilian proved his worth in 1490 when he managed to buy Tyrol out of the hands of his cousin

Sigismund. Maximilian made Innsbruck his capital because the city was halfway between the Burgundy and Austrian territories. By 1493, he had regained most of the Burgundy territory from France, and once Matthias Corvinus was dead, he helped his father regain the Austrian territories. When Frederick III died in August 1493, the only success he left behind was his successor, Maximilian, the ruler of both Austria and Burgundy.

As the king of the Romans, Maximilian became the de facto Holy Roman emperor, and he ruled as Maximilian I. Just like his father, he believed in the Habsburgs' divine right to rule, and he continued to spread that propaganda. Most of the Habsburgs' influence was spread through marriage, which Maximilian enjoyed setting up. The greatest marriage alliances he created were with the Spanish House of Castile and the Central European House of Jagiellon (they had Lithuanian origins but came to rule Poland, Hungary, and Bohemia in time). Thus, the Habsburgs spread their influence through Spain, Italy, the New World (the American continent), and much of Central Europe. This was possible because the Habsburgs were one of three emerging superpowers of Europe. They presented themselves as a balance between the French royal house and the Ottoman Empire. However, marriage was only one small part of the Habsburgs' dynastic success. Maximilian and his successors proved themselves to be capable leaders on the battlefield, too, and they waged many wars.

Maximilian was the first Habsburg who approached governance in a bureaucratic way. He attempted fiscal and administrative reform in his hereditary lands. He used the mineral and iron wealth of Styria and the copper and silver mines of Tyrol to finance wars and his imperial administration. To achieve this, he needed a centralized government, with regent councils in Tyrol, Lower Austria, Upper Austria, and Inner Austria. But his initiatives for more radical changes of the governance failed, as the Austrian noble houses resisted the expansion of new institutions and new executive bodies. The failure to execute this imperial reform happened due to the many wars, which distracted Maximilian. He fought the French (1498) and the Swiss (1499), intervened in the conflict between Palatinate and Bavaria (1504), and warred with Hungary (1507). But it was the hostilities of Venice that prevented Maximilian from being crowned by the pope as the Holy Roman emperor. With the pope's consent, Maximilian proclaimed himself as the "elected Roman Emperor" in 1508, ending the tradition that the emperor had to be crowned in Rome.

His proclamation didn't lead to the end of the various conflicts with which he was involved, though. Allying with Henry VIII of England, Maximilian led the English army against the French in 1513 and won the Battle of the Spurs. This was the second battle in what is known as the War of the Holy League, a conflict between France, the Papal States, and Venice. Although at first France and the Papal States worked together to alter Venetian influence, their differences were too great, and the league fell apart. The pope joined Venice against France, and Maximilian I sided with the pope. The conflict escalated into the broader Italian Wars (1494–1559), with many participants often switching sides, betraying their allies, and making new friendships. But all these wars took a toll on the Holy Roman Empire, and Maximilian was left without resources that would finance further campaigns. Despite his investment in the war, Maximilian gained very little and lost some of his Italian possessions.

At the end of his reign, Maximilian returned to what he was good at: marriage arranging. This time, he set up the marriages of his grandchildren, Mary and Ferdinand. Mary married Louis II, son of Vladislaus II of House Jagiellon (King of Hungary and Bohemia). Ferdinand was to marry Anna of Bohemia and Hungary, the older sister of Louis II. But Ferdinand only agreed to this marriage years later. The betrothal ceremony was performed in 1515, with Maximilian standing as a proxy to his grandson, and the actual marriage happened in 1521. Maximilian died in 1519 without securing the succession for his favorite grandson, Charles

V. Nevertheless, it was Charles who inherited all the Habsburg patrimonial territories, and with them came dynastic opportunities for this powerful European house.

Charles V (1500–1558) became the duke of Burgundy and the king of Castile in 1506. With the death of Ferdinand of Aragon in 1516, Charles became the king of Spain, ruling over both Castile and Aragon. But to gain the title of the king of the Romans, he had to resort to bribery. Charles spent so much money securing his election that he is known as the emperor who bought his empire. He ruled as Charles I from 1519 until his death in 1558. He was crowned by the pope in Bologna in 1530, becoming the last emperor to receive the crown directly from the pope's hands. His empire was vast, as he ruled the Habsburg hereditary lands, Germany, Spain, parts of Italy, and the Mediterranean coast, as well as colonies in the Caribbean, Peru, and Mexico. The Habsburg power spread far, and it looked as if Frederick III's motto of "A.E.I.O.U." was close to realization. Charles even came up with his motto, *Plus ultra* ("even further"), and with it, he proclaimed his intention to work toward a universal monarchy; there would be one ruler for all of Christendom.

But the Habsburgs' claim to a universal monarchy was never realistic. The kings of France had similar aspirations, and they stood in the way. France was too powerful an enemy and an unreliable ally. France's governmental administration was more effective than that of the Holy Roman Empire and Austria. The revenues they collected matched the Habsburgs, even with the income that the New World brought. The Habsburgs had problems managing their lands because of their vastness. Their hereditary lands were the first to protest the old regime in Vienna, with Austrians trying to set up their own government. The local ruling classes of other Habsburg territories started similar unrests. They wanted to preserve their autonomy, not become part of one universal monarchy. Aside from having to deal with the French threat and the local unrests, Charles V had to also be wary of the

Ottomans pressing on his southeastern border.

But the emperor's biggest problem wasn't a physical enemy, a country he could pacify with his army. It was the ideology of Martin Luther, who posted his *Ninety-five Theses* on the door of the Castle Church in Wittenberg in 1517 as a sign of protest against the corruption of the Catholic Church. Protestantism emerged as a result, and it presented itself as a mortal enemy of traditional Catholicism. And it was Catholicism that stood as a pillar of Habsburg imperial authority. Therefore, Protestantism was a direct threat to the Habsburgs' power and influence in the Christian world. Charles now had to deal with the Lutherans, Calvinists, Unitarians, and other emerging sects, and the idea of an empire united by faith seemed less and less plausible. The only logical course would be for Charles to suppress the new sects and confirm Catholicism as the empire's main religion. But the Ottoman attacks prevented him from acting, as he didn't have the resources to fight on two fronts.

A more charismatic and modest ruler might have united his vast empire to defend itself from the French, Turks, and Protestants. But Charles V was never loved among his people, and his pretentiousness inspired them to rebel. Charles was aware he couldn't be in every place at once, and to help manage his vast empire, he started partitioning it. He gave control over different areas to different Habsburg family members. Thus, he made sure the land stayed under Habsburg control while having the rebellions put down. But he also made sure that his cousins saw his generosity and stayed loyal. This was why Charles V gave the Austrian hereditary lands (Lower Austria and Tyrol) to his younger brother, Ferdinand. These were the most fertile areas, and with Tyrol, Ferdinand gained control over the silver mines.

Charles spent much of his reign warring with France in Italy. In 1527, his soldiers sacked Rome since the emperor was unable to pay them. In 1529, Charles was forced to accept the loss of

Burgundy, but he made France give up Milan. A year later, he was finally crowned as the emperor, and he felt the need to start concentrating on the empire's internal affairs. He succeeded in securing the title of King of the Romans for his brother Ferdinand in 1531. This meant that Ferdinand was his official successor as emperor. But what Charles failed to notice was the spread of Lutheranism through the empire's lands and estates. Many German princes converted to Protestantism, and in 1531, they formed the Schmalkaldic League, a military alliance of all the Protestant princes of the empire. The league had a political agenda as well, as it wanted to replace the Holy Roman Empire. The French supported the Schmalkaldic League because it was a direct threat to the Catholic Habsburgs. The next year, the Ottoman Turks started approaching Vienna, and Charles had no time to deal with the Protestants and their league. He had to appeal to the Nuremberg Diet, a deliberative assembly of the Holy Roman Empire, to send an army to defend Vienna. Unfortunately, Charles couldn't persuade the princes to give him an army and resources. Nevertheless, the Ottomans' second attempt (the first one was in 1529) to take the city failed.

Due to the pressure to accept the Protestants, who had the support of both France and England, Charles promised he wouldn't persecute them and recognized the Schmalkaldic League as legitimate. In return, the league promised it would fight for the empire against the Turks and the French. The religious issue of the empire wasn't solved, though, and Charles eventually lost interest in imperial affairs yet again. Instead, he invaded Tunisia, which was in the same region as Carthage, which was once an enemy of the ancient Roman Empire. Charles's victory was mostly symbolic, but he still continued the Roman tradition of a grand triumph into Rome to celebrate his success. By the 1540s, the empire had started gaining victories on different fronts, and Charles felt empowered by them. He attempted to break the Schmalkaldic League and restore the supremacy of Catholicism. In 1545, the pope summoned a council in Trent, which gathered an imperial army. In 1547, the Schmalkaldic League was defeated at Mühlberg.

The Protestant princes responded in 1552 when they allied with France. Henry II of France launched a surprise attack on Charles and almost captured the emperor at Innsbruck, but the city managed to defend itself. Nevertheless, Henry launched attacks on more German cities, which were more successful. Charles launched a siege of Metz as a response to the attack, but the siege failed in 1553. The emperor couldn't deal with the defeat, and he sent his brother Ferdinand to lead the negotiations. In 1555, the Peace of Augsburg was achieved, and the decision was made that each local ruler would assert his religion upon his subjects. That same year, Charles resigned as the ruler of the Netherlands. In 1556, he resigned from ruling Spain, and in September, he abdicated as the Holy Roman emperor, surrendering the office to Ferdinand. Charles V spent the remaining two years of his life in Spain.

With Charles's death, the idea of a universal monarchy also died. His son, Philip II, King of Spain, managed to secure a victory over France and gain Italy for the Habsburgs, but he came nowhere near becoming a universal ruler. However, with France declining into religious and civil wars, Philip became the most powerful European ruler. But Philip didn't succeed Charles as the Holy Roman emperor, nor did he succeed his uncle, Ferdinand I. If he did, maybe he would have continued the A.E.I.O.U. policy of his predecessors.

Religious unrest continued to shake the empire, and Ferdinand I, who became the Holy Roman emperor after his brother's death, had to deal with a largely Protestant Austria, the Turkish threat, and the division of the empire. However, the Habsburgs adapted their politics and successfully met these challenges by creating the Habsburg Monarchy.

Chapter 4: Bastion of Christendom

Siege of Vienna depicted by the Ottoman artists from the 16th century
https://commons.wikimedia.org/wiki/File:SiegeOfViennaByOttomanForces.jpg

The second half of the 16th century saw the decline in the worth of the lands of Germany and central Europe. The Habsburg hereditary lands that lay on the Danube were developing fast because of the trade routes of this great river. But when the trade shifted to the Adriatic Sea, the rest of western Europe started developing and became richer. The Habsburgs still had their Italian possessions, so this economic shift didn't pose a threat to the dynasty yet. But the Spanish and Dutch lines of the Habsburgs surpassed the hereditary lands. Trade to the east was blocked due to the Ottoman invasion, but there was still a highly developed mining industry in Tyrol. However, the revenues of these mines were soon undercut by the influx of gold and silver from the New World. Agriculture still prospered in the Danube Valley, but the land there was owned by rich landlords, so the peasants, unsatisfied with serfdom, caused much trouble in the region. Overall, the Austrian lands were economically declining while the rest of the Western world was prospering.

Nevertheless, Ferdinand I proved to be a remarkable ruler. Besides the economy's downfall, he had to deal with the religious problems that lingered after Charles's death and with the Turkish invasion. Although he didn't solve any of these problems, he managed to construct a monarchy that was strong enough to withstand them and a dynasty that was able to survive all the troubles that tortured the Habsburg domains. The initial years of Ferdinand's rule as the archduke of Austria were marked by bloody peasant revolts in Lower Austria in the mid-1520s. Ferdinand effectively put a stop to these revolts, but he could not stop the ideas of Lutheranism that were spreading through Austria. In 1526, Ferdinand managed to accumulate more power when the Hungarian army was defeated by the Turks, as their king, Louis II of House Jagiellon, was killed. Ferdinand then found himself being the heir presumptive to both Bohemia and Hungary because of the marriage alliance from 1515. However, both of these crowns were elective, meaning Ferdinand had to hope that the local lords would vote for him. He used his influence and fortune to bribe the electors. In Bohemia, his win was straightforward. But in Hungary, he was contested by John Zápolya, and a power struggle began.

In 1529, the Turks were back, and in September of the next year, Suleiman the Magnificent led his army to Vienna. The Siege of Vienna lasted for two weeks, during which 100,000 Ottomans attacked the city, which was defended by only 21,000 imperial soldiers. The attack was a response to the succession conflict in Hungary, as John Zápolya sided with Suleiman. Ferdinand took control of western Hungary and the city of Buda, but the rest of the country was under Zápolya's control, so it became an Ottoman vassal state. When the attack on Vienna was repeated in 1532, Holy Roman Emperor Charles V summoned all the Christians, including the Protestants, to defend the city. At the time, Vienna was the symbol of Christendom, and everyone felt responsible for its defense. The Ottomans were forced to retreat, but they remained in Zápolya's part of Hungary. The following fifteen years saw Ferdinand trying to take control over the whole of Hungary, with the Turks fighting back and even raiding neighboring Austrian lands. In 1547, Ferdinand was forced to agree to a ceasefire, and he had to pay the Turks an annual fee to preserve the peace. However, Hungary was now divided into three parts, so peace was impossible. The western and northwestern parts belonged to Ferdinand; Transylvania was given to John Sigismund, son of John Zápolya; and the rest was under the direct control of the Ottomans. The fighting resumed, resulting in a military frontier between imperial parts of Hungary and the Ottoman parts, with each side erecting fortresses alongside the frontier.

But Ferdinand wasn't on the losing side. At best, the situation was a stalemate. The archduke of Austria stopped the Ottomans' advance, and he expanded his hereditary lands to include Bohemia and parts of Hungary. Bohemia proved to be a very profitable acquisition because the lands there were fertile. Bohemia was so rich that it alone paid for two-thirds of the annual payment to the

Ottomans for peace. But all this expansion of the hereditary lands and the constant Turkish threat led Ferdinand to think about recasting the Habsburg government. He continued building on the reforms started by his predecessor, Maximilian, and he modeled the new government on the Burgundian one.

The centralized government was finally in place in Austria, although not fully. Ferdinand was aware of the power that the local princes had, and he didn't want to antagonize them. Therefore, he only introduced the core principles of centralization, such as the Privy Council as a supreme executive institution, the Aulic Council as the supreme court of justice, and the Court Chancellery, which administered Austria. Later, the Aulic War Council was introduced but only so it could manage the efforts to retrieve Hungary. Bohemian and Hungarian lands were exempted from the control of the Aulic Council, and they remained independent of the Court Chancellery. In 1556, the Court Chancellery became an imperial institution that now had to administer the whole empire. Ferdinand had to allow the existence of the local governments to persuade the local nobles to pay the taxes that financed the wars against the Ottomans and Hungarians.

Ferdinand also tolerated Lutheranism in Austria, and the message of Martin Luther spread through the Habsburg territories like wildfire. The new theology was taught at the northern Austrian universities, and it was particularly attractive to the new generation of the nobles. The constant Ottoman threat helped the Protestant cause, as it moved the imperial focus away from the religious problems. But the Protestants also used the war to blackmail Ferdinand into giving them religious freedoms. In 1541, when the archduke called all Christians to help against the Turks, the Protestant estates demanded religious concessions. Ferdinand's response was very complex. As a Habsburg, he was the bastion of Christendom, and his role was to defend Catholicism. But pressured by the Protestants, he realized it would be wiser to strive for accommodation within the church than for uniformity, which would risk a schism. The Spanish Habsburgs used military force to deal with religious unrest, as they preferred Catholic uniformity. But in Austria, the 16th century saw much more tolerance and freedom.

When Ferdinand signed the Peace of Augsburg in 1555, he proved to be more tolerant toward new sects than Emperor Charles V. And although the peace allowed each local lord to assert his own religion onto his subjects, this wasn't the case in Habsburg lands. Ferdinand continued his policy of tolerance, and by the 1560s, as the Holy Roman emperor, he advocated a reconciliation of the sects at the Council of Trent, which was a council the Catholic Church gathered as a response to the spreading Protestantism, but his recommendation was rejected. In 1563, the Council of Trent condemned Protestant teachings as heresy and assumed a militant stance against Protestantism. Ferdinand didn't welcome such a stance because he realized it would only deepen the divide between Protestants and Catholics. His greatest disappointment in life was that religious peace was never reached.

In 1554, Ferdinand had provided for the division of the Habsburg hereditary lands between his two sons after his death. His eldest son, Maximilian II, would inherit the Bohemian and Hungarian thrones, as well as Austria proper. Maximilian was also named Ferdinand's imperial successor. Maximilian's younger brothers, Ferdinand II and Charles II, succeeded the thrones of Further Austria (the Swabian regions, Alsace, Vorarlberg, and Tyrol) and Inner Austria (Styria, Carinthia, Carniola, and Gorizia), respectively. Once again, the Habsburgs divided the rule of Austria, throwing the state back into complex politics and a poor defense against the Ottomans.

As the king of the Romans, Maximilian II continued his father's politics of religious accommodation. Although the Habsburgs were Catholics, as a young man, Maximilian was attracted to

Lutheranism, and Ferdinand believed that if he was allowed, he would have converted. That was why Ferdinand provided a strict Catholic education for his sons. In the end, Maximilian II stated, "I am neither Catholic nor Protestant, I am Christian." This quote displays all of his resolve to push for accommodations within the church. Once he became the Holy Roman emperor in 1564, Maximilian rejected the aggressive tactics of the Counter-Reformation and continued the tolerance policy started by his father. The result was the *Religionsassecuration* of 1571, the legalization of Protestantism for members of the noble families in Lower Austria. A similar concession was made in Bohemia, as the majority of its population was Protestant.

Part of Maximilian's motives for this religious compromise was his need for revenues that would finance his struggles in Hungary. However, relative peace came in 1568, which allowed Maximilian to pursue his rights to the Polish crown. He was unsuccessful in Poland because he had to redirect his focus to the renewed Ottoman attacks, meaning he now needed to collect revenues to reinforce the borders of his empire. The majority of the imperial estates were now Protestant, though, and they didn't want to give their money to a Catholic ruler. Maximilian II had no other choice but to reconsider implementing the Counter-Reformation's aggressive doctrine. This wouldn't be a problem for Ferdinand II in Further Austria, as the population there was still largely Catholic. In Inner Austria, Charles II was the closest to the Turkish threat, and he was forced to acknowledge the *Religionspazifikation* in 1572, which was similar to Maximilian's *Religionsassecuration* of 1571.

Maximilian died in 1576 while preparing to continue his Polish efforts. He was succeeded by his eldest son, Rudolf II, who had already been elected the king of the Romans, as well as the king of both Bohemia and Hungary. Although Rudolf was raised in the court of the purely Catholic King Philip II of Spain, he preserved the Austrian view of the world. Thus, once he became the emperor, he was ready to continue the accommodation policy of his two predecessors, and he hoped that he would live to see the reunion of the Protestants and the Catholics under the same religious doctrine. Rudolf moved his imperial capital to Prague, located in Bohemia, partially due to Prague being the richest province of the empire.

Rudolf II was not interested in governing; he preferred arts and sciences, and he became one of the greatest patrons of both. He delegated the rule over the Habsburg lands to his brothers: Ernest, Matthias, Maximilian, and Albert, who were all educated at the Spanish court. By dividing the governance between his brothers, Rudolf decentralized Austria. This brought diverse religious policies to the Habsburg territories. In Tyrol, the Counter-Reformation was fully implemented, while in Upper Austria, it was never very active. Lower Austria was very successful in implementing a full Counter-Reformation due to the efforts of Cardinal Melchior Khlesl, who expelled Protestant preachers from Vienna and promoted peaceful reconversion to Catholicism. In Inner Austria, Charles II's son, Ferdinand II, began the forceful reconversion of Protestants. The Habsburg lands entered the 1600s with more Catholics than Protestants, although they had to make serious concessions toward Hungary, which kept its religious freedoms. This was allowed so that the dynasty could retain its succession rights in Hungary.

But all these religious quarrels in Austria resulted in the loss of some of the Hungarian territories to the Ottomans. The blame for this was put on Holy Roman Emperor Rudolf II. Some of the Austrian estates supported his brother, Matthias, wishing for him to become the head of the dynasty. In fact, they proclaimed Matthias to be the archduke of Austria in 1606. By 1611, Matthias was also proclaimed the king of Bohemia, as he managed to gather support there as well. Rudolf and Matthias openly competed and warred, and the emperor was forced to leave Prague with nothing more but his title. He died in 1612, and Matthias was elected as emperor.

He reestablished Vienna as the capital of the empire, but he had more trouble reestablishing the Habsburg dominion over the Austrian lands. Local Protestant lords increased their wealth and power, and they presented themselves as a serious threat to the dynasty. The religious balance of power was also still in crisis. The culmination of all this occurred in Bohemia in 1615 when the diet passed anti-German legislation and forced Matthias to accept it.

Ferdinand II was elected king of Bohemia in 1617, but he faced much resistance from the Protestant estates. The religious tension escalated on May 23rd, 1618, when Protestant representatives threw royal officials out of the window of the castle in Hradschin. No one was seriously hurt, but the act of defenestration was enough to spark a war.

Matthias and Ferdinand found themselves on opposing sides of the conflict. Matthias wanted to make a religious compromise, but Ferdinand wouldn't allow it. Ferdinand also had the help of the Spanish Habsburg line, and they managed to take over the governance of the empire right before Matthias's death in March of 1619.

The religious struggles in the Holy Roman Empire started the Thirty Years' War (1618-1648), one of the biggest and bloodiest European conflicts. However, the underlying cause of the war was not religion but rather the power struggle within the Habsburg dynasty. It began with the conflict between Ferdinand II and his opposition in Germany, but it soon grew to include France, Spain, Sweden, and other powerful allies or enemies of the emperor. The war had an enormous influence on the economy and demographics of central Europe, but Austria was largely spared. Nevertheless, the war had a profound influence on the Habsburg dynasty. Their ambitions of political hegemony and a unified rule under one scepter were crushed by the military superiority of France and Sweden. Ferdinand II overreached when he tried to assert the religious position the empire had held in 1555. Not only did his enemies, the Protestants, react violently but so did his Catholic allies. Ferdinand II died in 1637, just when the war entered its final phase. By this point, France had declared war on Spain, and much of Germany was under Swedish rule. Ferdinand III, the successor to Ferdinand II, had to salvage what he could of the Habsburg enterprise.

Ferdinand III was a more pragmatic leader than his father, and he had to continue the war alone because Austria's greatest ally, Spain, was pressed by France. Sweden occupied much of Germany and Bohemia, forcing the emperor to sign a peace in the fall of 1648. The war between Spain and France continued until 1659, but the Peace of Westphalia, which was signed on October 24th, 1648, ended Austrian involvement and secured peace in central Europe. Austria had to cede territories in Alsace to France and Lusatia to Saxony. The war also resulted in the diminution of the Holy Roman Empire and the Habsburgs' role in it. Switzerland and the Dutch Republic left the empire, and the estates that remained became politically independent. They actually changed their status from estates to states. The empire looked more like a federation of different states held together by the elective office of the emperor. The Peace of Westphalia also brought an increase of power to France, Denmark, and Sweden and allowed them to meddle in the imperial matters of the Holy Roman Empire, to which they didn't even belong.

On top of all this, the French Bourbon family rose to power and surpassed the prestige of the Habsburgs. The Austrian dynasty lost the power it had once held in Europe's political scene, but the war was a victory for them too. It brought the absolutist power of the dynasty in Austria and the victory of Catholicism over Protestantism. The Protestants that didn't want to convert left the empire. Over 200,000 Protestants from Bohemia and 100,000 from the Austrian hereditary lands migrated to countries that tolerated Protestantism. The remaining Protestant nobles gradually converted to Catholicism, which brought an image of a model

Baroque Catholic monarchy to the Habsburg territories.

The Peace of Westphalia was also the end of the Habsburgs' dreams of a universal monarchy. However, the dynasty continued to exercise its divine right to rule in a new way. The trinity between the dynasty, the church, and the aristocracy created the Habsburg Monarchy, a new regime that had a profound impact on Austrian history.

Chapter 5: The Habsburg Monarchy

Habsburg territories in central Europe

Unknown authorUnknown author, GFDL <http://www.gnu.org/copyleft/fdl.html>, via Wikimedia Commons https://commons.wikimedia.org/wiki/File:Growth_of_Habsburg_territories.jpg

The Thirty Years' War created a perfect setting in Europe for the Enlightenment to bloom. As an intellectual movement that dominated the continent during the 17th and 18th centuries, the Enlightenment had ideas of how states should be governed. People all over Europe demanded constitutional monarchies, but some kings proved more difficult to persuade than others. The Holy Roman Empire was reduced to the Habsburg Monarchy, and before the Habsburg rulers could even accept the Enlightenment's ideas, they had to consolidate their power. In central Europe, the age of Austria's Baroque began, a time of religious and cultural hegemony that resulted in success on the southeastern frontier against the Turks. By 1714, the Habsburg Monarchy had established itself as a great European power. But the monarchy still relied on the traditional notions of imperialism, and the Habsburgs resisted the changes that were engulfing their European neighbors, at least for some time.

The Habsburgs had such a hard time accepting the ideas of the Enlightenment because they used the Baroque ideas to consolidate their power. Salzburg, a city on the border of Germany and Austria, was where the Baroque cultural style and political thoughts developed. The Habsburgs tied their triumph to the Baroque age, and it was hard to abandon it. Baroque architecture is purposely imposing and grandiose as if to show off the privileged position of nobility, who looked down on the peasants. The Baroque age in central Europe was the age of second serfdom for the commoners. The rise of the high aristocracy at the expense of the lower nobility and the peasantry allowed the nobles to amass resources for building lavish palaces, cathedrals, and summer residencies for both the royal family and high church officials.

The formation of the Habsburg Monarchy started with Rudolf I in 1273. Even while the members of the Habsburg dynasty were ruling as Holy Roman emperors, the Habsburg Monarchy existed parallel with the Holy Roman Empire. It had territories outside of the Holy Roman Empire as well as within it. Through the 17th and 18th centuries, the Habsburg Monarchy was a union of different kingdoms, which was a common practice in Europe at the time. But this union was only formally unified in the 19th century and became known as the Austrian Empire (later the Austro-Hungarian Empire). The term "Habsburg Monarchy" was created by scholars to separate the Habsburg dynastic rule of their personal possessions from their imperial rule. The Holy Roman Empire continued its existence after the Thirty Years' War, but its role was diminished, and the Habsburgs' influence in Europe disappeared.

During the Baroque age, the dynasty chose to concentrate its efforts on the hereditary lands while still holding the imperial title. France became the main European power, and the Bourbon dynasty surpassed the influence of the Habsburgs. The perfect example of this French dominion came after the death of Emperor Ferdinand III of House Habsburg in 1657. His son, Leopold, was elected emperor in 1658 but only after he bowed to French pressure and refused to help their Spanish cousins in the war.

Still, Leopold proved he could resist French dominance. Although he stayed out of the War of Devolution, which lasted from 1667 to 1668, and allowed French aggression on Habsburg territories in Spain, he was ready to fight in the Dutch War (1672–1679). But he really didn't have a choice as not entering the war would mean full acceptance of French dominance. Instead, the Catholic Habsburg emperor joined forces with the Calvinists and Lutherans to fight Catholic King Louis XIV.

But the Habsburg influence wasn't marred only by the French expansion in the west. The problems on the empire's eastern border took their toll. Although Leopold's army defeated the Ottomans at Saint Gotthard, Styria, in 1664, he agreed to a peace that was so disadvantageous that the Hungarian lords rebelled. Leopold was distracted by the French advances on his western border, and he had to choose between preserving the Habsburgs' prestige and defending the empire from the Turks.

Leopold was quick to suppress the Hungarian Catholic magnates' revolt in 1671 and imposed an absolutist regime together with a strict Counter-Reformation campaign. This led to yet another revolt, this time in the north of the country, where Protestants started a civil war. It was fought between the Protestant *kuruc* ("crusaders") and the Catholic *labanc* ("long hair," as Austrian soldiers wore long wigs). In 1681, Leopold was forced to make large concessions to the Hungarian nobility, and Protestant rights were returned. But the revolt continued because it was the Turks who had orchestrated the conflict and supported the rebels. In turn, France encouraged the Ottomans to attack Vienna, and in 1683, Grand Vizier Kara Mustafa sent a large army to besiege Vienna. The siege culminated with the Battle of Vienna, which was fought on September 12th, and the Turks were soundly defeated. This battle was also the first time that the Holy Roman Empire fought beside the commonwealth to eliminate the Ottoman threat to the Christian world. The war continued, but Leopold I was successful in defeating the Turks and returning almost all of Hungary to the Habsburgs. The imperial army continued marching south, and in 1688, Belgrade was taken. However, two years later, it was again conquered by the Ottomans. The result was the First Serbian Migration, during which sixty thousand to seventy thousand Serbs retreated, together with the imperial army, into Habsburg-controlled lands.

Leopold I needed the Serbs as soldiers, so he issued the first *Chapter on Privileges*, which allowed the newly arrived Serbian people to remain an independent political entity within the Habsburg Monarchy. The diverse patchwork of ethnicities that would become the Austrian Empire was already in creation. The decisive moment of the war with the Turks came in 1697 with the Battle of Zenta (also known as the Battle of Senta in Serbia). Prince Eugene of Savoy led the imperial armies and crushed the Ottoman army with only half of the numbers that the Turks had. This battle was also the last Ottoman attempt to take back Hungary. The Treaty of Karlowitz was signed in 1699 in what is today Sremski Karlovci in Serbia. The conclusion of war brought great territorial gains for the Habsburgs: the whole of Hungary and Transylvania. Only the small strip of territory of Slavonia and Banat remained under Turkish control.

The return of the Hungarian territories brought Leopold new fame in Hungary. Learning from his past mistakes, the emperor wanted to reconcile with the Hungarian nobles who had previously rebelled against him. He granted recognition to the Hungarian constitution and religious freedoms to the Protestants. In return, the nobility confirmed the right of the male line of the Habsburgs to inherit the Hungarian crown. Leopold also soon recognized the constitution of Transylvania, and in 1691, he issued the *Diploma Leopoldinum*, which confirmed the traditional liberties of Transylvanians, except for the Orthodox Romanians. Leopold I greatly expanded the empire, and he won the undisputed rights for the Habsburgs to rule these lands.

The Spanish Succession

At the turn of the century, the Spanish Habsburg line lost its last male with the death of Charles II in 1700. There were only two serious candidates for the Spanish crown: the Austrian Habsburgs or the French Bourbons. Both of these dynasties had legitimate claims to the Spanish throne through family connections. Charles II had named Charles VI of Austria as his successor, and he stood by his decision until the last days of his life. Then, the nobles who gave their support to the French dynasty convinced him to change his will and name Philip of Anjou, grandson of Louis XIV, as his heir. King Louis XIV approached Leopold I and offered the partition of Spain, but Leopold refused to accept the division of land that had been previously ruled by the Habsburgs, even though it had been a different branch. Thus, the War of the Spanish Succession (1701–1714) started.

France stood almost alone against the rest of Europe, but it was still able to survive the war with much of the Spanish lands under its control. However, the alliance of England and the Holy Roman Empire proved that the Habsburgs were a vital force that balanced the political power in the continent. The alliance won significant battles at Blenheim (1704), Ramillies (1706), Oudenarde (1708), and Malplaquet (1709), although victories were achieved on many fronts, such as in the Netherlands, Germany, Spain itself, and Italy. Even the colonies in the distant lands were involved in the conflict.

Louis XIV was prepared to sue for peace that would be disadvantageous for France, but the allies were confident in their victory, so they didn't accept the peace. Leopold died in 1705 and was succeeded by his eldest son, Joseph I, who continued the conflict. He died in 1711, and the imperial throne was then succeeded by his younger brother, Charles VI, the same Charles that had been named the Spanish heir by King Charles II of Spain. Continuing the war was pointless because nobody wanted the Holy Roman emperor to rule Spain since the power balance would be greatly disturbed. England made peace with France, but it demanded that the French and Spanish crowns remain separate. That meant that a non-ruling member of the French royal dynasty would have to inherit the Spanish crown. The Habsburgs still wanted to rule Spain, and they would have continued the war, but all their allies abandoned them after England stepped out of the picture. Thus, they had no real option but to sign peace with France in Utrecht in 1713. Charles VI wasn't able to fight the Bourbons alone, and he finally agreed to sign the Treaty of Rastatt in 1714.

The Habsburgs gained large territorial acquisitions with the peace even though they were on the losing side. They had to accept that they would never rule Spain itself or its New World colonies, but they were given control over European territories that had previously been under Spanish rule: the Italian cities of Milan, Sardinia, Mantua, Mirandola, and Naples, as well as the Spanish Netherlands. The combined effects of the two peace treaties, Rastatt and Karlowitz, allowed Austria to extend its power and influence in Europe.

The Pragmatic Sanction

The Habsburg lands were a dynastic union, and since 1665, they had no common ruler. Tyrol was under the control of another branch of the family, and although various attempts were made to strengthen the bonds between the Habsburg territories, the division of the hereditary lands was never really dealt with. Hungary became a hereditary possession only in 1687, and the need to establish a legal basis for the de facto union of all of the Habsburg territories arose. The extinction of the Spanish Habsburg line prompted Leopold I and his sons, Joseph and Charles, to make a secret Mutual Pact of Succession. This document confirmed the right of primogeniture for the male dynastic line, but it also added the female line. This means that the daughters of Joseph and Charles would be able to inherit the Habsburg territories if there were no more males in the family. But the pact didn't resolve the question of which daughter would have the priority of inheritance. Would it be the daughter of the eldest brother or the younger one?

To clarify this, Charles VI made this secret pact public in 1713, and he added a statement that the Habsburg lands should remain indivisible and inseparable. He also made it clear that in the event of his death, the priority of inheritance would fall on his daughters, not the daughters of his elder brother, Joseph. This additional document is known as the Pragmatic Sanction, and it provided the legal basis for the permanent union of the territories ruled by the Habsburgs. For the first time, the Habsburg Monarchy wasn't only a regime based on the dynasty's divine right to rule. The Habsburg Monarchy had changed from an idea to a single legal entity. But to make the document legitimate, Charles had to acquire its recognition, which proved to be complicated. Still, Charles VI dedicated his life to diplomatic relations that would bring legitimacy to his Pragmatic Sanction, and he even did it at the expense of the empire.

Leopold I's and his sons' actions proved to be prophetic, as none of the brothers managed to provide a surviving male heir. Charles's son died in 1716 when he was only a few months old. The only two surviving children Charles had were both girls: Maria Theresa (born in 1717) and Maria Anna (born in 1718). The natural choice for the succession was Maria Theresa, and Charles worked hard to secure the throne for her. Joseph I didn't have any male heirs either, only one daughter: Maria Josepha (born in 1699). Of all the compliant estates of the hereditary Austrian lands, the Hungarians proved to be the hardest to convince to recognize the document. Bohemia, Croatia, and Transylvania gave their approval without any resistance. If you remember, though, the Hungarians had previously agreed to make their land a part of the Habsburgs' inheritance but only for the male line, and they didn't like this turn of events. However, Charles successfully fought off the renewed Turkish attacks, and in 1722, he secured Hungarian approval. On December 6ᵗʰ, 1723, Charles made the Pragmatic Succession law in the united Habsburg lands. Now he needed to secure the recognition of the European powers, and in order to do so, he had to make some concessions he would have otherwise never approved. France received Lorraine in exchange for the acceptance of the document in 1738, Prince Charles III of Spain was given Parna and Piacenza in the same year, and Great Britain and the Dutch Republic saw the dissolution of the Ostend Company (the Austrian rival to the British and Dutch East India Companies). King Frederick I of Prussia didn't want anything in return, and he approved the document out of the loyalty he felt toward the Habsburgs.

Although Charles VI secured the recognition of his Pragmatic Sanction from all the major European powers, he did it with negative effects for his monarchy. Aside from losing territories to the parties that accepted his document, he also lost Belgrade, northern Bosnia, and other parts of the monarchy in the Austro-Turkish War (1737-1739). The only territory Charles managed to gain and retain was Banat.

However, the loss of these territories was nothing compared to the loss of prestige. The effectiveness of the Pragmatic Sanction was now questioned by everyone, and when Charles died in 1740, Maria Theresa found herself exposed to attacks. She was the legitimate heir to the imperial throne, but she had to fight for her right to rule.

Chapter 6: Enlightened Austria

Emperor Joseph II plowing the fields in Moravia (1769 depiction)
https://commons.wikimedia.org/wiki/File;Joseph2pflug_1799.jpg

Charles VI neglected the empire and left it with a weak army and an even weaker treasury. It was this weakness of the Habsburgs that prompted France, Prussia, Saxony, and Bavaria to repudiate the Pragmatic Sanction after his death in 1740. Prussia acted first and invaded Silesia on December 16th, taking it away from Austria. This loss was great for the Habsburgs, who finally realized that a profound change needed to be made in the dynastic governance of their lands. The Pragmatic Sanction was unable to preserve the integrity of the dynastic lands, but Maria Theresa first had to secure her succession. The War of the Austrian Succession (1740–1748) started. While her enemies drew plans on how to divide Austria between themselves once they got rid of Maria, she managed to gain support in Hungary. This brought her an army ready to face all of her enemies. However, this army wasn't enough, and in 1741, she lost Bohemia to Bavarian prince-elector Charles Albert. He was then proclaimed Holy Roman emperor, and he ruled as Charles VII (r. 1742–1745), crushing Maria Theresa's dreams of becoming the first Holy Roman empress.

But Maria was persistent, and she launched a winter campaign against her enemies. The same day Charles had his coronation ceremony, the Austro-Hungarian forces entered Munich, his capital. This was a surprise attack, and the Austrian troops were able to occupy most of Bavaria. Bohemia was the next, and it fell in December of 1742.

Charles VII proved to be an ineffective emperor, and he couldn't prevent Maria Theresa from retaking the Austrian territories. And even though Prussia had signed a peace treaty with Austria earlier in 1742, it became anxious in 1743 when Maria Theresa pushed her army toward the Rhine. Prussia invaded Bohemia, and in 1744, they sacked Prague. Charles VII died in January 1745, shattering the French plans of defeating the Austro-Hungarian queen and dividing the Habsburg territories, but they continued to fight for three more years.

Francis Stephen, Maria Theresa's husband, was elected the next Holy Roman emperor, but to achieve this, Maria had to recognize the loss of Silesia to Prussia. The war ended with the Treaty of Aachen (also known as the Treaty of Aix-la-Chapelle), which was signed on October 18th, 1748. The treaty recognized Silesia as part of Prussia, and Maria Theresa had to cede the Duchy of Parma to Spain and the Austrian Netherlands to France. However, King

Louis XV of France wanted to put a stop to the animosity between France and Austria, and he returned the Netherlands to Maria.

The Reason Takes Hold in Austria

When Francis Stephen of Lorraine was elected as the Holy Roman emperor, all the traditional lands of the Habsburgs were returned to the dynasty, except for some small territories in Italy and Silesia, which had been conquered by Prussia. Frederick II of Prussia also took the Bohemian County of Kłodzko. Maria Theresa considered him her personal enemy. She even called him an "evil man." Silesia was one of the wealthiest regions of Austria, heavily industrialized with a developed trade. Silesia was also a very large territory that acted as a buffer zone for the heartland of Austria. Personally, Maria Theresa saw the loss of Silesia as a blow to her prestige, and she was determined to reverse it with radical reforms.

She introduced enlightened reforms to Austria, but she was a traditionalist, and in many ways, she ruled in the style of her predecessors. Her mother was a Protestant, but Maria was a zealous Catholic, and she had no love for the religious sects that were present in the empire. Maria Theresa was determined to banish all the Protestants from the Habsburg hereditary lands, and they started escaping to Transylvania. Although the Protestants were not safe even that far away, they started secretly practicing their faith while openly claiming they had converted to Catholicism. This was a Protestant practice that started in the Habsburg Empire but spread to other parts of the world where Protestants were persecuted.

However, Maria Theresa was aware she needed to learn how to tolerate Protestant businessmen and financiers because she wanted to get rid of her father's Jewish bankers. Maria hated the Jews, and in 1744, she expelled all the Jews from Prague and, in the following years, from all of Bohemia. Various European powers intervened, especially the British, and in 1748, the expulsion order was revoked. But nothing could stop Maria's hatred of the Jews, and she even openly called them the "plague race."

Maria was definitely stubborn in the traditional type of rule that stemmed from the Baroque age, but she also showed a remarkable ability to open her mind to novel approaches to government. But the Enlightenment was a period of change in all of Europe, and the traditional Habsburg Empire needed to adapt to these new circumstances or perish in the past. The empress was also prepared to do anything to return the prestige and power the Habsburg dynasty once had. She allowed low-born advisors into her court and listened to their ideas of reforming the empire's administration and financial structures.

Friedrich Wilhelm von Haugwitz, one of Maria's key advisors, led the first wave of reforms. Prussia's administration of Silesia proved to be very successful, and Haugwitz wanted to emulate it. In 1746, he established the *Directorium in publicis et cameralibus*, which supervised the economic changes in all the lands of the Habsburg Monarchy and suggested changes where they were needed. The results were good, and in 1749, Haugwitz was appointed as the head of the *Directorium*, the new central administrative agency. This economic system was a radical centralization. Before it, the Habsburgs would leave the local arrangements for funding to the local nobility. This nobility turned into a new class of government officials. By 1760, their number had grown to ten thousand, and they had to supervise the state's economic activities. If the revenues proved insufficient in a certain region, the monarch would intervene. But not all regions of Austria underwent this economic change. Lombardy, the Austrian Netherlands, and Hungary were excluded because their local lords refused to be part of such a system. Haugwitz was against coercion, so the centralization was mostly concentrated in the Habsburg hereditary lands and the Bohemian crownlands.

The Diplomatic Revolution also took place during Maria Theresa's rule. Maria Theresa was dissatisfied with the British as her allies, so she turned to France. At this point, Prussia rose to be the largest military threat in Europe, while French power was diminishing due to the incapability of King Louis XV. However, France was still strong enough to be a decisive force to overpower Prussia. In May of 1756, the First Treaty of Versailles was signed, and the Franco-Austrian alliance started. Both countries promised they would help each other if they were attacked by Prussia or Britain. Prussia wanted to dominate greater territories, so Frederick II allied with Britain. At the time, Britain was rivaling France for global superiority and readily jumped into the ensuing Seven Years' War (1756-1763). Prussia was the first to attack, with Frederick invading Saxony in August 1756. France responded to this aggression, and Sweden and Russia, as well as the Holy Roman Empire, soon joined in. The Seven Years' War was a conflict that started due to the unresolved issues left after the War of the Austrian Succession, and it included all the major European powers.

Maria Theresa was too cautious, and she didn't want to risk defeat, as it would lead to more blows to the Habsburgs' prestige. But her caution backfired, and Austria failed to achieve any major victories over Prussia. Austria succeeded in occupying Berlin two times, but Frederick survived on both occasions, which allowed him to gather his armies and retake it. Meanwhile, France and Britain fought, mostly in their overseas colonies. Due to French policy to have the colonies defend themselves, without even financial help from the motherland, and due to the superiority of the British navy, France suffered crushing defeats overseas. French enthusiasm for the war diminished quickly, but it was the events in Russia that sealed Austria's fate. The new tsar, Peter III, greatly admired Prussia, and he didn't want to fight against Frederick. Russia sided with Prussia, but in 1762, Peter III was assassinated, and Empress Catherine II (better known as Catherine the Great) opted for neutrality. The same year, Spain (on the Austrian side) and Portugal (on the British side) joined the conflict, but neither of them gained any territory, although the fighting was very bloody.

France stepped out of the war first. Having lost all the battles in the American and Indian colonies, it no longer had enough revenue to support its army. Louis XV made peace with Frederick II. Without its allies, Austria was unable to achieve much, and Maria accepted the truth that she would never take Silesia back. But the other gains Austria had won were enough to prove that the Habsburgs were once more a major force in Europe. The Peace of Hubertusburg was signed in 1763, ending the Seven Years' War.

The conflict didn't change the makeshift of Europe in any significant way. It was a stalemate between Prussia and Austria. However, the failure of the war led the Austrian Habsburgs to rethink how they were governing their lands. The *Directorium* was reshaped into the United Austrian and Bohemian Chancellery, with Wenzel Anton Kaunitz at its head. He became the main figure of Austrian politics and one of Maria Theresa's main advisors. Kaunitz pursued the policies of the aristocratic Enlightenment, and he reduced Haigwitz's centralization, allowing the local nobility more financial freedoms. He advocated education for everyone and the taxation of the church.

With the death of Maria's husband Joseph in 1765, Maria Theresa made their eldest son, also named Joseph, her co-ruler. Joseph II became the Holy Roman emperor, and Maria completely retreated from public life to mourn her husband in solitude. Nevertheless, she remained the driving power behind the emperor. Joseph II proved to be a true representative of the Enlightenment ruler. He wanted to change the empire, and he wanted it quickly. During his lifetime, he worked tirelessly, together with Kaunitz, to reform the empire's administration, religion, law, medicine, education, and foreign policy. His eagerness proved too much for Kaunitz, though, and the two often argued.

As co-ruler, Joseph was allowed to deal with foreign policy, in which he excelled. Together with Kaunitz, he approached a reconciliation route to the problem of Prussian animosity. Maria Theresa objected because she openly hated Frederick II. Nevertheless, Joseph's involvement in foreign policy led to the First Partition of Poland in 1772. Austria gained Galicia and 2.6 million new subjects. In 1775, Joseph employed his diplomacy skills yet again and acquired the Bukovina region (now in Romania) from the Turks without having to start a conflict. But Joseph wasn't so successful when he tried to swap Bavaria for the Austrian Netherlands, causing the War of the Bavarian Succession (1778-1779) to start. Austria gained almost nothing with this war.

Even so, Joseph II is remembered as a true enlightened ruler because of his domestic affairs. Although he was a Catholic, he worked on making Austria a secular monarchy, with the government taking full control over church matters. Joseph was mostly concerned for the people of his realm, and he would often travel Austria incognito, meeting the commoners and even working the fields with them to learn the true state of the society for which he was responsible. This created a legend of him being "the people's emperor." His devotion to the people and the state was sincere, and he was ready to sacrifice his personal interests for the good of the people. He genuinely believed in the prospects of the social contract between the people and their monarch.

Joseph II's enlightened approach to governance he had was later named Josephinism. He managed to make Vienna the European center of the Enlightenment and one of the largest cities, with over 200,000 citizens. The intellectual and cultural life of the city, as well as its industrialization, started blooming. A medical school was established, along with many new hospitals opening.

The atmosphere in the Habsburg lands once Joseph gained the sole rule in 1780 was optimistic. Now that Maria Theresa was dead, her son was free to implement all the changes he wanted. His first act as the sole ruler was to bring freedom of expression to the Habsburg lands, liberating the press from censorship. In 1781 and 1782, he issued the Edicts of Toleration for the Jews in Bohemia and Moravia, respectively. These edicts were followed by similar ones in other Habsburg territories in the years to come. However, Joseph never dared to allow Jews to settle in Habsburg hereditary lands, though he removed the oppressive taxes on the Jews who had their businesses there.

In 1781 and 1782, the emperor freed the peasants by abolishing personal serfdom. This brought forth many agrarian changes, which also brought new prospects to the empire. The changes Joseph II implemented were successful initially, but they didn't bring much freedom to his subjects. Even though Joseph was an enlightened autocrat, he regarded himself as an absolute ruler, as did all of his Habsburg predecessors. He believed he knew what was best for his people, but the inherited Habsburg autocracy was a poor match with the reforms he intended to implement. The full abolishment of press censorship proved to bring much criticism to his rule, and the nobles and church officials threatened an uprising. Joseph was forced to reinstall full censorship in order to prevent a revolution, but he was unable to stop the crisis that arose in different parts of his empire. Belgium resisted the administrative changes, and in turn, the emperor abolished its traditional constitution. This led to the Belgian Revolution (also known as the Brabant Revolution) in 1789. Hungary followed the revolutionary trend once Joseph tried to implement a different tax system there.

Aside from the domestic crisis, Joseph II also had to deal with a renewed war with the Ottomans that had started due to the failure of his foreign policies. The war started in 1788, and Joseph personally led his army, and it was on the battlefield that he first contracted tuberculosis, which would prove deadly. In 1789, Prussia allied with Turkish, Belgian, and Hungarian rebels in an attempt to exploit Joseph's personal weakness. Desperate, in 1790, Joseph recalled all the reforms made in Hungary to appease the local nobles, but he failed to avoid the war or to settle the revolutions in Belgium and Hungary. On February 20ᵗʰ, 1790, he died of the illness that had tortured him for nearly two years.

The Austrian Empire

Leopold II succeeded his brother Joseph II, and although he was an enlightened ruler himself, he was aware he had to undo many of Joseph's reforms to assure peace. In July 1790, he made peace with Prussia, which ensured him the title of Holy Roman emperor. Soon, he made peace with Turkey, and he made many concessions to tradition to appease Belgium and Hungary. However, he managed to preserve the educational and religious reforms, which remained under the state's control.

It is remarkable what Leopold achieved, especially since it was in a very short timeframe, but his deeds were overshadowed by the events in France. The Habsburgs had a link to the French royal family, as Leopold's sister, Marie Antoinette, was married to King Louis XVI. Leopold was prepared to make a compromise with French revolutionists in 1792, but before that could come to realization, the emperor suddenly died on March 1ˢᵗ of that year. The throne was succeeded by his son, Francis II, and a new era for the Habsburg Monarchy started, in which a response to the French Revolution became imperative.

The French Revolution brought about a rational rejection of the past and an insistence on national uniformity. As such, it was a threat to the Habsburg dynastic rule since it opposed all the ideas that the revolution promoted. A modern nation-based state was impossible in Austria, as it was an umbrella regime governing many ethnicities. If the monarchy would fall, there would be no more Habsburg unity, as each region would demand self-governance. This was not a moment to promote radical changes but to retreat to the comfort of absolutism and the divine right of the Habsburg rule. Leopold had to abandon his efforts to base his authority on modernity and the ability to serve the people. And although reverting back to the regime that ruled Austria in the Baroque era served Leopold for some decades, the revolutionary ideas of national liberty and progress penetrated the Habsburg Monarchy.

Although Francis II took a more conservative approach to ruling, he left the bureaucratic and administrative reforms implemented by Joseph in place. He also issued the Criminal Code of 1803 and the General Civil Law Code in 1811. Francis may have been a conservative Catholic, but he retained the state's control over the church as well. Everybody expected Francis to take the same route as his predecessors and implement new reforms, but that didn't happen. The French revolutionary ideas poured into Austria, and although they didn't have much effect during Francis's early reign, they still stirred unrest. The Jacobin conspiracy was discovered in 1794 among Austrian and Hungarian soldiers, and their leaders were immediately put on trial. The result was the execution of nine and the imprisonment of thirty-one military personnel. The Jacobins were members of a radical French political party that dominated politics during the French Revolution of 1789.

When Louis XVI was executed on January 21st, 1793, Austria became aware of the French threat and the possibility of its radicalism spreading through Europe. At that time, Prussia and Russia concluded the Second Partition of Poland, but Austria opposed this partition because Francis was aware that Europe needed to stand together to defeat France. Austria reacted first, and in March 1793, it led a coalition of many European monarchies against France. Prussia and Russia were not part of the alliance, though. Although the campaign was a success for the coalition, the French revolutionary authorities managed to reverse the situation by recruiting citizen armies. French military success became even more gruesome when Marie Antoinette was executed on October 16th, 1793. To the ruling class of the European elite, it seemed the French would stop at nothing to get rid of them. By the end of 1794, the French took the left bank of the Rhine and the whole

Dutch Republic.

A year later, Austria, Prussia, and Russia concluded the Third Partition of Poland, which ended the national sovereignty of Poland and Lithuania. The dissolution of one of the major historic states of central Europe was overshadowed by the events of the French Revolution, and except for small, disorganized uprisings over the next few years, there was no reaction to the partition. Still, Poles emigrated in masses, and many of them joined the revolutionary army of France so they could fight Austria and the Habsburgs in order to satisfy their personal need for revenge.

The war between France and the coalition continued, and Austria endured many losses. In 1801, it signed the humiliating Treaty of Lunéville, which marked the further decline of the Habsburgs. This was confirmed in 1804 when Napoleon Bonaparte proclaimed himself the emperor of France. This was a direct challenge to the power and prestige of the Habsburgs. At this point, the title of the Holy Roman emperor no longer seemed guaranteed for the Habsburg descendants. Also, the very survival of the empire was questionable. Because of this insecurity in the empire and as a response to Napoleon, Francis II proclaimed himself Francis I of Austria, the ruler of hereditary Habsburg Austria, on August 11th, 1804.

But this new title he assumed didn't create a united Austrian Empire. Instead, it referred to all the lands the Habsburgs ruled, even though the territories retained their original governments and constitutions, which often differed from one another. The Holy Roman Empire still existed, though, and the Austrian Empire based its emblems and symbols on the Holy Roman Empire, showing that the new imperial title Francis took relied on the existence of the old empire. Their colors were the same yellow and black, and both had a two-headed eagle. Francis ruled both as Francis I of Austria and as Francis II of the Holy Roman Empire. But the fact that he felt the need to assume a new title only proves that the traditional empire was changing, and there was nothing Francis could do but secure the hereditary lands for his descendants.

The War of the Third Coalition in 1805 confirmed French superiority. Napoleon entered Vienna on November 14th, and in December, he ended the war with a crushing victory at Austerlitz. The Peace of Pressburg was signed, and although Austria gained Salzburg, it lost Tyrol, Vorarlberg, and Habsburg Swabia. When Napoleon structured the Confederation of the Rhine in 1806, he effectively replaced the Holy Roman Empire. On August 6th, Francis II formally abdicated from the position of Holy Roman emperor and declared the dissolution of the empire. In 1806, France defeated Prussia, and Napoleon asserted his dominance over Europe. The Habsburgs now had to find their place in a world that had abandoned most traditional imperial institutions and authority.

Austria was also no longer fully independent, and it had to do France's bidding. In 1818, the Habsburgs were forced to join Napoleon's economic blockade of Britain, which had mixed results for Austria. The textile industry flourished due to increased demand, but the inflated prices that followed brought poverty upon its citizens. Nevertheless, the peasants were happy because food production increased to meet the army's demands.

It was at this point that the idea of Austrian patriotism and nationalism started. In 1805, a new foreign minister, Johann Philipp Stadion, persuaded Francis I that the best approach to France and Napoleon would be to start an uprising. He had the idea of gathering a nation and casting off the French yoke. But Stadion failed to define the Austrian nation, as the empire was populated by many diverse ethnic groups. Stadion was Swabian, a German, and he alluded that German-speaking Austrians would receive the idea of nationalism the best. He started working closely with propaganda writers, such as Friedrich Schlegel, to shape the messages that would inspire nationalism. But the reaction of the populace wasn't to embrace nationalism; rather, they found patriotism. After all, many different ethnicities of Austria shared the same history and felt compelled to unite against their common enemy: France. Military reforms were introduced, and by the end of 1808, Austria raised 700,000 troops that were ready to defend the country, as well as 300,000 more that were available for campaigns outside of Austria's borders. However, the reforms were not yet completed when Austria decided to declare war in 1809. And the Habsburg Empire stood alone against France since Francis I had failed to secure another coalition.

The Austrian campaign was a disaster, but Archduke Charles of Austria managed to inflict Napoleon's first defeat. Despite Austria's success, Napoleon occupied Vienna again, and in July, he won a decisive victory at Wagram, leaving Austria at his mercy. The Treaty of Schönbrunn, signed on October 14th, 1809, reduced Austria to a French satellite state. Napoleon was in the position of doing whatever he wanted with Austria and the Habsburgs. However, his advisors convinced him that if the civilized world was to survive, Austria needed to survive. Instead, Napoleon satisfied himself by removing the outer Austrian territories and making the empire a landlocked state with a limited military force, which ensured that Austria would never again pose a threat to France.

Francis I was humiliated, and he blamed the reforms for the debacle. He removed Stadion and put Klemens von Metternich in his place. Metternich was an enlightened man who believed in reform, but his obedience to his emperor was his most valued trait. He implemented sophisticated diplomatic efforts that were to bring forth a reconciliation between Austria and France. He cast aside the patriotic ideas of Stadion and worked on the marriage between Napoleon Bonaparte and Marie Louise, the daughter of Francis I. Metternich succeeded, and the marriage was concluded on March 11th, 1810. A year later, Marie Louise had a son, which only served to cement the alliance with France. This came at just the right time, as in that year, Austria was forced to declare bankruptcy due to the war expenses, French occupation, and the war indemnity it had to pay.

As a French satellite state, Austria was forced to join Napoleon's Russian campaign in 1812. But Napoleon lost, and his defeat reorganized the European balance of power. This meant a new outlook for Austria, but Metternich was slow to react. Instead of immediately joining the alliance against France, Austria hesitated and offered to be a neutral mediator. However, in 1813, there was no choice but to join the Fourth Coalition against Napoleon. In May 1814, France was defeated, and with Metternich's diplomacy and by good fortune, Austria ended up on the winning side.

When the Congress of Vienna ended on June 9th, 1815, Russia and Prussia had the largest territorial gains. Austrian gains were modest, but they were significant at this point of history because by swapping Belgium and Habsburg Swabia for Trent, Brixen, Salzburg, and Venice, Austria became a contiguous territorial bloc. The Holy Roman Empire was not resurrected, but Austria became the leader of the new German Confederation, despite Prussia being the more powerful choice. But the Congress of Vienna didn't restore the old Habsburg authority in Austria, and the regime wasn't allowed to come back. Francis I refused to adjust to the new world order, and Metternich had to work hard on putting out any possible revolutions within the empire.

Europe rushed forward to embrace economic and social change, but Austria stubbornly remained loyal to imperialism. The restoration of the old dynastic regime meant that Austria's system would eventually collapse.

Chapter 7: Revolutionary Austria and the Dual Monarchy

Austro-Hungarian coat of arms (1867–1915)

After the Napoleonic Wars, nationalism and liberalism were on the rise throughout Europe. But in the Austrian Empire, Francis I would not allow social or political changes. He continued to rule as an absolutist, even though he was the least efficient of all the Habsburgs before him. There were some reforms, but there were not enough to appease the masses who demanded change. The national bank was opened in 1816 with hopes that Austria could recover after its bankruptcy in 1811. However, there were no tax reforms, and the aristocracy paid the least amount of taxes. The burden fell on the commoners, and each province was left alone to manage its taxes as long as they were paid to the ruling Habsburgs. The result was an underfunded army, which directly influenced what could be achieved in the diplomatic field.

Francis I died in 1835, and Austria was left to wonder about the European political scene without a sense of purpose or direction. Due to the traditional values of the Habsburgs, the throne was succeeded by Ferdinand I, the eldest son of Francis I. Ferdinand I, however, was mentally incapable of ruling an empire, so his uncle, Archduke Louis, acted as his main counselor. As a result of this unstable rule, Austria's cultural, political, and social stagnation continued.

But although it was unable to catch up with the west, the Austrian economy was progressing. The northern provinces were the first to see industrialization, with the textile sector being the fastest-growing one. But other provinces of the empire lagged significantly, and Hungary saw very little to no industrialization. Bohemia and Moravia had a fast-growing iron industry, and the empire introduced steam-powered engines for transport and communication. In 1838, the first real railway company, the Emperor Ferdinand Northern Railway (*Kaiser Ferdinands-Nordbahn*), opened, and it established a connection between Vienna and the mines in Krakow and Bochnia.

Within Austria, the relationships of the many ethnic groups that inhabited it were very diverse. The Jews were still banned from settling in Vienna, although the corrupt government allowed their unofficial presence. In Bohemia, they were still oppressed by unfair workers' laws, and they were illegal in many parts of Austria. Yet, their numbers were constantly on the rise, and by 1848, they numbered thousands, although only in Vienna. Nationalism penetrated the Austrian borders, and the state could do nothing else but to allow its minorities to research their national cultures. The political activity of the ethnic groups was suppressed, but they were allowed to practice their culture. However, cultural nationalism led to a political one, and the intellectuals and aristocracy started discussing their ethnic historical rights. In Hungary, Magyar linguistic and cultural nationalism reached its peak with the political drive to restore Hungarian rights. In response, Austria started emphasizing its German heritage, and the government forbade the use of ethnic languages within the official administration of the state.

Austria never had a strong centralized civil society, and each region started developing its social consciousness independently. Because of that, the political life of the various provinces developed separately. But this was not fatal for the Austrian Empire because the state managed to plant the idea of supranational principle, a state capable of asserting authority over all nations within it. However, the Habsburgs' only excuse for asserting their authority above all nations within Austria was their divine right to rule. In pre-revolution 19th-century Europe, this excuse was not enough.

The Revolution and Progress

On March 13th, 1848, a group of students marched to the Lower Austrian diet to present a petition for reform. They protested in the streets of Vienna, but the revolution started when the troops fired on the crowd, killing five people. Mass rioting began, and by nightfall of the same day, the Lower Austrian diet demanded Metternich's resignation. On March 15th, a constitution was promised to the rioting people.

The unrest had been building in Austria for a long time, so the March revolution didn't occur out of thin air. After the Congress of Vienna in 1815, the Austrian Empire moved away from the Enlightenment and reforms, causing social and political tensions to rise. But the more direct cause of the outbreak of violence was the economic crisis and hunger that affected all of Europe between 1845 and 1847. The first unrest started in Paris, where Louis Philippe I had abdicated. Other European states saw the power of revolutions, and they started spreading like wildfire throughout the continent.

The events in Vienna sparked secondary revolutions in different parts of the empire. They were "national" in character, as different ethnic groups started demanding their national rights. Slowly but steadily, Europe started taking the shape of a patchwork of self-governing, constitutional states. And the people were surprised by how powerful and motivating the reform ideas were. The feeling of euphoric optimism grasped everyone as the ideas spread, mostly due to the speedy communication systems established by the industrialization of the European states. The censorship of the press was weak, although in place, and it allowed Austria to learn of the success of the French Revolution of 1848 in a few hours. And after March 15th, everyone felt confident enough to act immediately. The Jewish rabbis demanded the burial of the victims of March 13th, and the Poles in Vienna raised their flag next to the black, red, and gold German one.

The people were filled with hope, but no one knew how to convert those hopes into reality. There were still no flags of other nationalities living within the empire, and due to German nationalism, Austria was using the German flag. The Frankfurt Parliament elected Archduke John of House Habsburg as the regent of Germany, but there were no clear instructions on how much of the Habsburg territories were to be included in the new constitutional Germany. Should Galicia remain German, or should it be a part of the newly reconstructed Poland? Would Hungary be allowed into the constitutional state, or should it be abandoned? Many questions like these were left unanswered. Czech leaders refused to join constitutional Germany because Bohemia had always been a monarchy on its own.

There were many "nations without history," ethnic groups who inhabited the territories of the Habsburgs but who never developed their high society and culture. They were always regarded as peasants by the Austrian, Polish, and Hungarian aristocrats. Among them were the South Slavs, Transylvanian Romanians, Ukrainians, and Saxons, although there were many others. These people groups had no history of statehood in the territories ruled by the Habsburgs. These "non-historic" people had their own revolutionary leaders, but they were unwilling to rely on the generosity of their "historic" counterparts and wanted to fight for their own rights. Some of them regarded Austria, without Germany, as the perfect solution for uniting these non-historic nations. Many of them were Slavs, and they couldn't possibly imagine themselves belonging to the German world. Czech leader František Palacký invented Austro-Slavinism, a state with a Slavic majority ruled by Austria instead of Germany.

But because there was no unity among the many nations in Austria, the revolutions of 1848 collapsed. The multiple ethnicities and the failure of the different nations to work together and demand the same liberal and national freedoms caused the revolutions to die out without much progress being made on the state level. The insurgent ideology was impossible to maintain in Austria because it led to a conflict of interests among the different ethnic groups. Once the Austrian authorities took control of the situation, it became very easy to exploit the division between the nations to reassert power.

The key to doing this was the army, as the Habsburgs still had a superior military. The Habsburgs sent their troops to crush the revolt in Prague, where the German and Czech nationalists fought. The Prague Slavic Congress that gathered in June 1848 was dissolved, and the Germans celebrated their victory. However, they celebrated prematurely; since the Habsburgs didn't want nationalism to rise, their army was ready to attack the Germans too. By using their army, the Habsburgs easily renewed their authority throughout Austria.

The Austrian Parliament Reichstag, or the lower house (opposite of Reichsrat, the upper house), met on July 22nd, 1848, in Vienna. It had 383 deputies representing the whole empire, except Hungary. Almost half were Slavs, with 109 representatives. On September 7th, they passed one major legislative act that secured the full emancipation of peasants. Although this achievement was a result of the revolution, it didn't come without a drawback. The emancipated peasantry would no longer be allowed to unite and join the conflict between the monarchy and the revolutionary forces.

In Hungary, the revolution led to immediate reforms, and the April Laws changed the economy, as well as political and social life. The imperial court had trouble accepting the Hungarian demands, but it really had no choice. The Hungarians set limitations on the political involvement of the minorities that lived in their territories, such as the Croats, Serbs, and Romanians. Croatian Ban (local ruler) Josip Jelačić, who sided with the Austrian government, refused to step down from his position when the newly formed Hungarian government removed him. Civil war threatened to erupt, but Vienna acted and ordered the Hungarian government to abandon its plans of raising an army. Jelačić took the opportunity and attacked first, not waiting for imperial approval. This conflict led to more revolts in Austria, as the citizens of Vienna feared they would be sent to join the army. They chased the royal family to

Olmütz, and some of the Reichstag parliamentarians had to flee to Brünn. The second revolution in Austria was crushed by Ban Jelačić and his troops, and the execution of the revolution leaders ensued.

The Habsburgs celebrated their triumph, but Ferdinand was persuaded to abdicate on December 2nd, 1848, and was replaced with his nephew, Franz Joseph. The public saw it as the Habsburgs' willingness to reform the empire, but in reality, it was nothing more than the speculations of Prince Felix of Schwarzenberg, the Austrian minister-president, who quickly formed a new government with conservative politicians. Franz Joseph was intent on implementing changes in his empire, but as all the Habsburgs before him, he was an absolutist. With the use of the army, Franz Joseph dismissed the parliament and the constitution they were working on. The disbanded constitution was supposed to act as a compromise between the German-speaking centralists and the Slavs who wanted a federation within the empire. The parliament planned to pass the constitution on March 15th, 1849, and in it, they would proclaim equal rights for all the citizens of the empire, as well as the division of the provinces along ethnic lines. This was a subtle way of solving the nationality problem, and the constitution's destruction left the question of the nationalities within the empire unsolved for another two decades. Two decades were more than enough for attitudes to harden in such a way that no compromise could ever ease the tension.

The new emperor wanted to preserve the unity of his realm, and he knew that this was impossible with national division. So, Franz Joseph concentrated on restoring the Habsburgs' power, and he succeeded completely by 1851. In Italy, the revolts were suppressed in 1849, and the Habsburg hegemony was confirmed. The Hungarian rebellion ended in August of the same year, with the help of the Russian army, which Austria had invited to intervene. Thus, the end of the Hungarian revolt resulted in Austria owing a great diplomatic debt to Russia, and it also ended in the complete alienation of the Magyars, who found themselves occupied by the Austrian army.

In Germany, Prussia took leadership in February 1850, but by November, Prince Felix of Schwarzenberg managed to persuade the Prussians to give up the German union. The result was the creation of the German Confederation, with Austria gaining the presidency.

Schwarzenberg died in April 1852, and Austria gained a new, more capable interior minister with Alexander von Bach. He was formerly a revolutionary, and through his work, Austria became a land where everyone was equal but subordinate to the emperor. He pushed for the emancipation of the peasants and the equality of all citizens of the empire before the law. The tax privileges for the noble families were abolished, and the whole empire was run by the bureaucracy in Vienna. However, all state administration work had to be done in German, even in the distant parts of the empire. These changes and innovations in the Habsburg Monarchy came with the New Year's Eve Patent (*Silvesterpatent*) of 1851, which was approved by Emperor Franz Joseph I on, as you might have guessed, New Year's Eve. The only community left out of the patent were the Jews, although their emancipation would come at a later date, a move that would bring Franz Joseph a reputation as a Philo-Semitic emperor. But during much of the 1850s, Jews didn't have the right to own land or to reside in some of the provinces.

All the changes Franz Joseph implemented were a move forward, but the constitution was still far from being realized, and the absolutism with which he ruled only strengthened the regime's criticism. But the major problem Austria had wasn't its domestic policies. Foreign politics was where the real weakness of the Habsburg Empire could be seen. Franz Joseph had no confidence in his absolutism, and he had no courage to levy the taxes that he needed to supply the army. In fact, there was no successful reorganization of the army, and Austria managed to spend its whole yearly budget in the first three months of the Crimean crisis, which happened in 1854.

Russian Tsar Nicholas I wanted to remove Turkey from Europe, and he invited Austria, as his ally, to join the effort and share the spoils. Franz Joseph declined, as he saw Turkey's presence in the Balkans as positive for his own empire, and chose to remain neutral for as long as he could. Although Austria was neutral, it alienated its ally, Russia, which lost the war in 1856 and was deeply humiliated. Thus, Franz Joseph was left without an ally when, in 1859, France and Piedmont orchestrated a war with Austria. It took only two battles, Magenta and Solferino, before the Franco-Austrian War ended, with Austria on the losing side. A well-funded European power could have easily brushed off the two defeats, but the underfinanced absolutism of the Habsburg Empire led to the regime's collapse.

The military defeat also left the Habsburg Empire without Lombardy, its richest province. The citizens of Austria completely lost any confidence they might have in the regime, and Franz Joseph was forced to abandon the absolutism he had pursued.

He still had a considerable empire to govern, and he had to find a new method of doing so. However, it would take him several years before he could put Austria back on its feet. Jewish bankers were now the only realistic source of funds, which means they were now in a position to negotiate with the emperor. Their stance was clear: no constitution, no money. Because of this, in 1860, the emperor started emancipating the Jews by allowing them to own property and granting them the freedom to settle anywhere in the empire.

In Germany, the liberal ideas of the constitution were becoming commonplace, and Franz Joseph's conservatism couldn't stand in the way. That didn't stop the emperor from trying to reach a conservative, federalist solution, though. On October 20th, 1860, he issued the October Diploma, which would decentralize the empire and give the Hungarians their original autonomy. However, the October Diploma met resistance among the Hungarian and German liberals and their banker backers, who saw the document for what it was: a mock constitution that, in reality, wouldn't change the situation in the empire at all. As a response, Franz Joseph employed a German liberal named Anton von Schmerling as his prime minister. Schmerling drafted a February Patent that declared Austria a centralized and German-centric state but with parliamentary and constitutional freedoms for its citizens.

Although Germans comprised only one-quarter of Austria's citizens, they occupied the majority of the seats in the new imperial parliament. The parliament's duties were legislation and administration, while the army and foreign affairs remained the emperor's prerogative (although the Reichsrat, the upper house of the parliament, controlled the budget for everything). Although it was not a completely constitutional parliament, the liberals accepted it and planned to improve it over time. However, the imperial parliament remained the basis of the Austrian government until 1918.

Schmerling further secured the Austrian leadership of the German Confederation, which brought around seventy million people under the direct control of the Habsburg ruler. During the Frankfurt Fürstentag (an assembly of imperial princes outside of the Reichstag) in 1863, Franz Joseph celebrated his birthday, and all but one German monarch was present. Wilhelm I of Prussia and his new prime minister, Otto von Bismarck, worked to take away the leadership of the German Confederation from Austrian hands, and they didn't see fit to show up for Franz Joseph's celebration. At home, the Austrians didn't like the German-centered politics of their leaders, especially among the Magyars. Hungary was not accepted as part of the German Confederation, and a national revolt started when it was proposed that part of Austria should be included in Germany.

In 1864, Franz Joseph decided to adopt a more conservative stance regarding domestic politics. He started negotiating with the Hungarian nobles, and to reach an agreement, he fired Schmerling and suspended the February Patent. But events outside of the Habsburg Empire paused the negotiations as war broke out between Prussia and Austria in 1866.

Two years earlier, Bismarck had set a trap for Franz Joseph I to lure him into a war that would bring Prussian dominion over Germany. Under the pretense of cooperation, Austria joined Prussia in an attack on Denmark. Germany-oriented Schleswig became a Prussian territory, securing Prussian dominion over northern Germany. Austria received Holstein, but both territories were to be under the joint Austro-Prussian administration. Bismarck took the opportunity to protest the Austrian government of Holstein and start the Austro-Prussian War, which lasted just over one month. Prussia allied with Italy, which already was at war with Austria, as it demanded the unification of Italian territories. Franz Joseph wasn't ready to cede Venetia to Italy, and his stubbornness led to the total defeat of the Austrian troops.

The peace was signed in Prague on August 23rd, 1866. Austria lost Venetia, but Prussia didn't want any territory. Instead, Bismarck demanded the division of the German Confederation into the South and North German Confederations. Austria was to remain out of it. Franz Joseph agreed, but Otto von Bismarck's real intentions wouldn't be clear until 1871, when the German Empire was created under the leadership of Prussia. The Habsburgs' involvement in German affairs was effectively over. And since Austria was no longer part of Germany, the Austrian-German identity was in danger.

A Dual Monarchy

After the catastrophic Austro-Prussian War, Franz Joseph hurried to settle with the Hungarians. He was relieved that the Magyars didn't try to exploit the Habsburgs' weakness that followed the war, and he gladly accepted all of their terms stated in 1864. The result was the Compromise of 1867, or the *Ausgleich*, a dual monarchy of Austria-Hungary. The Habsburg Monarchy was transformed into a condominium (a political territory in which multiple powers share equal rule), in which the Magyars ruled Hungary, and the Austrian-Germans, with the Habsburgs on the throne, ruled the rest of the empire. However, Franz Joseph would be the constitutional monarch of both halves of the empire. In Hungary, he would be the king, but he would be an emperor in Austria. Austria as an official name disappeared. It was preserved in the name of the dual monarchy as Austria-Hungary. The German part of the empire was known as "the lands represented in the Reichsrat," or Cisleithania. It was only in 1915 that the name Austria became official again.

The Austro-Hungarian Compromise of 1867 obviously ignored the rest of the ethnic groups that inhabited the empire, but Franz Joseph was ready to take the risk of a Slav rebellion to quickly reach his goals. And his goals were to preserve the dynastic power and prestige of the Habsburgs by seeking revenge on Prussia. He was eager to re-enter German politics, but the ensuing Franco-Prussian War in 1870 and the proclamation of the German Empire in 1871 prevented him from acting. At that point, Franz Joseph became aware that soon he would have to face the domestic issues of the multi-ethnic monarchy he ruled.

In order to federalize Cisleithania, Franz Joseph installed Count Karl Sigmund von Hohenwart as the minister-president of the monarchy. Hohenwart's cabinet proposed the Fundamental Articles of 1871, which were supposed to give more control of Bohemia to the Czechs. However, the German liberals and the Magyars saw it as a threat to the duality of the monarchy, and they refused to support the articles. Since Franz Joseph was unable to solve the question of the Slavs, he confirmed the Compromise of 1867, which would remain the foundation of the dual monarchy until 1918.

The Compromise of 1867 was an agreement between the emperor and the Hungarian diet, and it consisted of two parts: the "pragmatic" and the "dualist." The pragmatic part was a permanent element based on the Pragmatic Sanction. It confirmed that the monarchy was inseparable and indivisible. Austria and Hungary were, therefore, linked together under the Habsburg rule. But the rule itself was dualistic. The Habsburg ruler was an emperor in Austria and a king in Hungary. This duality implied that there was a bigger empire still in place, with Hungary as a part of it but also as a separate political entity. The result of the Compromise of 1867 was the establishment of joint ministries of foreign affairs, war, and finance. Two separate parliaments presided over two parts of the monarchy, but they were to meet occasionally in Vienna or in Budapest. However, the Hungarians refused to recognize these meetings as the "imperial parliament," as that would mean Hungary belonged to the wider empire. Instead, a compromise was reached, and the meetings of the two parliaments were formally recognized as the Crown Council. The emperor still had his prerogatives of foreign and war policies, with separate ministries controlling the military and diplomatic budgets. The economic, financial, and military agreements that the two parts of the monarchy reached were to be renegotiated every ten years.

Liberal achievements followed the Compromise of 1867 in both parts of the dual monarchy. The December Constitution secured the complete emancipation of the Jews by providing equality before the law of all its citizens, regardless of their ethnicity or religion. In 1869, the rule of law was established for the first time in history. Austria became a true *Rechtsstaat* ("state of law"), with an independent judiciary and Imperial Supreme Court. In 1875, the Administrative Court was founded, and the people were allowed to appeal against the state and its officials.

In 1868, the Army Act was issued, and military reforms took place. However, Franz Joseph resisted full modernization, which resulted in the army being unable to defend its country against more modern enemies. For example, the emperor was unable to understand the superiority of armored vehicles against cavalry, and he refused to include them in the ranks.

The German liberals continued the Josephist policy of anti-clericalism, and the power of the church was significantly reduced. In 1855, Franz Joseph gave the power over education and marriage to the church, but the parliament reversed this in 1868. Education was now under state control, and significant progress was made when elementary school education became compulsory for all children.

The economy also started developing, mostly due to the investors who chose Austria as a place to develop their industries. In Hungary, similar progress was on the way. In 1868, the Nagodba ("Agreement") was achieved with the Croats, which stated that Croatia was a separate political entity within Hungary. Furthermore, the Hungarian parliament passed many more national and educational laws to catch up with Austria's progress, although Hungarian supremacy can be seen in these laws. At the time, Magyars made up only around 40 percent of Hungary, but they made their language the main language of education and all the state institutions and offices. The national rights of the Slavs were ignored, and the Czechs boycotted the Reichsrat in protest. But their absence from the parliament only served to confirm the German liberals' hold on power.

Even though Austria-Hungary was a constitutional monarchy, Franz Joseph was still very powerful. Article 14 of the December Constitution allowed him to issue emergency legislation by imperial decree whenever the parliament wasn't in session. All parliamentarians were responsible only to the emperor, and it was Franz Joseph who chose the ministers of Cisleithania. Although foreign politics and the military were his prerogatives, he still had responsibility for the domestic affairs in Cisleithania. In fact, he was formally in charge of domestic affairs but chose to leave it to his

German liberal ministers. The Cisleithanian government remained loyal to the emperor, not to parliament. The aristocracy was also loyal to Franz Joseph, and although they were not the center of Austrian political life, due to their wealth and prestige, they remained immensely powerful. It was from this social circle that the emperor chose his ministers, and they dominated the Reichsrat's upper chamber (*Herrenhaus*). The large landowners occupied the majority of the seats of the lower house.

In 1873, events outside Austria-Hungary's borders took center stage. Prussian Prime Minister Otto von Bismarck was aware of the French threat to Germany, so he decided to form an alliance with the Austro-Hungarian Empire and with the Russian Empire, making the so-called League of the Three Emperors. This way, France would be cut off, and it wouldn't dare attack Germany. In addition, the three emperors could concentrate on resolving the issue of their shared interests in the Balkans. Bismarck planned to let Austria-Hungary take control of the western areas of the Balkans, while Russia would take the eastern ones. However, the differences in opinions were too great, and there was no settlement until 1875, when a revolt against Ottoman rule started in Bosnia. Franz Joseph wanted to take control of the western Balkans, but he intended to leave the Ottoman Empire in control of the rest instead of Russia.

In 1878, the Ottoman Empire capitulated, and at the Congress of Berlin, Franz Joseph demanded Austrian occupation of Bosnia. But the Hungarian diet, as well as the German liberals in the parliament, opposed occupation because they didn't want to add more Slavs to the ethnically unstable empire. However, Franz Joseph didn't back down, and the Reichsrat ratified the occupation.

The Transformation of Austria

Franz Joseph realized that the German liberals, who were the majority in Reichsrat, were standing in his way of achieving his imperial goals. In 1879, he appointed his childhood friend, Count

Eduard Taaffe, as his prime minister. Taaffe started a new regime, one that would help the emperor rule Cisleithania on his terms. The new prime minister persuaded the Czechs to re-enter the parliament, gained Polish support, and relied on the aristocracy to give their support to the emperor against the liberals.

The elections of 1879 saw the liberals losing the majority of seats in the parliament, although their presence was never completely eradicated. Taaffe's new ministry was composed of Slavs, German clerics, German conservatives, and even Romanians. The coalition of those who were previously ostracized from Austrian politics remained in power until 1893. The government Taaffe created was similar to the Italian *Trasformismo*, a coalition that was able to rule out the extremes of both the leftist and rightist parties. The center coalition governed according to the emperor's wishes since it was composed of loyalists.

Taaffe imitated Bismarck's politics in Germany, and with advisors, such as Emil Steinbach, who was the minister of finance, the prime minister passed a series of social legislations dealing with questions such as child labor, women and workers' rights, sickness, and accident insurance for industrial workers. In 1882, he also implemented a strict regulatory code for trade and crafts. But when it came to workers in agriculture, the protections and insurances were much scantier. This was due to the influence the conservative landowners had on Taaffe and his government. In the education sector, the prime minister chose to satisfy his conservative friends instead of following the needs and demands of the modernized world. The Education Act of 1883 was a setback to the reforms that had been previously implemented by the German liberals. The new law allowed peasant children to end their education after only six years so they could go to their family's farms to work. Taaffe also wanted to satisfy the Czech nationalists, and in 1882, the University of Prague was divided into two linguistic halves: Slavic and German.

Czech was made one of the external languages of the imperial bureaucracy, but it was used only in Bohemia and Moravia. This satisfied the Slavs and secured their support of the government. However, all the communication the provinces had with Vienna and the German officials had to be done in the German language. But, in practice, things were different. Most of the Czech officials already spoke German, and the German officials who were in Bohemia and Moravia simply refused to learn the "language of the peasants." Most of the bureaucracy simply continued in German.

In 1882, electoral reforms took place, and the lower middle class gained access to Austrian politics. This, as well as the modernization of the empire, changed Austrian politics radically. The Linz Program was founded; this was a political platform that called for the complete Germanization of Cisleithania at the expense of the other nations within the empire. This program became the basis of German nationalism, and under the leadership of Georg Schönerer, the German nationalism movement embraced antisemitism. In 1885, he even added an Aryan paragraph to the Linz Program, which stated that only those of Aryan descent had the right to settle and start their business in German-dominated Austria. By the end of his political career, Schönerer became an extremist, and his attacks on the Jewish-run newspaper, the *Neues Wiener Tagblatt*, ruined his career. Luckily, his antisemitic views never reached other ex-liberals and the parties they later formed.

Still, the nationality conflict in Austrian domestic affairs continued. The next prime minister, Alfred III, Prince of Windisch-Grätz, summoned a parliament consisting of Poles, German conservatives, and German liberals. The representatives had nothing in common, as they each had their own national interests. The conflict tore through the Austrian political scene until 1895, when the Slavic language was introduced in the grammar school at Cilli (modern-day Celje, today in Slovenia). Previously, only the German language was taught here, and the

German liberals took this as an attack on German nationalism, so they abandoned the parliament. Alfred III felt obliged to resign. Franz Joseph was disappointed by the political development among the German liberals, and to solve the question of the Slavs, he employed Polish aristocrat Kasimir Felix as the next prime minister. Previously, Felix served as the governor of Galicia, a Habsburg territory, which had a Polish Rutheran majority. As such, Galicia was highly autonomous, and the appointment of Felix marked the end of German dominion over the Habsburg Empire. Germans didn't control any of the key positions in the Austro-Hungarian government, as the minister of finance and the minister of foreign affairs also came from Polish Galicia.

In 1897, Kasimir Felix opened up the question of the Slavic language again. He tried to introduce the Czech into the all-German "inner service," meaning that he wanted Czech to become one of the official languages of communication within government institutions. The German reaction to this was violent, with university professors writing letters of protest and German government officials refusing to perform legislative activities. In November of 1897, the protests reached their climax when the protest against Felix turned into a street riot in Vienna. The protests then spread to other parts of the monarchy, mainly in German towns in Bohemia. The military was called to appease the population, but the situation only calmed after some of the demonstrators were killed. Franz Joseph had no choice but to dismiss Felix and form a new government out of German parties under the leadership of Baron Paul Gautsch von Frankenthurn. But Gautsch's willingness to work in the interest of German political parties only sparked the Czechs' response. The demonstrations and violence that started in Vienna under the previous government now moved to Prague. Gautsch was replaced, and neither of his next three successors managed to solve the nationality problem that tore the Austro-Hungarian monarchy apart.

Finally, on January 18th, 1900, the emperor appointed Ernest von Koerber as prime minister. Koerber refused to concentrate his politics on the burning question of nationality and decided to implement reforms to the economy and enact social legislation. Under his term, the press was freed from governmental control. But although Koerber managed to keep nationalism out of Austrian politics, nationalism among the population continued to develop. Soon, the different ethnicities started demanding their own universities within the empire; Italians, Slovenians, Polish, and others demanded education in their native languages. The Czech-German conflict was now expanded to involve all ethnicities. Koerber was unable to avoid the politics of nationalities, and he was driven out of office in 1904.

The politics in the Austro-Hungarian monarchy were further complicated by foreign policy. Austria's decision to occupy Bosnia only put the empire in danger of conflict with Russia. Austria signed the Dual Alliance with the German Empire, which was ruled by the Prussian emperor, and promised each other support in the case of Russian aggression. This alliance remained in place until the end of the Austro-Hungarian monarchy. In 1881, Serbia became a satellite state of Austria-Hungary, as it sought protection from any possible conflict that might occur between the powers that wanted to dominate the Balkans (Austria, Russia, and the Ottoman Empire). Russia had no choice but to admit the Austrian predominance in the western Balkans. But the Serbian relations with Austria-Hungary deteriorated in 1903 when King Alexander Obrenović was assassinated. He was the last of the Obrenović dynasty, which was then replaced by the Karadjordjevićs. The Serbian government wanted to unite all the South Slavs under its umbrella and form the Great Serbian Kingdom. The Habsburg Monarchy needed to counter these expansionist politics, so Franz Joseph implemented economic restrictions on Serbia. The ensuing Pig War (1906–1908) didn't manage to crush the Kingdom of Serbia. Instead, Austria-Hungary only pushed Serbia under

Russia's influence.

In 1908, Austria tried to annex Bosnia, as it was afraid of the constitutional changes that were happening in the Ottoman Empire, and Serbia reacted violently. At first, Russia sided with Austria on the annexation question because it was promised access to the Strait of Constantinople. But Great Britain and France opposed the Russian plans for the strait, so Russia turned against Austria and sided with Serbia. Austrian politicians pushed for war, and in 1909, they sent an ultimatum to Russia, forcing it to withdraw its support for Serbia. Without an ally, Serbia had to accept the Austro-Hungarian annexation of Bosnia. Although the Bosnian Crisis was settled, the Bosnian Serbs, who were now part of the Austro-Hungarian Empire, felt their national needs were not met, and they continued to stir unrest within the empire.

Chapter 8: The First World War

Archduke Franz Ferdinand in Sarajevo
https://commons.wikimedia.org/wiki/File:Minutos_previos_al_atentado_en_Sarajevo.jpg

The Last Years of Peace

The annexation of Bosnia in 1908 caused other Slavic nations within Austria-Hungary to react. The Czechs were already attracted by the idea of pan-Slavism, and in July 1908, they organized a pan-Slavic congress in Prague, intending to pressure Franz Joseph into creating a federation of all the nationalities that would be ruled by a democratic Habsburg ruler. They thought they had the right to make such demands because, at the time, Slavs comprised two-thirds of the citizens of the dual monarchy.

During the diplomatic crisis that followed the annexation of Bosnia, the Czechs supported the Serbian cause by taking the streets and organizing violent demonstrations. Martial law had to be proclaimed in Prague, and the army was summoned to appease the protesters. However, the nationalistic strife spread through the whole empire, and the government fell. The new prime minister, Richard Freiherr von Bienerth, tried to settle the situation by forming a cabinet that would include representatives of all the nationalities of the Habsburg Monarchy. However, the government remained under the administration of German Austrians, who claimed that the monarchy was founded on German heritage. They were opposed by the Slavs who wanted to make space in Austria for themselves since the census of 1910 showed they represented 60 percent of Austria's population. Although the Slavs were dominant in numbers, they were weakened by the Poles, who remained loyal to the imperial government.

Nevertheless, Austria was able to manage the nationalistic aspirations of its many nations and concentrate on the rising threat from the outside: Serbia. Austria's expansionist policies made Serbia the main proponent of pan-Slavism in the south. If left to operate without control, Serbia would be able to unite the South Slavs and claim Bosnia and Croatia from Austria-Hungary.

From 1912 to 1913, Serbia fought in the Balkan Wars, and during this time, Austria tried to force it to give up the territories it managed to acquire. Franz Joseph even contemplated military action, but he was aware he couldn't win without Germany's support. Although Germany backed Austria due to its own aspirations, Germany wasn't ready for war yet, so the emperor decided to postpone the war. When Bulgaria started the Second Balkan War, Austria-Hungary gave its support. In the process, it alienated Romania, which also had a territorial conflict with Bulgaria. Thus, Romania joined the efforts of many ethnicities within the dual monarchy to restore its historic kingdoms that were, through history, consumed by the Habsburgs. To prevent the empire's dissolution, Austrian leaders were convinced they had to act against the foreign powers that supported the national claims of the ethnicities under the Habsburg Monarchy.

In June 1914, Archduke Franz Ferdinand of Austria, the nephew and heir of Franz Joseph I, decided to visit Sarajevo and participate in the army maneuvers in Bosnia. He was warned that his presence could instigate hostilities, but he ignored such claims and even took his wife with him. The couple was assassinated on June 28th by a young Bosnian Serb named Gavrilo Princip. The culprit shot Franz Ferdinand and his wife, who were riding in an open car through the streets of Sarajevo. Princip was immediately arrested, and the investigation determined he was a member of a secret nationalist organization called the Black Hand. Although some of its members held high positions in the Serbian government and army, the Black Hand was an illegal terrorist organization.

Austria had to respond to the assassination of Franz Ferdinand because the Habsburgs' reputation was at stake. Since Prussia took over the leadership of the German Confederation and transformed it into the German Empire, the Habsburgs' power had been in constant decline. Franz Joseph saw this as an opportunity to put Austria back among the great European forces. Although not everyone agreed that the assassination of the Austrian heir was reason enough to proclaim war, it was the perfect excuse the emperor needed.

First, he contacted Germany to ensure its involvement, and once he received a positive answer, Franz Joseph and his prime minister continued to plan the war. But the prime minister of Hungary, Count István Tisza, opposed it. The Hungarians had warned the emperor for a long time that there were too many Slavs and Serbs and that they would demand the federalization of the state. But once Austria's leaders assured Tisza that their only intention was to crush Serbia, not to acquire its territory and people, the Hungarian Parliament gave in and approved the proclamation of war.

From July 15th to July 19th, 1914, a series of ministerial meetings were held in which a provocative ultimatum for Serbia was drafted. The ultimatum was defined in such a way that there was no way Serbia could accept it. But after fighting the two Balkan Wars, Serbia wanted peace. In fact, the Serbian government tried to stop the assassination of Franz Ferdinand once it learned about the plot. Two weeks before the Habsburg heir even came to Sarajevo, Serbia tried to stop the assassins but failed. The only thing the Serbian government could do was hope Russia would back them if war with Austria ensued. Both Franz Joseph and the Serbian prime minister, Nikola Pašić, thought the war would involve only Austria and Serbia and their allies, Germany and Russia. However, the growing nationalism within the dual monarchy, the imperialism of Germany, and the many alliances Serbia and Austria had previously made led to a war of immense proportions. World War I pulled all the great world powers into the conflict.

The assassination of Franz Ferdinand was the notable event that started the war, but the conflict had been brewing long before Gavrilo Princip even joined the Black Hand. The shifting of power in Europe broke some old alliances and started new ones. To understand the cause of World War I and who started it, it is essential to understand what the world looked like in the decades before the conflict. After the death of Otto von Bismarck, Germany renounced its alliance with Russia in favor of Austria-Hungary. Later, this dual alliance was extended to include Italy. But Russia feared that it would no longer have access to the Strait of Constantinople once the Germans found other allies. Therefore, Russia approached France. At first, this Franco-Russian alliance was started because Russia needed a new trade market, but it grew into military support that would last until the end of World War I.

France and Germany had been enemies ever since the Franco-Prussian War (1870–1871) resulted in a Prussian victory and the unification of Germany with the annexation of Alsace-Lorraine. Since then, France resented Germany but had no military power to launch an attack and gain its territory back. Since that point, anti-German sentiment and revanchism ("revenge") grew in France. Bismarck's ingenious politics isolated France, and even though the French had the will, they didn't dare attack on their own. Even with Russia as its new ally, France felt insecure about going up against Germany. However, after the death of Bismarck, France succeeded in isolating Germany by forming the Triple Entente, which included France, Russia, and Great Britain. At that point, Britain had separate agreements with France from 1904 and with Russia in 1907. This alliance is what made Russia join World War I, not its support to Serbia.

The Franco-Russian alliance only strengthened during the Balkan Wars, as France came to realize the importance of the region. If the Balkans would fall under the Austro-Hungarian Empire, therefore becoming strongly influenced by Germany, France would never stand a chance against Germany. This was why France started supporting Russian interests in the Balkans and turned its alliance from a defensive one to full military support, even if Russia instigated the conflict. In fact, France started encouraging Russia to start challenging Austria so it could speed up the conflict.

In the meantime, a German officer, Otto Liman von Sanders, was appointed as the general of the Ottoman army in Constantinople. The Russians saw this move as a hostile act against their Black Sea harbors. An agreement was achieved in January 1914 to appoint Sanders to the lesser position of inspector general of the Ottoman army. Russia was satisfied for the time being, but its economy continued to fail, and it had to breach new markets. This could best be done by acquiring the Balkans and challenging Germany.

The Great War

When Austria-Hungary sent their ultimatum, Serbia had only forty-eight hours to respond. The main demand of the ultimatum was for Serbia to stop spreading separatist propaganda against the Austro-Hungarian monarchy and to suppress all criminal and terrorist propaganda within Serbia. Aside from this, the ultimatum had ten more demands, with one being especially problematic. Point six demanded that Serbia allow the representatives of the Austro-Hungarian government to investigate the assassination of Franz Ferdinand within Serbian borders. This ultimatum meant that Serbia had to give up its sovereignty, accept Habsburg rule, and become an Austrian protectorate. Serbia accepted all the ultimatum's points but this one, and it still tried to achieve a compromise. The Belgrade officials proposed to open negotiations about the disputed point, and they even approached Russia to ask for its support. They were declined, as Russia and France were not ready for military conflict yet. The Russian delegation in Belgrade advised Crown Prince Alexander of Serbia to accept the ultimatum.

Britain and Russia tried to postpone the outbreak of the war and urged Austria to give Serbia more time to respond to the ultimatum. Britain even offered to mediate in the negotiations. Austria declined, as its only intention was to provoke the war, not to prevent it. Serbia predicted the great European powers would fail in their mission to extend the peace and started mobilizing its army on July 24th, 1914. The next day, Franz Joseph signed the Austrian mobilization order and the declaration of war, which was to start on July 28th. France ordered its troops from Morocco to return home, and Russia ordered a partial mobilization, perhaps still hoping to avoid all-out war. Britain tried one last time to persuade Austria to a conference in which the dispute with Serbia could be solved peacefully. Austria declined.

When Wilhelm II, King of Prussia and Emperor of Germany, finally read the Serbian response to the ultimatum, he proclaimed that there was no reason for war anymore. He realized Serbia accepted the humiliating ultimatum, and he ordered Vienna to accept Belgrade's proposal for further negotiations. However, the chancellor of the German Empire, Theobald von Bethmann Hollweg, sabotaged Wilhelm by passing on the emperor's message and excluding the parts that called for Austria to stop the war. Thus, the war was declared on July 28th, 1914, at 11:00 a.m. Two hours later, the first Austro-Hungarian bombs fell on Belgrade.

Italy, although part of the Triple Alliance with Germany and Austria-Hungary, declined to enter the war. After all, Italy agreed to a defensive alliance only, and Austria was the aggressor in its attack on Serbia. The start of the war was a disaster, and by August, all the major European powers were involved. The Triple Alliance expanded to include the Ottoman Empire and Bulgaria. The Triple Entente expanded into a coalition that included Japan and the United States of America, with Serbia, Belgium, Romania, Portugal, Greece, China, Italy, and many more countries as associate members.

It was amazing that the multinational Austro-Hungarian Army, which had many Slavs in its ranks, held together during the war. The Czechs mutinied, but since they were outnumbered, the mutinies were quickly dealt with and didn't spread. Regardless, the army was badly prepared for the war, and its underfunding eventually led to disastrous losses in the Austro-Hungarian war effort, which was led by Field Marshal Franz Conrad von Hötzendorf. The dual monarchy had the worst-funded army of all the European countries. The emperor's reluctance to modernize it also affected the end result.

Austria-Hungary failed to conquer Serbia by August, which was when Germany planned to launch an invasion of France. In fact, Germany ordered Austria to abandon the Serbian effort and prepare for the defense of the German invasion of France, as Russia would surely react. But Austria's command decided to fight the war on two fronts, against both Serbia and Russia. This was a disastrous plan, and by early September, Austria had lost Lemberg (today's Lviv in Ukraine) to the Russians and had to retreat across the Carpathians. Germany had to send help to Austria to stop the Russians, which was hard to do. The Russians were stopped in December with the Battle of Limanowa-Łapanow.

The end of 1914 saw the stabilization of the Russian front, but the Habsburg Empire had to pay a grave price for it. Austria lost half of its officers and four-fifths of its infantry troops in the initial stages of the war. The poorly trained and underdeveloped Habsburg army was devastated on the battlefields of Galicia, and although Austria had its shining moments during the war, it never really recovered.

Italy joined the conflict in May 1915 after long consideration of which side to join. When Britain promised Italy parts of Austria-Hungary that it desired, Italy declared war on Austria-Hungary, breaking the Triple Alliance. But despite this betrayal, the Habsburg army had success both in Galicia and in the Balkans during 1915. Lemberg was retaken by June, and in November, Serbia was conquered, though not without the help of the German and Bulgarian armies. In fact, the German Army was responsible for all the Austrian victories and gains, plunging the dual monarchy into subordination.

Back home, Austria-Hungary didn't fare any better. The war only made internal problems resurface, and it also had to deal with hunger, the poor infrastructure in place for providing the army with food and equipment, and press censorship. Rumors started spreading, and the public opinion changed from pro-war to anti-war. The Habsburg regime started losing its credibility among the population due to press censorship, and the nationalist leaders started operating within the empire yet again. And when the militia started arresting these nationalist leaders, the people's resentment toward the regime only grew. Those who still supported the war effort did so quietly, afraid they would spark the anger of their neighbors.

In 1916, Field Marshal Franz Conrad von Hötzendorf ordered a May offensive on Italy, which ended in failure, and in June, the Russians started winning again in Galicia. Romania, resenting the Austro-Hungarian Empire for the oppression of the Romanians in Transylvania, joined Russia. Transylvania was lost by August, and German forces had to intervene again. The Russian front was broken in September, and in December, the German Army entered Bucharest. With a completely broken army, the Austro-Hungarian dual monarchy was hardly an independent political entity. Austria had to admit complete military subordination to Germany when the joint Austro-German High Command was formed under German leadership. At this point, Austria-Hungary was considered a German satellite state. With its independence eroding and its very poor economic conditions, the pressure on the monarchy to end the war increased. Aware that he would lose his patrimony, the Habsburg emperor demanded peace by the end of spring of 1917. When the Austrian prime minister, Karl von Stürgkh, was assassinated in October 1916, Franz Joseph considered returning to the constitutional government and ending the war. He even employed Ernest von Koerber, one of his most able politicians, as prime minister. However, before Koerber was able to gather a cabinet, Franz Joseph died, doing so on November 21st, 1916.

The successor to the Austro-Hungarian throne was Archduke Charles I of Austria. Charles, who was an inexperienced ruler, came to oversee an empire while it was in its most severe existential crisis. He didn't understand the complexities of the dual monarchy, and he was unable to battle the threat of the monarchy's dissolution. Charles wanted to introduce a constitutional monarchy, this time with recognized rights of all the minorities who lived within the empire. However, he wasn't aware of how badly the internal problems of the state had deteriorated since the war began.

Charles was influenced by his pacifist wife, Princess Zita of Bourbon-Parma, and he tried to end the war by secretly negotiating with the Triple Entente. The emperor sent messages to France, seeking a way to pull Austria-Hungary out of the war, but the results were crushing. The Allies demanded that Austria admit Italy's territorial claims, which Charles refused. The emperor hoped he could repair the domestic policy situation by summoning the Reichsrat in May 1917, but the session turned into a forum in which the representatives of the various monarchies and ethnicities demanded separation and the formation of independent national states.

A revolution in Russia occurred in February 1917, which led to the fall of the imperial regime. A new constitutional government was introduced, and although the Russians tried to continue the war, their further involvement only caused more revolts. In December 1917, the Bolshevik regime capitulated to the Central Powers provisionally and did so officially in March 1918. Thus, the Eastern Front was sealed with a German and Austro-Hungarian victory. On the southern Italian front, the prospect of victory was near due to the Austro-German victory at Caporetto. They forced the Italian army to retreat to Piave.

With the Russian Revolution and the entrance of the US in the war, a new ideology rose in Europe, a democratic liberation of the autocratic states, such as the German and Austro-Hungarian Empires. Due to the spread of these ideas, among other things, France and Britain stopped caring about the integrity of the Habsburg Empire. In April 1918, the Allies organized the

Congress of Oppressed Nationalities in Rome, in which the fate of Austria-Hungary's many ethnicities was discussed.

The end of the war came in the fall of 1918, with events rapidly developing on the Balkan and Western fronts. Germany managed to knock Russia, Romania, and Montenegro out of the war, and it occupied large parts of the Balkans, Poland, and Ukraine. Scholars don't agree if there was a single decisive battle that ended the Great War, but there was one that turned the tide of the war and made it possible for the Allies to win on all fronts. The Battle of Dobro Polje (in today's North Macedonia) started on September 15th, 1918, as an offensive of the combined Serbian, French, and Greek armies. The leader and the main tactician of this small but effective battle was General Louis Franchet d'Espèrey. In the course of three days, the combined army of the Entente managed to destroy the Bulgarian units that were entrenched at Dobro Polje. There were around five thousand victims on both sides of the conflict, but the Entente victory was such that the Bulgarian army's spirit was completely crushed, with soldiers starting to desert in masses. With their victory in this battle, the Allies managed to knock Bulgaria out of the war and cut Germany off from its Ottoman ally. Within two weeks after the Battle of Dobro Polje, Germany started suing for peace.

Emperor Wilhelm II of Germany was angered by the outcome of the battle, as he was aware that without Bulgaria and the Ottoman Empire, Germany had no chance to win the Western Front. He wrote to Tsar Ferdinand I of Bulgaria, saying how it was disgraceful that a small army of sixty thousand Serbs decided the war.

After the Battle of Dobro Polje, the British forces headed toward Constantinople, and there was nothing the Turks could do to stop them. On October 26th, the Ottoman Empire surrendered. The Serbian and French armies pushed north and freed the Kingdom of Serbia from German occupation. In November,

General d'Espèrey reached Hungary, and an armistice was signed. Germany was now completely alone in the war. In Italy, the Allied army pushed the Austro-Hungarians back, and on October 24th, the Battle of Vittorio Veneto started. The Italian victory not only ended the conflict in the peninsula but also brought the effective end of the Austro-Hungarian Army, marking the start of the empire's dissolution. One week later, World War I came to an end.

The End of the Habsburg Monarchy

The Habsburg Monarchy didn't collapse because the European powers, along with the US, supported the claims for independence of the various nationalities. In reality, the Allied forces changed their reaction to the already-formed nationalistic movements within the empire. In January 1918, the Czechs demanded self-determination and complete independence. Only one month later, Polish and South Slav officials presented their demands for the establishment of nationally homogenous areas within the empire to the Reichsrat. Although these moves were decisive, the rise of nationalism alone didn't bring about the downfall of the Austro-Hungarian monarchy. Since the beginning of the war, supply lines had been disrupted, causing a massive food shortage in the empire. The hunger and the inspiration that came from the Russian Revolution instigated strike movements within the empire. The government was heavily opposed by the people, who demanded more food and peace. They were joined by the nationalists, and together, the civilians took the streets of Vienna, Prague, and Budapest. This civil strife spread to the army, and mutinies started. The demonstrations and unrests were successfully suppressed in January 1918, with the government resorting to the use of its militia and army. But it was then that the various national movements gained momentum.

The Austro-Hungarian government concluded the peace in the Eastern Front with Ukraine in February 1918, Russia in March, and Romania in May. But this wasn't enough to appease the civil strife back home. The people demanded a full end to the war. The Poles were especially irritated, as the Treaty of Brest-Litovsk, which was signed with Ukraine, deprived them of some of their territories. The food supply situation didn't improve either, and people continued to feel resentment toward the emperor and the government. But the government was in a difficult position. With Charles's secret peace talks with the Allies now publicized, the emperor had to assure Germany that Austria was still loyal. This act was hailed by the German Austrians, but the Slavs were outraged. Charles and his government officials were oblivious of the effect the Slavs' dissatisfaction would have on the empire. In May 1918, a national Slavic celebration was organized in Prague, and the sheer amount of people on the streets should have been a warning to the emperor of the strength the Czech independence movement had.

By July 1918, the Austrian prime minister, Ernst Seidler, resigned, making room for Max Hussarek, who tried to reorganize the Austro-Hungarian monarchy. He proposed the creation of an autonomous Croatian state within the empire, but Charles already decided on complete federalization. On October 16th, Hussarek proclaimed Austria a federation of four parts: German, Czech, South Slav, and Ukrainian. The Poles and their territories were to be joined with a Polish state, and he met strong Hungarian opposition because the Hungarian lands were to be exempted from the program.

Provincial councils were established in all provinces of the empire, but within days, they started acting as national governments. The Poles were the first to proclaim the union with Poland on October 7th. The next was the Czechs, who proclaimed an independent republic on October 28th. A day later, the Croatian Parliament announced a union with Serbia. The Habsburg Empire had essentially dissolved before the Great War ended. By that time, the Austrian government was aware of the defeat that was about to happen. On October 27th, Foreign Minister Count Gyula Andrássy sent a message to US President Woodrow Wilson, asking for an armistice. In return, he recognized the sovereignty of the newly founded Czechoslovakian state. With the empire dissolved and an armistice in progress, Austria could only wait for the final moments of the war.

Still, the hopes of saving the Habsburg Monarchy lingered. Heinrich Lammasch founded a new cabinet on October 22nd. He was a pacifist, and he hoped he still had the time to persuade the many nations of the Austro-Hungarian Empire to stay in the federation. However, he ended up only supervising the empire's dissolution. The government and the emperor had no influence on the events that happened outside Vienna, and they signed an armistice on November 3rd, 1918. By this time, even the German Austrians had lost faith in the Habsburg dynasty and would no longer accept being ruled by its representatives. On November 11th, Charles took the advice of his new prime minister, Lammasch, and effectively abdicated the throne, though the word "abdication" was never formally used. Privately, Charles believed in his divine right to rule, and it seems he hoped that the loyal citizens of either Austria or Hungary would call him back.

But that didn't happen. The next day, the Republic of German-Austria was established, and on November 16th, Hungary announced its independence and the formation of the First Hungarian Republic. Yet, Charles continued to pursue his right to rule, and he claimed that the Republic of German-Austria did not impede his right to rule. However, on April 3rd, 1919, the German-Austrian government issued the Habsburg Law, which officially dethroned and banished the dynasty.

The Austro-Hungarian Empire wasn't the only monarchy that didn't survive the Great War. In Russia, the Bolsheviks overthrew the imperial Romanov dynasty; in Germany, the ruling Hohenzollerns fell; and the Ottoman Empire was effectively dissolved. However, all of these empires continued to live in different forms. Only the Habsburg Empire virtually disappeared with Poland's, Romania's, and Italy's restoration and with the formation of the Kingdom of Yugoslavia (also known as the Kingdom of the Serbs, Croats, and Slovenes). Czechoslovakia and Hungary were only interested in governing their historic territories, and the rest of Austria was integrated into German-Austria. This was a simple collection of German-speaking Austrian provinces, but they didn't see themselves as an independent nation. Their initial plan was to be absorbed by the German Republic since they didn't want to be associated with the Habsburgs anymore.

But the fate of Austria wasn't yet sealed, and these provinces would succeed and continue to bear the responsibility and heritage of the great power the Austro-Hungarian Empire once held.

Chapter 9: The Second World War

Soviet soldiers at Schönbrunn Palace in Vienna (1945)

The First Austrian Republic

The Republic of German-Austria was a leftover state, a piece of the Habsburg Empire no one wanted. Its existence was announced on November 12th, 1918, by the assembly of the German Reichsrat members. The Treaty of Versailles, which was signed on June 28th, 1919, rewarded the national leadership that sided with the Triple Alliance with the territories of the former Austro-Hungarian monarchy. Hungary was reduced to one-third of its previous territory. This left many ethnic Magyars outside of the borders of their home country. Transylvania was now Romanian, and Vojvodina belonged to the Kingdom of Yugoslavia. Much of Carinthia, Slovene Carniola, and southern Styria also became part of the Kingdom of Yugoslavia. Something similar happened in Bohemia, where many German Austrians found themselves living across the border, trapped in the newly formed Czechoslovakian state. But for Austria, the worst was its loss to Italy, which gained not only the Italian-speaking areas of the monarchy but also the German-speaking part of Tyrol (south of Brenner Pass) and part of Carinthia. At the time, the Austrian government claimed that only six million out of ten and a half million German Austrians lived within the borders of Austria.

What remained of the Austro-Hungarian Empire was now in a severe identity crisis. The German Austrians wished to distance themselves from their past and the Habsburg Monarchy, and in May 1919, Vorarlberg voted to join Switzerland. However, since Switzerland didn't want them and since Vienna disregarded the vote, they remained Austrian. Nevertheless, many of its citizens refused to identify as Austrian, and they claimed German or Swiss heritage instead. On March 12th, 1919, the newly elected national assembly of Austria even declared that Austria was a part of the German Republic.

But the Allies wouldn't allow that to happen. In the eyes of France, the blame for World War I was to be solely put on

Germany, and it would be absurd to allow it to grow past what it used to be before 1914. The Triple Entente forbade the union of Austria and Germany, even though it conflicted with their principles of creating nation states. The union of Austria and Germany, the so-called *Anschluss*, became the central point of Austrian politics, and it would be realized in 1938 when Adolf Hitler was in power.

And it seems the Allies weren't content on simply denying the German national basis for the new state, as they also banned the name the state assumed, "German Austria." Instead, the Allies persisted for the new state to be named the Austrian Republic, and it became the First Austrian Republic in September 1919. It didn't matter that its citizens renounced the Habsburgs and their rule and didn't want to be associated with the Habsburg Empire. The Allies saw them as heirs to the old Austrian monarchy, and that was precisely how they were treated.

The four years of war brought economic disaster to Austria. The result was poverty and social distress. Riots and demonstrations started, and the threat of a revolution became real. Bolshevism was now the greatest danger for the newly founded Republic of German-Austria, especially when the Hungarian Soviet Republic was established on March 21st, 1919. The communists within Austria attempted a putsch (coup) on two occasions, April 17th and June 15th. But the Austrian Social Democrats and their chancellor, Karl Renner, organized the Volkswehr (the People's Guard), a semi-regular army that actively suppressed the communists' attempts of taking over the republic. By mid-1919, the Communist Party of Austria was defeated, and political and social order were reintroduced in the republic.

On October 1st, 1920, the First Austrian Republic settled its constitution. The State Council was abolished, and a bicameral legislative assembly was formed. The upper house, *Bundesrat*, was elected according to the population of each state. It had the power to use a suspensive veto on all legislature. The lower house, *Nationalrat*, was elected by universal suffrage. Thus, the *Bundesversammlung*, or the Austrian Parliament, was founded. It had the power to elect the president of the republic, who would serve a four-year term. The federal government and its chancellor were elected by the lower house. But although the Austrian Republic finally took shape, the *Anschluss* remained its main policy. The activity of various political parties turned public opinion in support of the union, but according to the Treaty of Saint-Germain-en-Laye, which was signed in September 1919, Austria was not allowed to join Germany without the consent of the League of Nations.

With the constitution in place, new elections took place in the summer of 1920, and the Christian Socialists won. The Social Democrats came second and German Nationalists third. Since the Christian Socialists won eighty-two seats, they formed a cabinet, and the Socialist Democrats became their opposition. The political division within Austria hardened in the following years, but there were no major changes to the political scene of the First Austrian Republic. Although the urban middle class was at first dormant, it started gathering around the German Nationalist Party, and in subsequent years, the party was joined by many workers and peasants who felt they were German. During the 1920s, though, they were not strong enough to inflict major political and social changes.

The new Austrian government's main task was to recover the economy. After the war, the Austrians lived on relief supplies they received from Britain and the United States. Production within Austria improved, but the demand was so great that in 1922, inflation occurred, threatening a financial collapse. Chancellor Ignaz Seipel secured a large international loan to stabilize the Austrian economy. In return, he promised Austria would remain an independent republic for at least the next twenty years. A period of stability and economic recovery started, and the Social

Democratic Party, which was in control of Vienna, started a housing and education program for the worker class.

Three major political parties existed in Austria during 1920, and although they had very democratic platforms, each prepared for the possibility of civil war. The Christian Socialists believed in a strong government and believed they had to maintain the social order against the Marxist revolutionaries. In the provinces, a Home Defense Force (the *Heimwehr*) was organized to defend themselves against the Slavs, but they slowly started becoming a fascist organization. The Social Democrats believed their social program was endangered, and they started their defense by transforming the People's Guard into the Defense League (the *Schutzbund*). The Home Defense Force and the Defense League often clashed, and their first innocent victims were an old man and a child who died during a riot in Schattendorf in 1927. Members of the Home Defense were accused of the murder, but they were freed by the Vienna jury. In response, the Social Democrats organized protests and mass demonstrations. The result was the burning of the ministry of justice, and one hundred people were killed in the exchange of blows between police and demonstrators. The Social Democrats escalated the situation by launching a general strike and prompting Seipel to answer with violence. The social order was restored, but the relations between the socialists and nonsocialists in Austria continued to deteriorate.

In December 1929, the parliament issued a series of constitutional changes that elevated the position of the president of the republic. The president now had the power to appoint ministers and issue emergency decrees. The next year, the Social Democrats won the elections, and they formed their cabinet. However, the events in domestic politics were overshadowed by the emergence of the Great Depression, an economic crisis that engulfed the whole world. In the spring of 1931, the government's leaders, Johann Schober and Otto Ender, tried to push for a union with Germany in the hopes it would help them avoid economic collapse. But the strong opposition of the foreign forces (mainly France, Romania, and Serbia) prevented the union from happening. In May, Austria's most influential bank, the Creditanstalt, declared bankruptcy, and with this, the financial and economic disaster of the republic was imminent.

The German National Socialist Party gave financial support to the Austrian Nazi Party, which resulted in the growth of the party. In 1932, they started demanding general elections, which were organized on May 20th. But the Christian Socialists won, and Engelbert Dollfuss filled his cabinet with conservatives.

Authoritarianism on the Rise

The Great Depression forced Engelbert Dollfuss to obtain another national loan from the League of Nations, but he had to make a promise that Austria would not seek any form of unification with Germany. That meant that even a customs union was out of the question. Austria started recovering in the financial sector, but it was unable to fully rise out of the economic disaster that was the Great Depression. Dollfuss's promise only served to divide the country on a political level. The Social Democrats, German Nationalists, and National Socialists (Nazis)s protested Dollfuss's decision, calling it a "surrender to the western powers." The political parties' private armies continued to cause mayhem on the streets of major cities, with shootings and bombings often occurring. Even though things were bad in the Austrian political scene, it was overshadowed by the events in Germany, where the Nazis were on the rise. The economic misery in Austria led people to believe the country wouldn't be able to sustain itself, and a union with Germany became ever more attractive.

When Hitler became the German chancellor on January 30th, 1933, the threat of Nazism breaching in Austria became real. In response, Dollfuss decided to exploit the constitutional crisis that occurred on March 4th when all three presidents of the assembly resigned. Dollfuss proclaimed that the parliament was no longer in function. The Christian Socialists abandoned parliamentary ideals and started instituting an authoritarian form of government known as "Austrofascism." This was Dollfuss's attempt to form an anti-Nazi government, but Hitler responded by implementing a tax on all Germans who wanted to enter Austria.

Dollfuss proved to be courageous with his dealings with Nazi Germany. Instead of giving in to bullying, he modeled Austria in the image of Italy's and Hungary's fascism. He used the pro-fascist *Heimwehr* to fight the Social Democrats. In February 1934, a four-day-long civil war broke out, and the *Heimwehr* won, allowing Dollfuss to proclaim the Social Democrats illegal. Soon enough, all political parties, except the Fatherland Front (*Vaterländische Front*), were abolished. But the Fatherland Front was nothing more but Christian Socialists in new clothes.

In the parliament session of April 1934, an authoritarian constitution was accepted. All the elected assemblies were disbanded, and democratic human rights policies were removed. This authoritarian parliament had both executive and legislative powers. The First Austrian Republic also changed its name, becoming the Federal State of Austria.

On July 25th, 1934, Dollfuss was murdered by a group of Nazis, who breached the Chancellery and proclaimed their own government. The assassination of the Austrian leader caused international outrage, and the Austrian Nazi leaders were compelled to surrender. They were all executed. Hitler was unable to react because Italy's leader, Benito Mussolini, and the leaders of other European nations threw their support to Austria. Regardless of the world's condemnation, the economic success of Hitler's Germany led the Austrian population to become loyal to the Nazi movement. The Third Reich seemed far more impressive than the authoritarian government of Dolfuss's successor, Kurt Schuschnigg. The development of the Austrian economy was slow. Although the shilling was strong, the financial state of the citizens barely improved, and there were no new job openings in sight. The unemployment rate had remained around 20 percent since the end of World War I.

In foreign politics, Austria mostly relied on fascist Italy, which was ideologically similar to Austria. Britain and France were supportive of Austria's denunciation of Hitler's Nazism, but they did little to support Austrofascism. Italy, France, and Britain formed the Stresa Front in April 1935 to oppose Hitler's mobilization of Germany, which violated the Treaty of Versailles. But in October 1935, Italy invaded the Ethiopian Empire and lost the support of the Western powers, and the Stresa Front collapsed. Mussolini started approaching Hitler, and an alliance was formed a year later, in October 1936.

Austria was trapped between the two powers. Unable to leave its ally of Italy, Austria had to consider approaching Germany peacefully. Mussolini managed to persuade Schuschnigg to consider collaborating with Hitler. In reality, Schuschnigg had to comply, as Austria was bound to Italy by the Rome Protocols of 1934. On July 11th, 1936, Germany recognized Austrian sovereignty and lifted the tourist tax. But Hitler never intended to keep his promise that he wouldn't intervene in Austrian politics, which means Austrian independence was coming to an end. In return for the recognition of sovereignty, Austria promised that it would stop all anti-Nazi propaganda and that it would release all Nazi prisoners, roughly seventeen thousand of them. Schuschnigg also allowed the *Heimwehr's* influence to diminish in favor of German nationalism. This led to Hitler's acceptance into Austria's fascist political and social circles. By October, all the militias were dissolved, including the *Heimwehr*.

After Italy became a German ally, it was no longer concerned with keeping Austrian integrity. When Germany promised South Tyrol to Italy, it became obvious that Hitler intended to occupy Austria and that Mussolini would allow it. Schuschnigg was aware he had no foreign support, so he formed the Volkspolitisches Referat with the intention to preserve Austrian national interests. However, the majority of the Referat's members were loyal to Germany.

Hitler's Four-Year Plan to prepare Germany for World War II was well underway by this point, but it became obvious Germany didn't have enough resources to supply its army. The Germans needed access to the Austrian steelwork industry and raw resources. The chief-in-command of the Four-Year Plan, Hermann Göring, pushed for the union of Austria and Germany. On February 12th, 1938, Schuschnigg met Hitler, hoping he could persuade the German leader to abandon his unification plans. But in return, he was presented with a set of demands. For Hitler to reaffirm the national integrity and sovereignty of Austria, Schuschnigg had to allow Nazi officials to take over key governmental positions within Austria. Police were to be under direct Nazi command, and Nazi supporter Arthur Seyss-Inquart would become the minister of national security. When Schuschnigg announced his plans of organizing a referendum to deal with the question of unifying with Germany, Hitler demanded his resignation as chancellor. Under the threat of German invasion, Kurt Schuschnigg sought help from France and Britain, but he received none. To avoid bloodshed, he was forced to resign on March 11th, 1938, allowing Nazi Germany to take over Austria.

There was no more Austria. It was completely absorbed into Germany, and it was renamed Ostmark ("Eastern March"). Upper and Lower Austria were also renamed to completely eradicate the name of Austria, becoming the Upper and Lower Danube instead. Hitler ordered an invasion, but it became a triumph march as there was no one in Austria left to oppose the German troops. His political opponents were immediately arrested, in particular, the Socialists and Communists. Austrians, in general, supported the *Anschluss.* But although many wanted the union with Germany, not all of them wanted it to happen under Nazi rule. In fact, contemporary Austrian historians often skip the period between 1938 and 1945, saying that Austria didn't exist at the time and that all the events that happened in the state were a part of German history. Nevertheless, the *Anschluss* happened, and the plebiscite of April 10th showed that 99.75 percent of Austrians supported the union. This support might have been extorted, but the acceptance of the Nazi takeover shows that the nation was content to go along with the inevitable.

The new Nazi leaders of Austria started the economic recovery of the country, which was now a region of the Third Reich. In Linz, the steel industry came under the supervision of Hermann Göring, and the unemployment percentage started falling. The Nazis certainly brought prosperity to Austria but not without victims. The first to suffer were the Jews, as their expulsion started almost immediately. Thousands of Jews lost their jobs, which artificially created job openings. They were forced to sell their property to survive, often for a much lower price. Some Jews were arrested under trumped-up charges, and their property was confiscated by the state. Jewish children were expelled from Aryan schools, and the availability of higher education was severely reduced for them. Because of the hardship that awaited them in Vienna, many Jewish families decided to leave Austria. This later proved to be a life-saving decision.

World War II

On the night between November 9th and 10th, 1938, the pogrom of the Jews began. It is remembered as the "Night of the Broken Glass," or *Kristallnacht.* The name refers to the broken glass all over the streets of German cities, left behind in the violence inflicted upon Jewish families and their homes. The *Kristallnacht* extended to Austria. The violence was even more severe in Vienna, where thousands of Jews were killed and many of their homes and temples were burned. In Austria, antisemitism took a new shape, known as the *Wiener Model* (Viennese model), in which Jewish families were murdered or expelled from the city, their property either confiscated or destroyed. Nazi Germany would adopt this model and use it not only in their own country but also in all the other countries it would come to occupy.

Kristallnacht came as a response to the assassination of a German diplomat in Paris, Ernst vom Rath. He was murdered by a young Jew, Herschel Grynszpan, who was angered by the treatment of his people by German officials. In Austria, antisemitism was especially attractive to the younger population, who believed in Hitler's propaganda that the Jews were to be blamed for the disaster that was the Great War and for the economic downfall that followed. Even before World War II began in 1939, Austria exiled roughly 125,000 of its Jewish population. Around 650,000 Jews were killed by the end of the war. But the Jews were not the only victims of the Nazi regime. Hitler also thought Slavs were inferior, and many of them were deported to labor camps. Another ethnic minority that suffered was the Roma people, as well as mentally and physically disabled Austrians and those belonging to the gay community. Most of them were killed in the euthanasia center established at Hartheim Castle, near Linz.

The exodus of the Jews meant that all those people needed to find a new home. The United States, Britain, and British-controlled Palestine had already implemented refugee restrictions and took only a small number of Austrian Jews. The rest had to search for an opportunity in any country that was deemed safe and would take them in. Among those who escaped during the early stages of Nazism in Austria were Jews who would become the backbone of the western European intellectual world, such as Sigmund Freud and Victor Weisskopf, the latter of whom worked on developing a nuclear bomb in the US during World War II. However, those who found refuge in continental European countries, such as France, Czechoslovakia, or Holland, were again caught up in the Nazis' web once the Axis forces occupied those lands. It is estimated that almost one-third of all the Jewish refugees of Austria didn't survive World War II.

In Vienna, the remaining Jews were forced to live in ghettos and eventually in concentration camps since their neighbors resented living next to them. The first concentration camps were to be near Vienna, but the swift victory of the Axis Powers in Poland changed those plans. The Jews were sent to the east in masses. There, they labored as prisoners and awaited their eventual annihilation. By 1941, all remaining Jews in Vienna were deported to Poland.

When Hitler occupied Austria, he was welcomed almost as a savior. The young people saw him as their deliverer from the economic disaster of the Great Depression. And indeed, the Nazi regime elevated Austria's industry and economy. Most Austrians gave their support to the regime, actively or passively. It is not surprising to learn that although they represented only 10 percent of the population of the Third Reich, Austrians played a major role as soldiers and concentration camp guards. The estimation is that almost half of the Holocaust camps personnel were Austrians, and they were directly responsible for the deaths of approximately three million Jews. The greatest blame for the Holocaust is put on Germany, but Austrians share the responsibility, even though it is a very painful part of history.

The Nazi regime didn't only invest in Austrian industries, which it did so it could use Austria's resources, but it also set up its main German military camps there. This was because Austrian territory was well guarded by the Axis Powers, and the Allied bombers had difficulty reaching cities such as Vienna or Hitler's hometown of Linz. Wiener Neustadt became the largest aircraft factory of the Third Reich, and it was connected with Vienna and Salzburg with the Autobahn.

It took only several months after the German occupation for Austrian unemployment to virtually disappear. But with the economic changes came social ones. Farmers and house servants had to look for their fortune in cities that lacked industrial workers.

They regarded this phenomenon as emancipation for many social classes, particularly the peasants. The new well-paying jobs, the improved infrastructure of Austria, and even the Aryanization of the nation were welcomed by the populace. But not all of the modernization efforts were welcomed. The Nazi regime restricted the Catholic Church and imposed new taxes on religious institutions and the people who attended masses. As profound Catholics, the Austrians, especially those in conservative circles, disapproved of the attacks on the church. Many were forced to abandon the church just because they couldn't afford to pay the tax.

Another reason Austrians resented the annexation and the *Anschluss*, as well as the Nazi regime, was the fact that all the key governmental, educational, and institutional positions were now occupied by German Nazis instead of Austrians. Those who helped the regime were rewarded, but they were given positions either far away in the Netherlands, Croatia, or Poland, or they were given key positions in concentration camps. This might be one of the reasons why Austrians were the majority to commit the Holocaust atrocities. Eventually, the Austrian Nazis and Austrians, in general, started to stir unrest against their German counterparts. It didn't help that the newly arrived German Nazis managed to collect all the material fortunes left behind by the fleeing Jews. It was this resentment toward the German Nazis that kept the Austrian identity alive. To differentiate themselves, the Austrians insisted on preserving their Austrian heritage, and they did so through art and culture, claiming national fame for the works of individuals such as Gustav Klimt (painter) and Josef Weinheber (poet).

The Axis Powers were successful in taking Europe with their innovative blitzkrieg tactics. By 1941, they dominated central and western continental Europe, and the Axis armies were taking over the southeastern territories as well. To the Austrians, it must have seemed as if the Nazi regime was proving the Aryan race's right to having a cultural and military dominion. When Hitler's forces took territories in North Africa, it seemed that there was no stopping him.

But Britain proved impossible to conquer. Since it was isolated, the island country resisted and became the bastion of opposition to Hitler. However, compared to the might of the Axis Powers and what it did in Europe and beyond, even Britain looked like a puny power. In the summer of 1941, the Eastern Front was shattered, and the German Army rushed to Moscow. The Nazis' triumph was imminent, and the Austrians shared in the triumph, as many of the soldiers were, indeed, Austrians. By that time, the Germans considered the Austrians to be a fully trustworthy and completely German nation. They were completely integrated into the German Army, and it is hard to discern their real numbers. But this would not have happened if the Austrians weren't willing. It was their sense of belonging and sense of duty that allowed the world to see them as one German nation. This is why it is hard to make a difference between German and Austrian history during the World War Two period.

However, there were Austrians who would not give up their separate national identity. They resisted, and they helped the Jews, for which they were severely punished. Around thirty-two thousand Austrians who were not of Jewish descent died in prisons or concentration camps. More than one hundred thousand Austrians were arrested as political enemies of the Third Reich. Around twenty thousand more were executed on political grounds. Given the Austrian population was around seven million, these numbers are not insignificant. Even so, the Austrian resistance was dwarfed by the Austrian army that served the Third Reich. They were crucial for taking over the Balkans, as well as the mountainous regions of Norway (where the Austrian Mountain unit proved invaluable).

But when the situation turned and the Axis Powers started losing the war, the Austrian troops were the first to suffer. At

Stalingrad, during the winter campaign of 1943, more than 50,000 Austrian soldiers were lost. Of the whole regiment, only 1,200 returned home. Over 247,000 Austrian soldiers died during World War Two.

The defeat at Stalingrad in 1943 made many Austrians regret ever supporting the Nazi regime. This was the point when Austrians started remembering their Austrian heritage. Many joined the resistance movement, but the majority still continued to support Hitler until the very end. In August 1943, the Allies started advancing in Italy, which allowed the bombing of Austria to finally be possible. On August 13th, the first bombs fell on Wiener Neustadt. On the Eastern Front, the Russians drove back the Germans, and in the west, on June 6th, 1944, the D-Day invasion was launched.

It became apparent to the Axis that it would lose the war, even though Hitler survived an assassination attempt in July, allowing the war to continue. The final wave of defeatism spread when the US bombed Vienna in September 1944. Baldur von Schirach, the Nazi German governor of Vienna, pleaded to Hitler to make the Austrian capital a demilitarized zone, but the Führer declined. By October, the resistance grew, and it took its final shape under the codename "O5." The number five stands for the letter E, as it is the fifth letter in the alphabet. Thus, the codename spells "OE,' which stands for *Österreich* (Austria).

In February, the Russians were closing in on Austria. They took Budapest and continued bombing Vienna. The culmination of these events came on March 12th, 1945, when the raid on Vienna was launched. Many city landmarks were damaged or destroyed, and the citizens started openly resenting the Nazi regime for its failure to protect them. Nevertheless, the regime still had the support of the majority of Austrians. A plot to surrender Vienna to the Soviets was discovered in April, and the main culprits were immediately executed. Nevertheless, the Soviets tried to take

Vienna in a battle that took place between April 6th and April 13th. The Austrian troops made their last stand at Marchfeld, but they did not engage in combat. By May 8th, the American and Russian troops met on the Enns, ending the hostilities in Austria. Hitler had already committed suicide in his Berlin bunker, and on May 7th, Germany had capitulated.

The Austrian resistance, the "O5," was effective only during the final stages of the war and after the fall of Vienna on April 13th. The western branch of the resistance launched their rebellion plan on May 1st, attacking the German forces. When the US troops entered Innsbruck on May 5th, the resistance already held the city. But the success of the resistance in western Austria was due to the people's preference of American rather than Russian occupation. The Russians were all alone, and they had to fight for the territory they took. The Americans, on the other hand, didn't put up much resistance, and the Austrians surrendered to the US troops willingly, joyful that the Americans got to them before the Russians.

With the end of the war came the question of what to do with Austria. Should it remain German? Or should it become independent once again? British Prime Minister Winston Churchill advocated Austrian independence but not because he believed in a self-determined Austrian nation. He wanted to use Austrian independence to undermine Austrian loyalty to Germany and the remnants of the Nazi regime. In fact, the Allies already agreed on the restoration of Austria in 1941 when the US and the Soviet Union entered the war. The narrative at the time was that Austria was the first victim of Nazi Germany and that it should be liberated. Nevertheless, Austria had to be reminded that it willingly took part in the war and that it should take on its share of the responsibility.

Chapter 10: Modern Austria

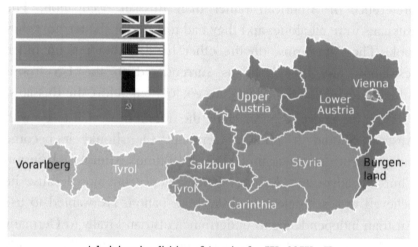

Administrative division of Austria after World War II

Austria Occupation Zones 1945-55.svg: Master Uegly (talk · contribs)derivative work: Hanzlan, CC BY-SA 4.0 <https://creativecommons.org/licenses/by-sa/4.0>, via Wikimedia Commons https://commons.wikimedia.org/wiki/File:Austria_Occupation_Zones_1945-55_en.svg

Post-War Austria

The Second Republic of Austria was proclaimed on April 27th, 1945. It was a restoration of the old republic, but it wasn't celebrated by its people. Instead, they were devastated and morally degraded by the loss of World War II and the overthrow of the Nazi regime. Physical, moral, economic, and political ruin followed the Third Reich's disintegration. But, according to the Allies,

Austria had been occupied by the Third Reich, which means it was never really a part of Germany. And although the Austrian people saw the Allies as the occupiers, the Allies called themselves the liberators. Confusion followed, and people had to suddenly change their political and social worldviews. They realized quickly, though, that a liberated Austria would be much less responsible for the war atrocities committed by the Third Reich than if it remained a German province under the occupation of the Allies. Nevertheless, the period between 1945 and 1955, when Austria was finally proclaimed independent, is still called the occupation period. Even so, the myth of the Second Republic's founding in 1945 preserves the narrative of Austria being the first victim of Nazi Germany.

This myth of Austria's innocence was supported by the Allies, who wanted to remove Austria from the German sphere of influence and enlist it on their side for the upcoming Cold War. Austria grabbed the opportunity to avoid the consequences of participating in the Second World War. The First Control Agreement, signed on July 4th, 1945, put Austria under the direct control of the Allied Council. The council was composed of four military commissioners, who set up distinct occupation zones. The troops had to be repositioned, and the American soldiers had to leave the Mühlviertel region in Upper Austria, as it was to be under Soviet control. Vorarlberg and Tyrol were under French control, and Americans controlled the rest of Upper Austria and Salzburg. The British took control of East Tyrol, Carinthia, and Styria, while the Soviets were given Mühlviertel in Upper Austria, all of Lower Austria, and Burgenland. Vienna, as Austria's capital, was divided into four districts, and each Allied power controlled one. Only the inner city was under joint administration.

Out of the four Allied powers, only the Soviet Union treated their part of Austria as occupied territory. They removed heavy industries and shipped them to Russia. They also hijacked the eastern Austrian economy and used its resources as if they belonged to the Soviet Union. The Soviet administration became notorious for its ruthlessness. However, the other occupied zones were different. The French were well received by the Austrians because they were the most benevolent. The British were appreciated because they served as protection against Yugoslavian efforts to gain some of Austria's territory. The Americans were also valued because they quickly adapted and adopted the same tone as the French. US President Harry Truman's administration of the occupied zone brought economic prosperity and benefits. After the end of the war, the Americans advocated for humanitarian help for liberated Austria, and by 1946, they set up food relief, as well as fuel for the cold winter.

The United States' Marshall Plan was a program designed to recover the European economy. It started in June 1947, and Austria benefited from it, receiving roughly one billion dollars over the next few years. Most of these funds were invested in infrastructure, while the rest was used to help recover the Austrian economy. By the summer of 1947, the Americans also paid three hundred million dollars as reimbursement for their occupation. This money was also put to good use and propelled the Austrian economy.

But the Western benevolence toward the Second Austrian Republic didn't come without a cost. Austria was to have a pivotal role in the Cold War, as it was a central European country that bridged the East and the West. Austria willingly embraced its role in the Cold War, as its new leaders were aware of the benefits it could bring them. Elections were organized as early as November 25th, 1945, and its success allowed Austria's new government to persuade the Allies to grant them considerable autonomy.

The elections were won by a coalition made out of Christian Democrats and Social Democrats, and together, they took over 90 percent of the votes. The fear that Austria would become another communist country was dispersed, as the Communist Party received only 5 percent of the votes. Karl Renner became the president of Austria, and he appointed Leopold Figl as his federal chancellor.

The Second Control Agreement, which took place on June 28th, 1946, granted so much autonomy to Austria that the Allies took the roles of mere supervisors. Nevertheless, the Allied administration still had the power to veto Austrian legislation but only if all of the powers agreed. By July, the banks had been nationalized, as well as heavy industries. The Soviet Union was no longer able to exploit the occupation zones and send resources back to Russia.

But many years would have to pass before Austria was able to persuade the Allies to grant them complete freedom and end the occupation. The negotiations started in 1947, and eight years passed before the Austrian State Treaty was signed. The main reason for the prolonged occupation was the Cold War. The Western powers were not ready to give up on strategically placed Austria, nor were the Russians. The Cold War standoff lasted through the whole of 1948 and 1949, and Austria was unable to move in the diplomatic field until the death of Russian leader Joseph Stalin in 1953.

Julius Raab became the Austrian chancellor in 1953, and he explored the idea of Austria becoming a neutral country, just like Switzerland. This would resolve the standoff that was the center of Austrian politics. But it would take years of diplomatic maneuvering for Austria to finally break the chains that locked her into the Cold War. With the rise of Nikita Khrushchev as the leader of the Soviet Union, Austria finally had the chance to break off. Khrushchev was eager to repair Russian relations with the West, and he was willing to let Austria leave the Soviet sphere of influence. In fact, Austria first made an agreement built around its promise it would become a neutral country with Russia. The Austrian State Treaty followed on May 15th, 1955. It was signed at the Belvedere Palace in Vienna by the foreign ministers of the four powers that occupied Austria. Three months later, all the military occupation troops left the country. The Austrian Parliament passed the law of state neutrality on October 26th, 1955.

The Austrian State Treaty finally left Austria a completely independent and free country. The neutrality that was promised brought the republic even further away from Germany and allowed its citizens to assume their lost Austrian identity once again. Neutrality also brought challenges, especially in economic spheres, but it was its price to pay for independence. But the main benefit of the neutrality was that the Allies agreed to relieve Austria from its share of responsibility for World War Two. The republic was able to shake off the horrors of its past and look forward to future social and economic stability.

Progress

After regaining its independence, up to the 1970s, Austria had to go through a series of economic and political struggles to become the model of domestic peace and prosperity that it is now. The industrial crisis that ensued during the 1950s gave momentum to the communists, who took to the streets and organized general strikes. Although the strikes failed, the economy continued to suffer due to runaway inflation. The social market economy was introduced with the Raab-Kamitz economy reforms, named after Chancellor Julius Raab and his finance minister, Reinhard Kamitz. They dealt with the unemployment rate by starting major building projects, such as the further development of the Autobahn and the construction of a hydroelectric plant. By the mid-1950s, the first foreign workers were introduced (from Greece and Italy) to the construction sites of Austria to help fulfill the labor demand.

With the Soviet takeover of Hungary in 1956, Austria received around 180,000 Hungarian refugees. This improved the Austrian image in the West and boosted the economy even more. Vienna was a meeting place between the East and West, and in 1961, Nikita Khrushchev and John F. Kennedy met there during the summit where the fate of Berlin was discussed. When the European Economic Community (EEC) was founded in 1957, Austrian leaders were worried their country would be excluded from the market due to its neutrality. But in 1960, Austria joined the European Free Trade Area (EFTA), demonstrating that its political neutrality no longer stood in the way of its economy.

While the economic and political growth of Austria continued during the 1960s, one burning question made all the political parties work together. Should the Habsburgs be allowed to come to visit their homeland after they renounced their right to rule? The Administrative Court decided in 1963 that Otto von Habsburg, the eldest child of the last Austrian emperor, Charles I, should be allowed entry. This decision was opposed by the Social Democrats and the Freedom Party of Austria, and although formally he was allowed to enter Austria, Otto von Habsburg was persuaded not to do so.

During the 1960s, Austria didn't have any major crisis, but there were some concerns raised due to the presence of ex-Nazi professors at the University of Vienna, as well as ongoing corruption within the government and the state administration. But these were scandals, easy to deal with, and nothing that needed international intervention. Austria proved it could take care of its domestic politics.

Political stability pushed the republic to its spectacular economic rise and the improvement of the citizens' lives. Linz steelworks, which was founded and developed by the Third Reich, remained one of the best performing steel industries in the world. Through smart domestic politics, industry was nationalized, and it led the republic to its economic boom. Austria further invested in infrastructure and enterprise, and it soon became one of the richest European countries.

With this prosperity and increased living standards, Austria became attractive to tourists. The first visitors were the Germans, but the government continued to invest in the tourism sector and started working on attracting British and American visitors. Annually, Austria receives around thirty-two million foreign tourists, with fourteen million of them visiting Vienna alone. The Austrian cultural heritage is enormous, and it mostly displays a nostalgia toward the Habsburg rule. But the government has also developed many sport centers, and Austria is known for being a winter wonderland, with its ski resorts and picturesque villages nestled among the high ranges of the Alps.

In 1971, the question of South Tyrol was resolved when the Austrian president, Franz Josef Jonas, visited Italy. After World War II, the Italians merged German-speaking South Tyrol with Italian-speaking Trentino, and ever since, the Austrians had felt tricked. The resentment toward Italy even led to some terrorist attacks. However, in 1969, South Tyrol was promised its autonomy as long as it stayed within Italy. Franz Jonas's state visit led to the improvement of diplomatic relations between Austria and Italy, and in 1972, Italy finally lifted its veto on allowing Austria to join the EEC. However, Austria remained neutral, and its leaders used this status of being a non-aligned state to benefit from its neighbors in both the West and the East. Luckily, Austria's neutrality was never militarily tested, and the country was able to continue its steep economic rise. By the 1980s, Austria became the most attractive state to which to emigrate due to its good social program, family and equality laws, and stable and ever-rising economy.

Austria became a full member of the European Union (EU) on January 1ˢᵗ, 1995, but the major political parties couldn't agree on what Austria's military status was going to be in the future. Should it remain neutral, or should it align itself with its fellow EU countries? Austria was a member of the United Nations since it gained independence in 1955, but although its army served as blue helmet peacekeepers, it kept its neutrality. Social Democrats continued to advocate neutrality, but the People's Party pushed for total integration in the EU's security program and even hoped for future NATO (North Atlantic Treaty Organization) membership. But to this day, Austria remains neutral, and it is one of only six EU member states that are not part of NATO. In 1998, Austria took the EU presidency, and the Second Austrian Republic reached its pinnacle in prestige. The next year, Austria supervised the introduction of the EU currency, the euro.

Modern-day Austria has a secular cultural and social life. With the integration of many war refugees and asylum seekers, as well as with Muslim economic migrants, Austrian society became multicultural, cosmopolitan, and open to international influences. But in recent years, xenophobia has returned to state politics, threatening to end an era of peace and prosperity. The conservatives still hold a skeptical view on welcoming so many immigrants, and they claim that European and Austrian values are in danger. Nevertheless, the conservatives haven't managed to sway the majority of Austria's population, and the Second Austrian Republic remains one of the most democratic and open societies in Europe.

Conclusion

Modern Austrians are a nation without history. Or maybe it would be correct to say that Austrian history is one without a nation. A multiethnic hodgepodge, the people of Austria struggle to construct their national identity even today. Maybe even more so today than in the past, with all the migrants and refugees they have received. But Austrians received them with open arms, proving they are no longer stuck in their past conflicts. They are a tolerant, open, and truly modern nation, capable of accepting its past, such as it is, and boldly look into the future.

Austria is a Central European state, and as such, it was a place of many conflicts. Protected by the mountains and by the mighty Danube River, it was often unapproachable, secluded, and untouched by enemy forces. The Ottomans had trouble approaching Vienna in the 16th and 17th centuries, and so did the Allies during World War Two. Although the city was finally raided in 1944 and continued to be bombed fifty-two more times, it somehow managed to preserve much of its history. Around 20 percent of Vienna was destroyed, mostly residency buildings and strategic points, such as oil refineries and storage facilities. Historic landmarks, such as Saint Stephen's Cathedral and Schönbrunn Palace, were also damaged, but they were lovingly repaired and returned to their old Habsburg glory so every city visitor would be able to see it in all its splendor.

Austria is composed of many ethnicities, and while this fact used to be a point of conflict, now it is something of which Austrians are especially proud. However, that doesn't mean xenophobia is not present. It still lingers, mainly in the political circles of the far-right and conservative parties. But today, these parties have a very low percentage of followers and are mainly presented as being opposed to the democratic government. Austrian society remains open and cosmopolitan, as well as tolerant and completely Western in its values. In 2019, Austria legalized same-sex marriage, continuing to prove its intention to be a fully modern and democratic state. Austria is also the fourth safest country to live in, as it has an extremely low crime rate. In addition, no terrorist attacks have been committed in its territory. However, modern society has proven it would not stand idly by when faced with corrupt and scandalous governments, so social protests still occur in major Austrian cities.

Although it is a country of many conflicts, Austria managed to rise above its turbulent and rich past to become a peacekeeper of Europe. The country has maintained its military neutrality since the end of the Second World War, and with its European politics, it is a moral beacon of the continent. Perhaps this is why it attracts so many people, tourists, and immigrants.

Austria is a nation composed of Germans, Slavs, Magyars, Turks, Indians, Moroccans, and so many more. Since the early medieval times, it continues to prove that one nation doesn't have to limit itself on an ethnic basis. A nation is a concept that reaches far beyond one's place of origin. It is a sense of belonging, acceptance, and prosperity. Austria may have not always been this "island of the blessed," as Pope Paul VI described it in 1971, but it is something even the enlightened Habsburg rulers tried to make. And it has certainly become the "island of the blessed," even though it continues to struggle with the issues of the modern world.

Part 2: The Habsburg Empire

A Captivating Guide to the House of Austria and the Impact the Habsburgs Had on the Holy Roman Empire

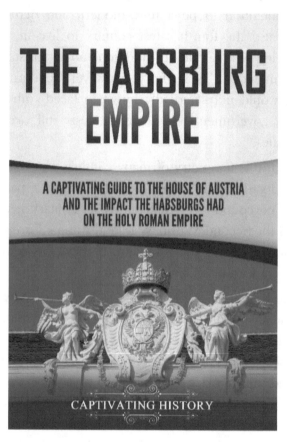

Introduction

The vowels AEIOU perfectly summarize and symbolize the ambition of the House of Habsburg. They are the dynasty's motto, but in their full form, it's *"Austriae est imperare orbi universo"* ("All the world is subject to Austria"). The family shared the European idea of the divine right to rule, but unlike other European dynasties, the Habsburgs ruled much longer and had more grandiose ambitions. For almost 650 years, the sons and sometimes even the daughters of the Habsburgs ruled central Europe. There are very few European countries that can say they were never ruled by a Habsburg. The family domain spanned from England in the north to Serbia in the south, from Portugal in the west to Poland in the east. They touched even other continents, at one point ruling almost all of the Americas, as well as some Asian and African territories. The dynasty had the highest European rule in its possession: the crown of the Holy Roman Empire. But even when they lost it, they didn't stop believing their destiny was to rule the world.

But such a high family's regard of itself came at a price. The belief of the Habsburg superiority led the family on a path of interbreeding. The marriages of the Habsburgs were kept within the family for a long time, and the result was a very diluted genetic pool. Many Habsburg rulers were marked by a very distinct genetic trait, a protuberant jaw known as the "Habsburg lip" or the "Habsburg jaw." This physical trait can be easily seen in many portraits of the Habsburg family members. But on occasion, the inbreeding led to more serious health conditions and even madness. Charles II, with his many illnesses, is a prime example of this. Some modern scientists even believe he could have been a hermaphrodite.

Nevertheless, the Habsburg dynasty remained the most prestigious one in Europe. To achieve and maintain such status, the family had to develop a series of strategies. They were extremely bound to tradition, and they were conservative to the core. Nothing less could be expected from a dynasty whose motto is the aspiration to rule the world. Even the enlightened autocrats, like Maria Theresa, only allowed the Enlightenment movement to influence their rule to a certain extent. They used the trendy political and cultural movements to strengthen their rule and to present themselves as modern leaders, but in reality, they were far from it. The only Habsburg willing to bring liberal changes to the empire was Maria Theresa's son, Joseph II. However, he couldn't contain his ambition, which displayed itself through constant innovations and reforms. But his subjects were not yet ready for these reforms, and his good intentions were met with strong resistance, which ultimately led to his downfall. While some believe Joseph II was ahead of his time, history remembers him as a visionary who did not know how to lead a state.

Joseph was followed by another series of conservative rulers who firmly grasped the dynasty's prerogatives. But when faced with international enemies, such as the French Revolution and later Napoleon Bonaparte, they had a choice to make: preserve the empire or preserve the family. The Habsburgs had to make that choice twice, and both times, they chose family. This loyalty to the dynasty is outstanding, but it brought about the end of the Holy Roman Empire. Out of fear that Napoleon would remove him from the Holy Roman throne, Francis II proclaimed the Austrian Empire, with himself as its first emperor. In 1804, the Holy Roman Empire ended. Francis II's unwillingness to allow Napoleon the same prestige as the Habsburg dynasty brought the end of one of the mightiest European empires. Almost a century and a half later, this same family loyalty would bring about the end of the Austro-Hungarian empire. To defend the Habsburg honor and the right to rule as a European superpower, Franz Joseph started World War I, which he was aware he couldn't win. The Habsburgs lost their right to rule in Europe, but they saved the dynasty and its honor and prestige.

However, the end of the monarchy didn't mean the end of the Habsburgs. They continue to live and dominate European politics even today, although their aspirations to rule the world changed into the ideals of a unified Europe. Although they are no longer the rulers but rather the leaders into the future of European integration, the Habsburgs today stand as a symbol of Europe, one that is capable of unity.

Chapter 1: The Hawk's Castle

Old ruins of the Habsburg Castle

The place where the great European Habsburg dynasty originates is a modest castle on a hill above the Aare River, in today's Switzerland. This castle was built in the early 11th century by one of the progenitors of the dynasty, and he named the castle "Habichtsburg," the "Hawk's Castle." The legend says that the first inhabitants of the newly built castle saw a hawk sitting on its walls every morning. Thus, they named the castle, unaware that soon it would become a name of one of the greatest dynasties that ruled Europe. The family was named after the castle, but the truth is that not much is known about the early days of the Habsburgs. History is often mixed with the legends of old, and it is quite possible that the story about the castle's and family's name is nothing but distant echoes of a story passed down through the generations. Modern linguists even believe that the name Habsburg wasn't derived from Habichtsburg, but from "Hablhap," which is High Middle German for ford, and Aare River has a ford near the castle.

But even in the haziness of the early Habsburg history, there are glimmers of truth. Its earliest members known to us were a certain Guntram the Rich, who lived sometime during the 900s. But it was his son, Lanzelin, who acquired the land where the castle would be built at a later date. Lanzelin was the count of Altenburg, and it is possible he had three sons. One of them was named Radbot, and it is believed that it was he who started building the castle, together with the bishop of Strasbourg, who might have been Lanzelin's brother or third son. Lanzelin and his family were minor nobles of Swabia, but they acquired the land that guarded the transalpine trade routes, meaning they had the right to collect tolls on whoever passed through their land, usually traders from Alsace, South Germany, and Switzerland. Thus, Radbot and his brothers grew rich, as well as their sons and grandsons. With these riches came appropriate authority and titles. It was Radbot's grandson, Otto, who was first named "count of Habsburg" in approximately 1090.

During the 1100s, the Hohenstaufens were the most prominent European family because they ruled the Holy Roman Empire, and the Habsburgs realized they should build political relations around this family. But the title of the Holy Roman emperor wasn't hereditary; it was elective. The council, which was made of the highest-ranking German princes, would gather to vote for the new emperor, and the Habsburgs proved to be loyal to the Hohenstaufens. As a reward for this loyalty, Emperor Friedrich

(Frederick) II took Rudolf the Benevolent's grandson, of the Habsburg family, as his godson. Thus, the Habsburgs were introduced to the highest imperial political and social circles. By the end of the 13th century, the Habsburgs rose in power and became known as the wealthiest and most influential family of southwestern Germany. But the end of the Hohenstaufen rule over the Holy Roman Empire led to a period of interregnum, lasting almost twenty years, as Germany was split between multiple claimants to the Holy Roman throne. Finally, in 1273, the princes gathered to vote for a new king, and Rudolf von Habsburg, thanks to his family's ties and political influence, became the new Holy Roman emperor.

Reign of Rudolf I (r. 1273-1291)

Rudolf I was the fourth count of Habsburg with that name, but he was the first elected Holy Roman emperor. He was chosen for that role because the twenty years of interregnum brought chaos to Germany, and the Habsburgs were the only family rich and powerful enough to bring back peace. However, they hoped that Rudolf wasn't too rich and too powerful, as the electors didn't want him to overstep his imperial boundaries and touch on their princely sovereignties. Rudolf was already fifty-five years old when he was elected, and he was often described by his contemporaries as wise, modest, and a decent person. However, these epithets might be prescribed to him because he was the head of the Habsburg family. Nevertheless, Rudolf gained fame as an excellent politician with a great sense of humor, and he proved his modesty by dressing in less than was expected from lords. The stories started circulating that the new emperor sewed his own clothes and liked to indulge in physical work with his men.

But whatever stories his admirers or political opponents shared, nobody can dispute that his reign was very successful, even though the empire was unrestful since the interregnum period. In truth, Rudolf I was never crowned by the pope, and his official title was king, not an emperor. But this didn't stop him from acting to preserve the whole empire and save it from disaster. Rudolf was aware he had to concentrate his efforts in Germany, where the rogue knights needed disciplining and where petty princes were fighting each other for various territories. Rudolf also realized the importance of the German princes, and he never tried to assert his dominion over them. He worked together with them, and to build relationships even further, he decided to marry his four daughters to these princes. But to restore law and order throughout the empire, Rudolf needed military and monetary support from the imperial cities, and he worked hard to establish good relations with them too. Because of this, Rudolf often traveled across the empire to bring order and justice. He would personally combat the rogue knights who robbed and harassed the civilians, he abolished the taxes implemented by the local lords, and he dealt with the feuds between the noble families in an effort to appease them. During his rule, the cities and their citizens felt safe returning to the empire, and they were glad to serve a king who could deliver what he promised. Therefore, they were glad to provide him with men for the army, as well as tax money that would be spent to maintain that army.

Rudolf I's most important achievement was the acquisition of Austrian duchies for his family. Austria was a territory that belonged to the Holy Roman Empire, but since Emperor Friedrich gave it a series of privileges in 1156, the territory gained considerable independence. The ruling family of Austria was the Babenberg dynasty, which was extinguished in 1246 when its last male representative died, leaving no heir. During the interregnum period, Otakar Premysl of Moravia took hold of Austria. To consolidate his rule in Austria, he even married a Babenberg daughter, and he hoped he would be chosen as the Holy Roman emperor. When Rudolf was elected, Otakar refused to acknowledge him, leaving no choice but for Rudolf to declare war. Luckily, Rudolf I had the support of other German princes, and he wasn't alone in his fight against Otakar. The decisive battle occurred on August 26th, 1278, in which Otakar was killed, and Rudolf claimed the Austrian territories for himself. At this moment, nobody dared to oppose him, for he grew in both power and might. Austria would remain a Habsburg possession until 1918, and because of their long reign there, the Habsburgs would become known as "the House of Austria."

Rudolf died on July 15th, 1291, at the age of seventy-three. It is said he was such a meticulous man that he even planned his own death and rode to the city of Speyer, which he believed was a burial place of his ancestors. Rudolf even hired an artist to decorate his future tomb, and he produced what is believed to be the first realistic portrait of the Holy Roman emperor. It was displayed in the Speyer Cathedral on the day of his death. Rudolf contributed not only to the Habsburg family but also to the Holy Roman Empire by bringing back peace and order after the unruly years of the interregnum. But aside from the king's duties, which he performed almost flawlessly, Rudolf also took it upon himself to personally arrange the marriages of all of his children. Thus, he bound the lords of Bavaria, Saxony, and Hungary, as well as Moravia, to the Habsburg dynasty, cementing the lofty status of the family. With careful planning, he organized family alliances that could not be broken easily, and he established inheritance claims for the future, the ones the Habsburgs would use to acquire even more land for themselves. But Rudolf I had one major failure; he was never crowned emperor by the pope. Thus, he never really had the imperial prerogative of naming his heir. He failed to promote his son as the candidate for the next Holy Roman emperor, and the electoral princes were already against voting for another Habsburg because they thought the family had acquired too much power during the reign of just one of their members.

Albert I (r. 1298-1308) and His Three Sons

Albert's seal
https://commons.wikimedia.org/wiki/File:Albrecht1_habsburg.jpg

After the death of beloved King Rudolf I, the German princes were reluctant to elect another Habsburg. Rudolf's successor was Adolf, Count of Nassau, and he ruled between 1292 and 1298. The princes preferred a king without much political influence or enormous wealth, which he could then use to gain supporters. Adolf was a perfect candidate, but when he started meddling in the domestic affairs of war-torn Thuringia and Meissen and even started buying land in these areas to set up his power base, the German princes started recognizing he was a threat. Adolf was deposed in 1298, and Albert I Habsburg was elected king in his place.

Albert was the oldest son of Rudolf I, and the general opinion of him was that he was very energetic, fierce, intelligent, and competent. He had only one eye, which bolstered his frightening look, and he had a reputation as a harsh and brutal person. Albert started ruling Austria while his father was still alive, which only served to give him training in royal administration. His official title was the duke of Austria, but when he started ruling the territory in 1282, he had to confront many challenges. For one, he wasn't welcomed there, as the people saw him as a foreigner from Swabia. As a result, Albert had to put down a rebellion in Vienna in 1289, in Styria in 1291/2, and a revolt of the nobles of Austria in 1295/6. But even while quelling these rebellions, Albert tried to be modest when punishing the main culprits because he hoped he could win them over. He even named his sons Friedrich and Leopold, names that were commonly used in the previous ruling family of Austria, the Babenbergs.

When Albert became king in 1298, his reputation as a harsh person came to light even more. He ruled for ten years, and in that time, he constantly tried to strengthen his authority as a king. He pursued the same goals as his predecessor Adolf: Thuringia, Meissen, and some other key territories. In his efforts to make the Habsburgs hereditary successors of the German throne, he pursued an alliance with Philip IV of France. This disturbed the German electoral princes because Albert was ready to give up some of the German territories to gain French support. Three of the electoral princes—the Archbishops of Cologne, Mainz, and Trier—plotted to dispose of Albert, but the king used force to convince other princes to stay loyal to him. The rebellion of the three princes was fruitless, ending in 1302, but it did manage to put Albert on the bad side of Pope Boniface VIII, who also sought to install his own man as the Holy Roman emperor. But Albert managed to make peace with the pope by swearing allegiance to him and by renouncing some of the Italian territories so they could become part of the Papal States.

During Albert's reign, Bohemia came into the hands of the Habsburg dynasty. After the death of the Přemyslid dynasty's last king, Albert made sure to put his son, Rudolf, on the throne of Bohemia. He even sent an army to Prague to confront the duke of Carinthia, who also claimed this region of the empire. The very presence of the Habsburg soldiers persuaded the Bohemian nobles to choose Rudolf as their new king. At the same time, Albert worked hard on getting Thuringia too, although his luck turned against him. Rudolf died in 1307, and the Bohemian crown went to the duke of Carinthia, who then allied himself with the Wettin dynasty of Thuringia to defeat Albert's army. The battle occurred in May 1307, and Albert was crushed.

There is evidence that Albert planned to secure the succession of his sons to the German throne, but before he could act on it, he was murdered. The culprit was none other than his nephew, John Habsburg (also known as Johann Parricida), who wanted to enlarge his lands and possessions at the expense of his cousins. He claimed that Austria and Styria should belong to him, and he went so far as to claim that he should be the rightful heir to the empire's throne instead of Albert's own sons. In May 1308, John conspired with four other nobles, and together, they attacked Albert while he was on the road to the city of Brugg. This internal family conflict cost the Habsburgs the crown, as they would not be elected kings and emperors for the next 130 years. Nevertheless, the dynasty continued to exist and to meddle in state affairs.

However, it wasn't only the death of Albert that caused the Habsburgs to lose their prestige and the crown. His sons, Friedrich and Leopold, were as ambitious as their father, but there was not a trace of his competence within them. When Rudolf died in Bohemia, Friedrich, known as the Handsome (or the Fair), was sent to lead the army and take the crown for himself, but he failed. After the death of his father, Friedrich was also unable to persuade the German princes to vote for him during the next elections, with the winner being Henry (Heinrich) of the Luxembourg family.

When Henry died in 1313, the new elections were held the following year, and Friedrich once again tried to gain the crown for the Habsburgs. But once again, he lost, this time by only one vote. The new king of Germany was Louis of Upper Bavaria, and even though he was crowned, he couldn't receive the original imperial crown, as it had been in Friedrich's hands since the death of his father. Friedrich took the opportunity and crowned himself as the king of Germany with the proper imperial crown. However, he wasn't accepted as the legitimate ruler, and the double crowning resulted in an eight-year-long war between Louis and Friedrich.

During the war, the Habsburgs lost their prestige in their home territory in Switzerland. There, the cantons of Uri, Schwyz, and Unterwalden formed the Eternal League in 1291, and even though they were loyal to Rudolf I and Albert I, they changed their stance and became hostile toward the Habsburgs during the eight-year war. Friedrich's brother Leopold was tasked with suppressing the unrest in these areas, but in 1315, at the Battle of Morgarten, the Swiss farmers ambushed the Habsburg army and butchered their men. Leopold failed to rally his troops, and he was forced to run for his very life. In 1322, another battle occurred, which was the decisive battle that resolved the conflict between Friedrich and Louis. During the Battle of Mühldorf, Friedrich fought alongside his men. Even though he displayed all the chivalric ideals of a knight by personally leading his army, this proved to be a fatal decision. He was defeated and captured. The Battle of Mühldorf remains one of the most memorable battles fought on German soil because it was the last knightly battle and also the last battle in Europe in which no firearms were used.

Friedrich spent only three years in Louis's prison, and during that time, it seems the relations between the two men improved. He was released in 1325, but he had to promise he would persuade his brother Leopold to give up on fighting for the German crown. However, Leopold refused, and Friedrich once again stood up to his chivalric ideals and returned to Louis's prison voluntarily. Louis was impressed by Friedrich's values, and he befriended his old enemy. Eventually, he even proclaimed him a regent of Bavaria, and in time, the two friends would rule together, sharing the administration of the empire. Louis allowed Friedrich to use the title *rex* (king), and this unique situation was the only example of co-rulership in German history. Unfortunately, this arrangement only lasted for one year, as Leopold died in 1326, and Friedrich had no one to support him anymore. But instead of even trying to keep the crown, Friedrich renounced it and returned to being only the duke of Austria and Styria. He died in 1330.

After losing their authority over Switzerland, the Habsburgs focused their efforts on Austria, where they built many monasteries and churches to consolidate their power there. But on an imperial scale, the Habsburgs played only a marginal role. With the deaths of Friedrich and Leopold, there was no one brave enough to claim the crown. These two left no male heirs, so it was up to their younger brothers, the sons of Albert I, to continue the dynasty. Albert II (1298-1358) became the head of the family, but he had no desire to rule the empire, as he was content with Austria. His efforts to consolidate the dynasty's power in the duchy made him the first true Austrian Habsburg. However, he wasn't the only remaining child of Albert I with political influence in Germany. Agnes Habsburg (1281-1364), the widowed Queen of Hungary, was one of Albert I's daughters, and she distinguished herself with bravery, intelligence, and energy. She became the main advisor to her brothers, and she often acted as a mediator when settling disputes within the family and outside of it. Agnes was only nineteen when she was widowed, but she refused to remarry. Instead, she opted for a quiet life in a country house in Tyrol. She lived there until the end of her days, leaving the house only to act as her brother's official on different political matters.

As was the custom among the noble families of the Middle Ages, Albert, one of the youngest children of Albert I, was prepared for a career in the church. He had several older brothers, so it was very unlikely he would rule the family. However, Albert gave up on his church office even before Friedrich and Leopold died, as he was unable to withstand the rivalry within the religious order, but the education he received from the church he later used to rule. This is why he is known as Albert the Wise, though he is also remembered as Albert the Lame, as he was almost paralyzed due to a disease he suffered as a child. Albert shared the rule over Austria with his younger brother, Otto the Merry, who was widely known for his lavish lifestyle at court. Nevertheless, it was Albert who acted as the head of the Habsburgs, and he made a series of decisions that secured the family's influence in the empire. In 1335, he recognized King Louis IV, and he even ensured family ties with the ruling house. He betrothed his son with the daughter of Louis's successor, Charles IV of Luxembourg. But this wasn't the only marriage Albert organized to expand the political and territorial influence of the Habsburgs. He also married one of his daughters to the last count of Tyrol, hoping that after the count's death, this territory would come into Habsburg hands. Louis was pleased with Albert's loyalty, and as a recognition of it, he granted him the rule over Carinthia and Carniola (in today's Austria and Slovenia), making them Habsburg lands. Unfortunately, during Albert's life, the family's ties with Switzerland weakened, as he lost major battles with Zürich and Bern during the 1350s.

Still, Albert is sometimes considered the true founder of the Austrian state because he revised the duchy's economy and administration. He employed only professionally trained people as jurists, and he promoted the growth of the cities and towns through trade. In turn, he was able to collect more taxes and fill the treasury. He planned to create Austria as one people under one ruler from one house. This meant he intended to keep Austria as a Habsburg possession, and in 1355, he issued a set of rules that would secure dynastic solidarity and make the family unable to divide the territory. These rules were never fully implemented, but the Habsburgs often referred to them when discussing the dynasty's unity. For Austria, Albert managed to do more than his elder brothers ever hoped to achieve. But it was his son, Rudolf IV, who cemented the Habsburgs as *the* Austrian dynasty. For this, he would remain known as Rudolf the Founder.

Rudolf the Founder (1339–1365)

Rudolf IV
https://commons.wikimedia.org/wiki/File:Rudolf_IV.jpg

Rudolf ruled Austria very briefly. He was only eighteen when his father died in 1358, and he followed his father in death not even seven years later. Rudolf was young, bold, and energetic, and that reflected in his politics. He was also raised as the future son-in-law of Charles IV, a crown prince who had no sons of his own. This greatly influenced Rudolf's attitude and self-esteem. Rudolf IV was alone in making the decisions for Austria and the Habsburg dynasty, as his brothers were still children, preoccupied with games instead of fraternal jealousy. The only person on whose advice he could rely was his aunt Agnes. But Rudolf's young age, nor his short life, didn't stop him from achieving great things for Austria. His main concerns were the acquisition of Tyrol, building Vienna as the dynastic capital of Austria, reforming the government and the tax system of the duchy, and raising the status of the Habsburgs to the equal level of prince-electors, to which they didn't belong. Rudolf raised Austria from being a simple duchy to an archduchy.

But one of the first tasks Rudolf had to deal with was the taking of the Tyrol area. His father already secured the succession of Tyrol by marrying his daughter to its last count, but after his death in 1363, it was his sister, Margaret of Tyrol, who inherited the rule. Rudolf's claim over the county was also challenged by the Bavarian House of Wittelsbach, so the Austrian duke was forced to cross the Alps with a small military contingent to claim it. Rudolf first stopped at the city of Bressanone, where Margaret resided, and he managed to persuade her to agree to the Habsburg suzerainty. The Habsburgs finally had Tyrol under their claim, and it was a valuable territory, as it contained rich mines. Tyrol also connected the Habsburg lands in Austria with the family estates in Further Austria, commonly known as Vorlande (southwestern Germany).

Aside from Tyrol, Vienna was the main symbol of Rudolf's reign. He looked up to his father-in-law, Holy Roman Emperor Charles IV, who transformed Prague into the capital of the empire through numerous building projects. But Rudolf didn't only build the city to display it as a pearl among the major cities of Europe.

He also started many new institutions that nationalized the Austrian administration, separating it from the rest of the empire. He also founded the University of Vienna in 1365, where all the government administrators could receive higher education. This university still exists, and it is the third-oldest university in central Europe, founded right after those in Prague (Czech Republic) and Krakow (Poland). Sadly, Rudolf didn't live long enough to finish all of his planned projects for his capital city, and although he did compete with Charles IV, Vienna wasn't able to come close to Prague's glittering prestige as the capital of the empire and the third-largest city of Europe.

But while he was alive, Rudolf was impatient in building Austria's prestige and the Habsburg dynasty. He tried to speed the matter up by forging a document known as the *Privilegium maius*, the "greater privilege." This document was similar to the one issued by Emperor Frederick Barbarossa in 1156 when he elevated Austria to a duchy. This time, Rudolf wanted to elevate his country to the status of an archduchy. The document was created sometime between 1353 and 1359, and it allowed the rulers of Austria to call themselves archdukes. It also gave them various other privileges and titles, such as "Master of the Imperial Hunt" or "Duke of Swabia." The document also exempted the Habsburgs from imperial military operations unless they specifically wanted to get involved. The *Privilegium maius* put the Habsburgs above the status of any other noble family of the Holy Roman Empire. To legitimize the document, Rudolf claimed it was ancient, dating it back to the time of Julius Caesar and Nero, whose letters accompanied the document. Rudolf was "lucky" to rediscover these papers, but to trained historians, the *Privilegium maius* is an obvious imitation of Barbarossa's *Privilegium Minus*, which he had granted to the Babenbergs of Austria in the 12th century. Rudolf even removed the imperial seal from Barbarossa's document and attached it to his forged one.

However, Rudolf had to send the *Privilegium maius* to Charles IV for affirmation, and the emperor had a professional ready to examine the document. This professional was none other than the famous scholar and poet Petrarch, who immediately knew he had an imitation in his hands. Although Charles IV refused to acknowledge Rudolf's *Privilegium maius*, the document shaped the landscape of Austrian politics for the centuries to come. While Charles couldn't forgive Rudolf for the usage of imperial insignia in the Habsburg display of power, he allowed him the usage of the title archduke. Nevertheless, the first Habsburg to use the title in an official manner was Ernest the Iron (1377–1424). Although the emperor never confirmed the *Privilegium maius*, the Austrians took the document to heart because it regulated the duchy's internal administration. Through it, the Austrian lands were inseparable, and the title of the archduke was hereditary, though it was never specified that it should pass from father to son; rather, it would go to the next eldest male of the house. It also gave the Habsburgs the right to administer not only their courts but also the courts of other noble Austrian families and to enjoy the taxes collected on the whole Austrian territory. They also had the right to use any of the forests in Austria, whether they were privately owned by a landlord or other nobles.

Rudolf died in 1365 while traveling to Milan to attend his brother Leopold's wedding. He arranged this marriage himself to acquire the Italian territory for the Habsburgs, and he also promulgated the inheritance treaty with the Luxembourgs and the Angevins, which would, centuries later, lead to the Habsburg acquisition of their lands, setting the family as the rulers of Bohemia and Hungary. Duke Rudolf IV was probably the most important Habsburg who lived between the time of his grandfather, Albert I, and his great-grandson, Friedrich III, who would become the emperor and finally legitimize the *Privilegium maius* in 1452. But Rudolf's own life was too short to achieve his aspirations. Nevertheless, he set the Habsburgs on the path to glory, and it was only a matter of time and competence of his successors to fully utilize the prestige Rudolf had left for them.

Chapter 2: The Division of the Dynasty

Rudolf's younger brothers, Albert III and Leopold III, showed a glimpse of competence at the beginning, but ultimately, they were the ones responsible for the eventual partition of the Habsburg dynasty. Albert was only fifteen and Leopold fourteen when Rudolf died, and they were of strangely different characteristics. While the younger brother was competitive, ambitious, and prone to combat, the elder brother was reserved, passive, and shy. Each of them went too far in their direction, which led to their ultimate doom. They attempted joint rulership after the death of their older brother, and they even managed to gain some important territories for the Habsburgs during those years. In 1368, they acquired the thriving city of Breisgau, and in 1382, Trieste and parts of inner Istria submitted to them. But due to Leopold's ambitions, the joint rule came to an end in 1379, and the brothers decided to ignore Rudolf's instructions of *Privilegium maius* and split the family territories between themselves. In September of 1379, they signed the partition treaty at Neuburg in Styria. The result was the creation of two family branches: the Albertinian and the Leopoldian. Albert took over Upper and Lower Austria, as well as the territory of Salzkammergut. Leopold took Vorlande, Tyrol, Carinthia,

Carniola, and Styria, as well as the Adriatic areas, which were then opposing the power and might of the Venetian Republic.

The Albertinian branch of the Habsburgs continued to pass the rule from father to son, but the Leopoldian line split into the Styrian and Tyrolean lines. Eventually, by 1496, only the Styrian Leopoldian line had survived, and it united all the Habsburg lands under a single ruler once more. The Neuburg Treaty claimed that the division of the territories between the brothers wouldn't influence the administration of the united realm, but the reality was that Leopold and Albert rarely worked together, and they distanced themselves during their rules. Even in the Papal Schism of 1378, the brothers took opposite sides, with Albert supporting the election of Pope Urban VI while Leopold supported Antipope Clement VII. The brothers managed to divide the Habsburg family, which only led to its weakening and loss of many chances to advance the house's prestige.

One of the brothers' common interests was the Habsburg territory in Switzerland. The confederacy of the Swiss cantons still showed hostility toward the family, so Leopold went to war. However, he lost his life in the Battle of Sempach in 1386 while leading his army, which was decimated. Albert tried to undo the loss his brother's war had caused and sent 6,000 men to battle the Swiss Confederation at the Battle of Näfels in 1388. Once more, the Habsburgs and their army were defeated by the villagers and peasants, who wielded crude weapons such as axes, pitchforks, and spears. These two battles drove the Habsburgs out of Switzerland, although they continued to claim the old Habsburg territories there until 1415 when the Swiss symbolically took over the place of the dynasty's birth, Hawk's Castle. After the defeat and death of Leopold, Albert took over the care of his brother's four sons. They grew up to be much like their father, and their individual ambitions led Austria into a civil war, which also involved Albert's own son, Albert IV. They fought during the first decades of the 1400s, which is considered to be a very gruesome time for the Habsburg lands, as they were ravaged by the knights' marauders. There was no one to insert judicial authority, as the Habsburgs had stepped into a time of anarchy. Famine, disease, and natural catastrophes hit the countryside hard, and the noble families did little to help. Instead, they took the opportunity to assert their interests against the Habsburgs.

The civil war within the Habsburg territories wasn't at all fought between the brothers who divided the lands between them, although it does explain the different interests the different branches of the family had. The Albertinian line in Upper and Lower Austria fought the Hussite rebellion, which spread through Bohemia after religious leader Jan Hus was accused of heresy and was executed by the Catholic Church in 1415. Loyal to the Holy Roman Emperor, the Albertinian line fought on the side of the Catholics, and their efforts grew into a crusade against the Hussites, which was given papal permission. But the rebellion proved to be much tougher to break than it seemed at first, as the conflict continued in a series of crusades until 1434. The Styrian branch of the Leopoldian Habsburg line was preoccupied with the rising power of the Ottoman Turks, which ravaged the Balkan lands and posed a serious threat to central Europe. The Tyrolean branch of the Leopoldian line continued to pursue family interests in Switzerland and was soon to experience its final defeat. The Leopoldian line was divided between the two sons of Leopold III; Ernest the Iron ruled Carniola, Carinthia, and Styria, while his brother, Friedrich IV, ruled Tyrol.

Ernest the Iron was the most competent Habsburg of the time, and he was responsible for elevating Graz and Wiener Neustadt, making them the seats of his government. He became the head of the family in 1411 after the death of his older brother, Leopold IV, who left no male heirs. At this point, Ernest started calling himself an archduke and started signing official documents using this title. Ernest was the first Habsburg who fought the Ottomans, and after him, the successors of the dynasty repeatedly had to deal with the

Ottoman problem. But Ernest the Iron is probably most famous for consolidating the family's rule over Inner Austria (Styria, Carniola, and Carinthia), as he worked hard on establishing its economy through iron production. However, this was not why he was nicknamed "the Iron." Like all other medieval rulers, such nicknames are closely connected to the physical and characteristic appearances of an individual.

Ernest's younger brother, Friedrich IV (1382–1439), wasn't as successful in ruling Tyrol. In 1415, he managed to antagonize Holy Roman Emperor Sigismund by firmly supporting Antipope John XXIII at the Council of Constance (1415), an antipope the Catholics had been trying to dispose of. Angered by Friedrich's meddling in the matter, the emperor had him outlawed, and he even went so far as to forfeit all of his possessions in Tyrol and Vorlande. Sigismund promised that whoever conquered a part of Friedrich's territory would be able to keep it. The young Habsburg was attacked from all sides, and even his brother Ernest tried to get a portion of Tyrol for himself. In 1417, Friedrich paid a considerable sum of money to Ernest for him to surrender the parts of Tyrol that had accepted him as their duke. Through 1418, Friedrich used even more money to bribe people in certain positions so he could clear his name and lift Sigismund's ban. This endeavor cost him everything he had, which was why he earned his nickname "Frederick of the Empty Pockets." When Ernest died in 1424, Friedrich became the head of the Habsburgs, and he managed to reconcile with Sigismund. As if the experience of the previous year served its purpose, Friedrich became wiser, and he even managed to repair some of the damage he had caused during the Council of Constance. Upon his death, he left the Habsburg territories in better condition than when he got them.

Albert V (1397–1439)

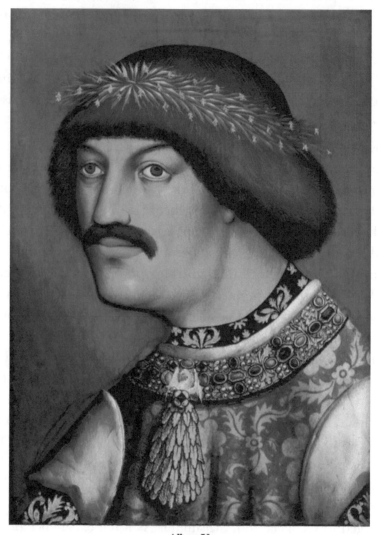

Albert V
https://commons.wikimedia.org/wiki/File:Albrecht_II._von_Habsburg.jpg

The son of Albert IV, Albert V was a member of the Albertinian family branch, and after the death of his cousins, he became the duke of Austria in September of 1404 when he was only seven years old. He ruled his territories with the help of advisors, but after the death of his last regent, Leopold IV, Albert V started administering Austria on his own. He proved to be an able ruler, tying himself into an alliance with Holy Roman

Emperor Sigismund by marrying his daughter. Because of these ties, he was able to gain the imperial crown back for the Habsburgs, the first time in more than 130 years. Albert didn't only give his ultimate support to the old emperor; he also actively took part in the Hussar Rebellion and the Ottoman wars. His brilliant military mind was put in the service of the empire, and as a reward, Sigismund decided to make Albert his heir in 1422. When the old emperor died in 1437, Albert was accepted as the king of Hungary, and in the spring of 1438, he was crowned the king of the Romans, starting his rule as Albert II. It should be noted he was never actually crowned as the Holy Roman emperor. From this point on, the Habsburg family would hold that title until 1806, with only a short interlude between 1742 and 1745 when a member of the House of Wittelsbach was chosen as the Holy Roman emperor.

Albert didn't plan on becoming the king of the Romans, and when he was offered the crown, he took his time in making the decision. Modern scholars believe he was indecisive because the Luxembourg family, who had held the position previously, managed to empty the royal treasury and alienate the imperial possessions from which the taxes were drawn. If Albert chose to accept the crown, he knew the task of rebuilding the empire would be enormous. He had to weigh his options and decide if he was capable of ruling and repairing the whole empire. Aside from the economic disadvantages, the empire was also under the constant threat of the Hussites and the Ottomans. Still, Albert knew he couldn't reject the empire, and he must have believed himself strong enough to deal with all the problems that came with the imperial title. The first task he needed to deal with was in Bohemia. While the nobles and the Catholic Church of Bohemia accepted him as the ruler, the Hussites rejected him. In 1438, Albert marched his army to battle, in which he defeated his opponents. He took the crown of Bohemia, but he didn't remove the Hussite problem permanently. For the time being, though, he was satisfied with the situation, and he turned his attention to the

Ottomans. Albert was a soldier by training and by spirit.

Albert's reign as the king of the Romans lasted for only a year and a half. While leading an expedition against the Ottomans in Hungary, he died of dysentery in October of 1439. He didn't manage to do much for the empire, but he secured the crown for the family, which is considered his greatest achievement. However, Albert did much good when it came to the family territories in Austria. He managed to heal the duchy after the civil war of his brothers ravaged the land. He strengthened the Habsburg army and expanded the defense of the duchy. Through the implementation of special taxes on townspeople and Jews, Albert managed to keep the Austrian treasury full even during the hard times of the Hussite wars. But Albert's reign over Austria wasn't prosperous for everyone. The special taxes on the Jews were the least of their problems, as Albert attempted to forcefully convert them to Christianity, with the long days of the Jewish exodus from Austria starting in 1420. They ended only when Pope Martin V intervened, but over half of the Jewish population had left Austria by that time. The rest were arrested, and those who refused to convert were executed, with their family and business possessions being confiscated by the state. When Albert realized he couldn't continue his Jewish policy, he decided to burn the remaining Viennese Jews on stakes outside the city walls.

Friedrich III (1415-1493)

Coronation of Friedrich III depicted on a tapestry

TribalDragon1, CC BY-SA 4.0 <https://creativecommons.org/licenses/by-sa/4.0>, via Wikimedia Commons https://commons.wikimedia.org/wiki/File:Frederick_III_Coronation_Tapestry.jpg

The Habsburg rule in Austria continued undisturbed, but the family now had the imperial crown in its possession too. During the next two centuries, the Habsburgs would produce a plethora of characteristically different rulers, and through schemes and careful, strategic planning, they would elevate the family to the position of the most important noble house of Europe. With this status, it was easy for the family to spread its dynastical influence on other kingdoms, and through marriage ties, it would acquire the distant territories of modern-day France and Spain. The oddest pair of Habsburg rulers of the time were a father and son: Friedrich III (1415-1493) and Maximilian I (1459-1519). They were very different from each other, but they had one common trait, the inability to fulfill imperial objectives. While Friedrich had no desire to move the empire forward, as he constantly waited for things to happen, his son was the complete opposite. Maximilian had grandiose plans and tried his best to improve the empire's circumstances, but his efforts constantly failed and were fruitless. Friedrich ignored his duties in the empire, while Maximilian gave his best to do something meaningful. In the end, his efforts paid off in some ways, as, during his rule, the Habsburgs became the biggest players in European politics.

Friedrich III was the son of Ernest the Iron, and he is considered one of the worst rulers in German history. His period is marked by anarchy in the governmental system, as well as by the complete atrophy of imperial power. But while his rule may have been disastrous for the empire, he did benefit the Habsburgs by uniting the Austrian lands under a single ruler and by arranging a marriage between his son Maximilian and the princess of Burgundy, the daughter of Charles the Bold (1433–1477). This marriage was important because it brought Burgundian inheritance to the Habsburgs. Friedrich was elected emperor in 1440, and his rule can be divided into two periods. The first one lasted until 1471, and during it, Austria was tormented by the family's internal conflicts. They were so intense that Friedrich had to fully devote his attention to the House of Habsburg and neglect his imperial duties. But from 1471 until he died in 1493, he returned to rule the empire with full attention, and he even attempted to restore the central authority.

Friedrich lacked initiative, and he was often criticized for his lack of energy. His contemporaries even gave him a nickname, the *Erzschlafmütze* (the Arch-Sleepyhead). However, he was never that disconnected. The documents left behind testify that he was very much involved in the decision-making process. Friedrich was well educated and profoundly intellectual. At the same time, though, he was convinced that the Habsburgs had a divine mission and that God would guarantee them success in the end. Because of that, he was an inactive ruler, as he believed in God's plan for the family. But this conviction may have been just his personal effort to rationalize the weakness of his imperial rule. He chose to be inactive because he believed that there was nothing he could do to improve the empire. Still, the fact still stands that he managed to bring all the Habsburg possessions into his hands, which should be proof enough that if Friedrich intended to do something, he would see it to the end. He was a stubborn ruler, which proved to be a beneficial trait, especially when it came to family feuds.

The first family feud started in 1435 when Friedrich became the duke of Inner Austria, while his brother, Albert VI, got the leftover territories at the fringes of the duchy. At this point, Friedrich started using his famous motto, "A.E.I.O.U.," and he started signing documents with it. There are many speculations to the meaning of this motto because the explanation found in Friedrich's personal notebook is somewhat strange. It is written in completely different handwriting; therefore, scholars believe it's a forgery. Nevertheless, it is the only known explanation of the acronym motto, and it claims that A.E.I.O.U. stands for both the German and Latin versions of "All the world is subject to Austria." Another problem with this explanation is that at the time Friedrich started ruling Inner Austria, there were no signs that the whole of Austria could be united. It was fragmented and by no means close to becoming a single entity. This is why it is believed that by Austria, Friedrich meant the House of Austria, which were the Habsburgs.

In 1439, Friedrich became the warden of Tyrol because his uncle, Duke Friedrich IV, died, leaving behind a minor son named Sigismund. Tyrolean nobles demanded Friedrich give up his wardenship in 1443 when Sigismund turned fifteen, as the rightful heir of the duchy was now old enough to rule on his own. But Friedrich refused. In fact, he developed a strategy to hold Sigismund as a personal prisoner until the young duke agreed to hand over at least part of Tyrol's territories to him and his Styrian line of the Habsburgs. This plan would cause Friedrich problems over a decade later, but for now, Friedrich considered it a good plan, as he could use Sigismund as a source of income and as a shield against his brother Albert, who continuously tried to grab more territory for himself. Friedrich persuaded young Sigismund to grant some of his lands to Albert so he wouldn't have to sacrifice his own territories of Inner Austria.

Friedrich repeated this pattern of holding the young Habsburg heir as a pawn for his plans. In 1439, Holy Roman Emperor Albert V died while his wife was pregnant with a son. When the boy was born, the widow chose Friedrich as the warden of her son, Ladislaus Postumus (named this because he was born after his father's death). Ladislaus was the heir of the Albertinian line of the family, as well as the heir to the Bohemian and Hungarian crown, which made him extremely valuable. Because of this, five different influences loomed over the boy his whole life: his mother, Friedrich, and the nobles of Austria, Bohemia, and Hungary. But when Albert's widow chose Friedrich as Ladislaus's guardian, he essentially kept the boy captive and ruled Upper and Lower Austria in his name. When the Hungarian nobles proclaimed Ladislaus their king in 1444, Friedrich refused to hand him over, repeating the pattern he had devised with Sigismund, the heir of Tyrol. In 1452, the Austrian nobles joined the Bohemian and Hungarian nobles to wrestle the control over Ladislaus from the hands of Friedrich, but when the duke refused to even talk to them, they sent an army. Friedrich found himself under siege in Wiener Neustadt. To alleviate the situation, in September of 1452, he agreed to hand the boy over. Ladislaus was immediately taken to Prague to be crowned king of Bohemia.

Ladislaus didn't reign for long as he died in 1457, and his death ignited further family feuds. He was the last male of the Albertinian Habsburgs, which made the remaining family heads—Friedrich, Albert, and Sigismund—fight over Ladislaus's inheritance in Austria. Sigismund and Albert soon made a deal in which Albert promised he would compensate him if he gave up his claims on Ladislaus's possessions. Sigismund agreed, and Friedrich and Albert divided these territories between themselves; however, the conflict continued because the people of Upper and Lower Austria refused to acknowledge either of them as their rulers. Law and order disappeared from these lands, as there was no authority to enforce them. The chaos that ensued from this situation suited Albert, who used his alliance with the king of Bohemia, Jiří z Poděbrad (George of Poděbrady), to get rid of Friedrich in 1461. Friedrich also had the Viennese rebellion to deal with, and by the next year, he was running out of food while living under siege at Hofburg Castle. One of his loyal diplomats used all of his power to persuade the Bohemian king to switch sides, who then helped Friedrich lift Albert's siege. However, the conflict was at its peak in 1463 when Albert suddenly died. In 1464, Friedrich and Sigismund made a deal about Albert's inheritance, and the former became the ruler of Upper and Lower Austria and Vienna.

Friedrich ruled for fifty-three years, but he wasn't elevated to the rank of the Holy Roman emperor due to his political power or ability to rule. He proved he was a passive ruler who achieved very little. Rather, the electors chose him because of the geographical position of his lands. They were situated in such a way that gave Friedrich the ability to deal with both the unrest within the empire as well as the incoming Ottoman invasion. His lands also bordered Hungary, which, at the time, started growing into a powerful kingdom under the rule of Matthias Corvinus. But unlike his predecessors, Friedrich secured the succession of his son, Maximilian. In 1452, he traveled to Rome, where he was crowned by the pope, becoming the last Holy Roman emperor (and the first Habsburg) to do so. By 1470, Friedrich started taking an active role in administering the empire, but it wasn't because he suddenly came to his senses. Rather, it was because the Ottomans were slowly advancing toward his lands, and he needed to prepare the defense. For that, he needed the empire's army. But to efficiently use the army, he had to implement some governmental reforms, which would allow him more freedom to make decisions on his own. However, Friedrich wasn't able to persuade the imperial council to grant him command over the whole imperial army.

They only allowed him a small force of a few thousand men, which was enough to mount a defense of his immediate household and crucial border points. However, during his reign, it wouldn't be the Ottomans Friedrich had to worry about.

At this time, during the 1470s, the Hungarian king, Matthias Corvinus, fought the Turks, and together with Romanian and Serbian nobles, he defended the empire and the whole of Europe from further Ottoman invasions. In 1482, he made a truce with the sultan and used this armistice to attack Friedrich. He overran Lower Austria, Carinthia, and Carniola, and in 1485, he even conquered Vienna. In 1487, he took Friedrich's imperial residence of Wiener Neustadt, making the emperor search for refuge in Linz. Matthias even named himself the archduke of Austria, and there was nothing Friedrich could do to dispose of him at that time. In fact, Friedrich used these events to deal with his succession issues. He led very careful politics to ensure that his son Maximilian was elected as the king of the Romans. This title was traditional, as it simply meant he was the official heir of the empire. But it wasn't only Friedrich's political achievements that secured Maximilian as his heir; it was also the willingness of the German electors, who hoped that the emperor's young and energetic son would perform much better than his father.

Friedrich hoped that he could influence the German council to grant him the army to regain the territories he lost to the Hungarian king. But once again, he was refused the command, so he had no other choice but to wait. Matthias Corvinus died in 1490, leaving no male heir behind him. After his death, no ruler was rich enough to maintain his Black Army, the most powerful and numerous mercenaries of the period, and they dissipated. Maximilian led the Austrian army to retake the lands, and he was successful. However, he ran out of funds quickly and had to abandon his intentions to push even deeper and take more Hungarian territories. But instead of choosing the Habsburg, the Hungarian nobles elected the Bohemian king as their next sovereign. Instead of admitting defeat in the Hungarian elections, Maximilian persuaded his cousin, Sigismund of Tyrol, to sell him the ruling rights over his possessions. Maximilian took over the governance of the Tyrol area in 1490, but it was only in 1492 that other Habsburgs acknowledged and approved of this transition of power. Once again, the entire Habsburg patrimony was ruled by one individual—well, two to be precise, as both Friedrich and Maximilian, father and son, ruled as the head of the family. But by 1493, Friedrich's health had deteriorated, and he suffered a fatal stroke that August. Friedrich didn't achieve much, but he certainly laid the foundations for the successful rule of Maximilian I.

Maximilian I (1459-1519)

Emperor Maximilian I with his family
https://commons.wikimedia.org/wiki/File:Bernhard_Strigel_003b.jpg

Habsburg lore presents Maximilian I as the "Last Knight." The truth is, he ruled during the early Renaissance when the old chivalric ideals started to wane, and he was the type of king who would lead his own troops. Another aspect of his rule and life that puts him closer to the medieval knights than to the Renaissance princes was the constant movement of his government, much like the itinerary courts of the past, as his government had no permanent capital city. But in all other aspects, Maximilian was a true Renaissance man. He was constantly occupied with new ideas and projects, as well as new innovations in science and art. Even his military ideology wasn't completely stuck in the past, as he wholeheartedly approved the use of modern artillery. He is considered to be one of the most advanced rulers of his time, and he often indulged in the humanistic trends of art, philosophy, engineering, and science. Therefore, Maximilian I wasn't the "Last Knight" as his family tried to present him, but he also wasn't fully a Renaissance prince. He walked the fine line between those two worlds, and the success with which he did so speaks much about his character.

Niccolò Machiavelli, a famous Italian philosopher, met Maximilian on a few occasions, and he described him as a perfect ruler with only one flaw—he didn't know how to manage his funds. This is true, as Maximilian's grandiose plans were often held back by the lack of funds. He spent most of the royal treasury on conflicts with France after he married the daughter of Burgundy's ruler, Marie the Rich, in 1477. With this marriage, Maximilian gained the right to the Burgundian inheritance, but King Louis XI of France held great interest in these territories. The French monarch wouldn't allow part of his empire to go into the hands of a German king. By 1481, Maximilian resolved the issue he had with Louis XI by surrendering Artois and the original duchy of Burgundy. But these conflicts were costly, and the people of the Low Countries (today's Netherlands, Belgium, Luxembourg, and the French Calais region) rebelled. The lack of money wasn't the only reason for a rebellion, though it helped its spread through the various social classes. They also protested against the new ruler, Maximilian. When his wife died in 1482, the resistance of the people became even stronger. The Flemish nobles demanded to take his son, Philip, under their custody so he could become Princess Marie's heir rather than a Habsburg heir. Maximilian was forced to go to war against the nobles to preserve his status as a ruler, and in 1485, he managed to defeat them.

However, his victory didn't bring the end of the conflict. He raised the taxes again so he could pay the foreign mercenaries he had employed, and the people revolted once more. But during this revolt, the representatives of Bruges and Ghent managed to take Maximilian as their prisoner. In 1488, he was held hostage in a pharmacy building on the main square of Bruges for several weeks. Afraid for his life, Maximilian smuggled a letter to his father, in which he begged him for help. Only when Friedrich organized an army to help rescue his son did the nobles of Bruges, Gent, and the city of Ypres sit at the negotiating table. Realizing they had installed fear in Maximilian, they decided to treat him with respect and acknowledge him as a ruler, but this was not the end of his troubles in the Low Countries.

Burgundy, or at least some of its territory in the Low Countries, remained a Habsburg possession until 1797. These were rich lands that brought wealth to the family, but they also played a cultural role in the Habsburg rule of the empire. They were the bridge between Germany and France, and through them, art and intellectual ideas were often exchanged. The cultural influence of France on the Habsburg dynasty cannot be denied, but the influence traveled both ways, as France adopted some of the German values and ideals of the Habsburg court. Politically, the Burgundian lands drew the Habsburgs into the orbit of French and English influence, but it also sparked the conflict between France and the Habsburgs, which would shake Europe for more than two centuries.

Back in Austria, Maximilian's rule brought peace and order. The Habsburg lands were finally unified under one ruler, whose main base was in Innsbruck, Tyrol. Maximilian chose Tyrol as his base because Vienna was too far east, while his personal and political interests lay in the west and the newly acquired Low Countries. Thanks to its silver and salt mines, as well as the fact that the main transalpine trade route went through it, Tyrol was the golden goose of Austria and the Habsburg dynasty, whose revenues

Maximilian used to fund his wars and political schemes. But unlike his father, Maximilian didn't concentrate all of his energy on Austria. He wanted to be the perfect emperor. He was aware his empire was threatened by both the French and the Ottomans, and he wanted to make the whole of Germany strong so it could resist these threats. To achieve this, Maximilian needed to reform the imperial institutions, such as the administration, justice system, and financial sector. However, the nobles, the prelates, and the independent cities had a different idea of what these reforms should include. The main problem was that Maximilian was never able to differentiate between his personal interests and state interests. For him, he was the empire, and everything he considered good for himself was by default good for the state. But the rich and noble of Germany did not agree. Maximilian wanted to make the central power more effective; he did not want to strengthen the state but rather bolster his power and spread his influence through the empire. In the end, the nobles agreed to negotiate with Maximilian, and it took several assemblies, known as the *Reichstag*, to finalize the reforms.

However, the differences between the king and his counselors were so great that, in most cases, the reforms were only partially applied. For example, during one of the assemblies that took place in Worms in 1495, the new imperial high court, the *Reichskammergericht*, was created. It had the role of accepting the appeals of lower courts, which helped centralize the empire's justice system. However, the nobles did everything in their power to minimize the influence the emperor would have in the high court, and Maximilian was even banned from electing the judges. But the Worms assembly did approve the creation of the so-called "common penny," a new tax that raised revenues with which the imperial defense was funded. This was positive from Maximilian's point of view, as the new tax created steady means of funding the army for conflicts he instigated. But Maximilian didn't expect there to be resistance to the new tax. Even four years after its installment, the "common penny" wasn't being collected.

For the next two decades after 1495, Maximilian was mired in a series of wars that didn't bring him much success. A large part of the conflict was against the French ruling family, the Valois. But this time, they didn't fight about Burgundy but rather who would assert influence on Italy. Maximilian was eager to continue the empire's influence in its former territories of northern Italy, but the French kings, namely Charles VIII and Louis XII, started taking an interest in the region. To keep his authority alive, he agreed to marry Bianca Maria Sforza, a daughter of the Duke of Milan. Another reason behind this marriage was her dowry, which would bring Maximilian much-needed finances to keep the conflict alive. But there was never anything else in this marriage other than financial interests. Maximilian treated his new wife very poorly, making her live as a commoner in a small household. She was forced to let go of her servants and all of her ladies-in-waiting. At one point, she even pawned her underwear at the local creditors to buy food. All of this just to finance her husband's expensive wars, wars that brought him nothing but humiliation. In Italy, Maximilian was repeatedly defeated by the French, and in 1500, his father-in-law was captured, which gave the French king control over Milan. The imperial estates in Burgundy, Germany, and Austria refused to send money and men to Maximilian, as the council saw them as pointless.

But Maximilian wasn't willing to give up his plans. After 1500, he began using diplomacy more often than arms. His luck seemed to turn around, as he proved to be more successful in diplomacy than in warfare. He managed to break the alliance of France and the Republic of Venice, and in 1508, he organized the League of Cambria, which included the Papal States, France, and Spain, and pitted the league against Venice. Eventually, France broke off and resumed a hostile attitude toward Maximilian. The emperor searched for help in Britain, and together, they attacked Paris. However, the war was fruitless, and in 1514, Maximilian and Louis

XII signed a truce. Due to the debts he had created to keep the wars going, Maximilian had to give up on his efforts in Venice in 1518, but the war against the French in Italy resumed. During the last years of his life, Maximilian made sure his grandson, Charles V, would be elected the next Holy Roman emperor. He started bribing the German electors, but he died before his endeavor was complete. Charles V had to continue his father's efforts by himself.

Chapter 3: The Superpower of Europe

The Imperial Banner (1400–1806)
David Liuzzo, eagle by N3MO, CC BY-SA 3.0 <https://creativecommons.org/licenses/by-sa/3.0>, via Wikimedia Commons
https://commons.wikimedia.org/wiki/File:Banner_of_the_Holy_Roman_Emperor_with_haloes_(1400-1806).svg

During the reign of Charles V and his immediate successors, the Holy Roman Empire became a European superpower. The rulers of the 16th century are rightfully called "the greatest generation of Habsburgs." Every head member of the family born in this time was either a king or a queen. They ruled the Holy Roman Empire, Hungary, Bohemia, Austria, and more. Female members of the Habsburgs were married off to be queens of some of the greatest European kingdoms, such as Portugal, the Netherlands, France, Denmark, Sweden, and Norway. Charles V chose his motto "Plus ultra" ("further beyond"), as it symbolically described his greatest achievement, the extension of the borders of his empire to the Gates of Gibraltar. He had heard these words when he was a youngster from his Italian advisor, who believed the Christian world would expand beyond Europe. Charles's empire was globe-spanning, larger than any European ruler, past or present, could ever claim. It was this 16th-century empire that brought Austria the closest to its destiny of ruling the world.

There was one family to rule them all during this time. Maybe not in name alone, but by its presence. The Habsburgs gained so many European crowns because they were seen as the answer to the problems of the time. The Habsburgs were extremely wealthy, had many powerful allies, were influential, and, above all, were a family. As such, they were regarded as a unique body that would be strong enough to defend the lands from external threats. In Bohemia and Hungary, the Habsburgs came to rule because they were willing to spend their family resources to mount the defense against the Ottoman invasion. This generation of Habsburgs also proved to be very cosmopolitan and adaptive to the various cultures of Europe. As a family, they were brought up in the same manner but in different parts of the empire. They were given a unique opportunity to learn about the world that surrounded them. Because of this, when they became rulers of Poland, Sweden, Portugal, or even Sicily, they had no trouble adapting to become an efficient king or queen. However, this doesn't mean they were extraordinary people. For example, Charles V was not a brilliant ruler or a military strategist. He was simply a man who, by luck, came to wield extraordinary power and wealth. But he proved to be competent enough to fulfill the responsibilities that came with the imperial titles.

Once the family parted ways to take up their titles, they would rarely meet. Charles and his younger brother, Ferdinand, the king of Hungary, Croatia, and Bohemia, met for the first time in 1517. They had spent very little time together, so they never really knew each other. As rulers, their interests were often different, but they managed to form a close and cordial working relationship. The explanation for this must be in the family ties and the sense of loyalty the Habsburgs cherished. The rules were simple: Charles was not only the emperor but also the head of the family, so Ferdinand owed him his allegiance. Gradually, the brothers developed a mutual trust, and Charles even allowed Ferdinand to take the affairs of the Holy Roman Empire on himself while he was busy with his personal interests. At the same time, Ferdinand was aware of his brother's expectations, and he didn't try to take the initiative when it came to the empire's administration. He knew his task was only to carry out Charles's orders. However, the brothers had disagreements over various matters. For example, they couldn't agree on how to deal with the Ottomans or who would succeed the imperial throne after Charles's death. Still, Ferdinand proved to be patient and wise. He never openly disobeyed or voiced his considerations. He learned how to stall, misdirect, and persuade his brother to change his mind.

Charles V (1500-1558)

Emperor Charles V from 1519
https://commons.wikimedia.org/wiki/File:Barend_van_Orley_-_Portrait_of_Charles_V_-_Google_Art_Project.jpg

Charles was raised by his aunt, Archduchess Margaret, who governed Habsburg Netherland. She was the daughter of Holy Roman Emperor Maximilian I, and she took in young Charles and hired his first tutor, Adrian of Utrecht, who would later become Pope Hadrian VI. These two guardians installed chivalric values, the love for God, and a sense of duty to the Church in the young prince. He adopted these attitudes very early in his life, and they would continue to mark his entire reign. At the age of sixteen, he came to rule Spain, even though he had never set foot in the country before. The Spanish nobility resisted him at first because they saw him as a foreign ruler. His own brother, Ferdinand, was born and raised in Spain, so they preferred him. To remove the threat his younger brother posed, Charles sent Ferdinand to Germany to take care of the family estates.

Not very long after becoming the king of Spain, Charles's grandfather, Emperor Maximilian I, died in 1519. To secure his election, the previous emperor had started buying votes. Through his proxies, Charles continued to do the same, spending so much money on bribes that he remains known in history as the emperor who bought his empire. The other two competitors for the title, Francis I of France and Henry VIII of England, had no such funds to compete with the young Habsburg. Charles spent, borrowed, and received approximately 851,000 florins, whose value is hard to estimate today. To paint the picture, the rich families, nobles, and merchants who lent the money to the king had to put themselves and their businesses in debt. However, the investment was worth it because once Charles became the emperor, they rose to become major merchants and nobles, and their businesses grew tremendously. The price of the German crown speaks about the prestige it brought to the person who wore it. But after Charles V's reign, that prestige started diminishing, never to rise to those heights again. Although being the Holy Roman emperor was restrictive in the sense of executive power, one had to protect the Christian world from the Atlantic Ocean in the west to the eastern Austrian frontiers, from the Low Countries in the north to the Mediterranean Sea in the south. During the 16th century, the empire was the largest since Charlemagne had initiated it in 800.

The empire's enormous size meant Charles had to rely on governors, viceroys, and diplomats to control it. Although the Holy Roman Empire was a German empire, Charles only spent nine years of his forty-year reign in Germany proper. Charles spent the first years of his reign in Spain. He learned Castilian, adopted his government to the traditional Spanish, and he started acting like a Spaniard. These efforts finally brought him popularity in the Iberian Peninsula. In return, he secured peace and prosperity for the Spanish kingdom. However, Charles's start of the imperial rule is marred by the Spanish rebellion, known as the Revolt of the Comuneros, during which the nobles who were against the imperial rule formed a communal government (hence the name Comuneros). At the time, Charles wasn't in Spain, and he had left the kingdom under the regency of his tutor, Adrian of Utrecht. The rebels demanded more freedom for certain cities, the king's presence in the country, and the ousting of foreigners from the royal offices. The conflict lasted for only one year, and the imperial loyalists won the decisive Battle of Villar in April 1521. The leaders of the revolt were arrested and executed. The end of the revolt brought security to the Habsburg succession of the Spanish crown and the strengthening of the monarchical rule.

The rebellion in Spain wasn't the only one Charles had to deal with during his reign as Holy Roman emperor. His native Netherlands rose against him because he extensively used its riches to fund his imperial ventures. Just as with Spain, Charles was absent from the Netherlands when the rebellion occurred. The whole region was under the governorship of his aunt Margaret, and the first troubles there occurred much earlier in 1515 when Maximilian I had raised the taxes to fund his wars. Charles inherited this rebellion from his grandfather and dealt it a final blow in 1523 when his army captured and executed two of the most prominent leaders of the rebellion.

Although these regions were problematic for Charles, the most troublesome was the governance of the whole Holy Roman Empire, as this was the period when the Reformation started, which was one of the most disruptive times in European history. The emperor was a defender of Christianity, but this doesn't mean Charles was extremely orthodox in his beliefs. He lived during the Renaissance, so he was influenced by the ideas of great religious and secular leaders, which led him to believe that the Church indeed needed reform. During his reign, Germany was torn apart by the religious conflict between Catholics and Protestants, with Martin Luther demanding the reformation not only of the Church but also of the pope's authority. Charles hoped he could end the conflict peacefully, but he considered Luther's ideas to be heretical, and he even admitted he would personally be ashamed if he allowed their spread through his empire. The main reason why

Charles was against the Reformation was that he saw it as means of breaking the unity of all Christians. But this wasn't the only reason. Charles was an intelligent man, and he realized that with the break of Christian unity, the unity of the Holy Roman Empire would end too. German princes had already begun using Protestant ideas against the emperor's power, but Charles refused to make a compromise. His stubbornness in the matter only resulted in even stronger resistance to his rule. Christianity ended up splintered, and Charles's reign as emperor fell apart.

At the Reichstag (or Diet) of Worms, in April 1521, Charles met with Martin Luther and heard his famous speech in which he explained his principles and demanded reformation of the Church. However, Charles wasn't swayed, and he saw no other solution but to outlaw Luther. The ideas of the Reformation continued to spread through the empire, and the famous priest found refuge at the court of the Saxon prince. By 1530, when the next Reichstag was to be held, the Protestants had split and started gathering in two factions, one based on the teachings of Luther and the other one around Ulrich Zwingli, a Swiss leader of the Reformation movement. But Charles's main goal of the Reichstag wasn't only to find a religious compromise but also to raise money and an army against the Ottomans. However, he failed in both. The only thing he managed to achieve during this meeting was to secure his brother, Ferdinand, as his successor. The younger Habsburg brother was given the title of king of the Romans in 1531. Charles promised he would not use force against the Protestants, but the religious conflict continued to rage, and for the next decade, Charles continuously tried to appease both the Catholics and Protestants to no avail. Finally, when he realized there was no other solution, he turned to the military. During the Reichstag of Regensburg in 1541, the negotiations were going well, but the final form of peace was rejected by both the pope and Martin Luther.

The pope finally started a council for the Counter-Reformation in 1545, but this time, the Protestants refused to attend. Instead, they organized the Schmalkaldic League, an alliance of several German princes and cities whose task was to mount a defense against the Catholics. The 1540s saw several German prince-electors convert to Protestantism, and by 1547, the majority of the imperial electoral college belonged to them. This was a major threat to the Habsburgs, especially because the German Protestants allied with Charles's enemy, Francis I, King of France. The emperor saw no other choice but to war against his enemies, although he was careful enough to specify that not all Protestants were considered enemies, just the treacherous Schmalkaldic League. Charles started organizing his supporters into an alliance, which mainly included the German nobles who wanted to replace the existing electors. The decisive battle occurred at Mühlberg in April 1547, and Charles won. This victory was Charles's high point of his rule, but it didn't really help him solve the empire's internal problems. He tried to push for even stronger centralization of the government, but even the Catholic princes refused him, seeing it as just another excuse to grab more power.

The next several years were disastrous for Charles, as the events that occurred led to his abdication. He publicly declared his wish to make the imperial crown alternate between the Spanish and Austrian branches of the Habsburg family, but both Catholics and Protestants resented the idea of being ruled by a Spaniard. The Protestants again allied with the French king, who was now Henry II, and in 1552, they launched a surprise attack on Charles. Charles managed to defend his position in Innsbruck and made the Protestant army retreat across the Alps to Carinthia. That same year, Henry II launched an attack on German cities in Lorraine, defeating Charles. Ferdinand took over the negotiations with the Protestant princes, and in 1555, he achieved the Peace of Augsburg. It was a religious peace that brought rulers the power to decide whether their territories would be Protestant or Catholic. Charles refused to sign the document because it degraded the imperial authority, leaving each king to make such a decision without consulting the emperor. Nevertheless, Ferdinand finalized the peace and signed it with imperial authority as the king of the Romans and Charles's heir.

When it came to foreign policy, Charles's main problem was the constant conflict with France, and, in particular, its king Francis I (r. 1515-1547). But this conflict was much older, as it started during the reign of Maximilian when he took Burgundy. Since then, the French kings were eager to reclaim Burgundy back, as well as to end the Habsburg superiority in Europe. After all, France was surrounded by the Habsburg territories, in the north with the Low Countries and Calais, Germany to the east, and Spain in the south. Charles and Francis mainly competed for control of Navarre, Burgundy, and northern Italy, particularly Milan. Francis also resented Charles because he lost the imperial election to him, and he took the opportunity of the unrest caused by the Revolt of the Comuneros to attack Navarre in 1521. However, the Spanish Army managed to deal with the French without having to invoke imperial protection. The conflict then moved to northern Italy because it was the richest region of Europe at the time and a worthy prize. Charles defended Milan with vigor because he saw the region as a link to his territories in the south of Italy, which he had inherited from his Spanish side of the family. But France wasn't the only one trying to assert its influence in northern Italy. At the Battle of Pavia in 1525, Charles defeated Francis and even took him as a prisoner. The next year, in Madrid, the French king signed a peace treaty in which he renounced his claims in Italy and Flanders, but as soon as he was freed, he reputed the treaty, mainly because he had the support of Pope Clement VII and the Papal States. Charles sent an army to Rome to intimidate the pope, but his army rebelled against him because he failed to pay the soldiers. The mutiny within the Habsburg army resulted in the sacking of Rome and the pope's exile for nine months. Charles apologized for the unfortunate events, but the scandal shook Europe and ruined his good image. For several more years, the French attacked the Habsburgs in Italy, but Pope Clement eventually forgave the emperor and even agreed to crown him on February 24th, 1530, on Charles's thirtieth birthday.

Despite this, the conflict with France continued, especially in 1534 when Francis made an agreement with the Ottomans against the Habsburgs and attacked Italy again. Charles wanted to avoid the deaths of his people, so he offered to personally fight Francis in a duel, but Pope Paul III strictly forbade such a fight. Peace was finally made in 1537 when both monarchs exhausted their funds and had no means to continue the war. In 1542, Francis made another offensive, this time attacking both Italy and the Netherlands. For this fight, Charles managed to persuade the council to grant him the imperial army, and he was also joined by Henry VIII of England. Together, they invaded France, reaching Paris. In retaliation, Francis attacked Naples in 1544, but his further advance was stopped by his death in 1547. His son and heir, Henry II, resumed the conflict with the Habsburgs in 1552.

Two major events occurred during Charles V's reign that he didn't consider important enough to occupy his imperial attention. However, from the point of history, these events are striking. The first one was the Ottoman advances in Europe, which Charles's brother Ferdinand had to deal with, and the second one was the conquest of the Americas. By 1519, the subjugation of the Aztecs had started, just a few months before Charles became emperor. In 1535, a major naval battle with the Ottomans occurred in the Mediterranean Sea, off the shores of Tunis. In the same year, the conquest of the Incan Empire happened, and the spread of the Christian lands was achieved in the name of the king of Spain and emperor of all Christians, Charles V. Though Charles had little to do with it personally, everything that was achieved was in his name and glory. New Spain (modern-day Mexico) and Peru were both organized as separate kingdoms under Charles's rule but were overseen with the help of special viceroys and councils known as *audiencias*. Charles only meddled in the overseas colonies to secure the human rights of the conquered natives. This was very progressive for the time. Charles couldn't allow slavery to rise in the newly acquired territories, especially since Spain made slavery illegal in its proper territories in 1492, even though it remained fully legal in the colonies. Regardless, Charles believed that natives, at least those who were born free, should remain rightful citizens of his new kingdom, even though they were often described as nothing more than savage animals. In 1542, he brought about a series of laws that abolished slavery in the Spanish territories of the Americas, but his decision to do so wasn't completely humanitarian. He needed free people who could keep the viceroys in check and prevent them from making the new kingdoms hereditary lands and creating a new dynasty that would overthrow the Habsburgs. However, Europe and the emperor were far away, so the laws Charles brought forth were not always enforced.

Charles was aware his empire was too big to be governed by one person or even as one unified political entity. Because of this, he appointed his younger brother Ferdinand as the regent of *Erblande*, the Austrian Hereditary Lands, in 1522. But what Charles really did was set the stage for yet another division of the family, this time in the Austrian and Spanish branches. Later in life, Charles feared Ferdinand wasn't strong enough to keep all of the family possessions together, especially Burgundy, so he awarded the Low Countries to his son Philip, who already had Spanish wealth as the heir of the Spanish crown. Eventually, Charles wanted Philip to take over Germany and to secure the imperial crown for the Spanish branch of the Habsburg family, but he quickly gave up on this idea because he realized the German princes would never allow a Spanish king to rule them. Charles did all of this with the intention of abdicating the throne. He had planned to do so since 1553, but he took his time to secure his son's position in the political world. In 1555, with a very emotional speech and tears in his eyes, Charles passed the control over the Low Countries to his son Philip. In January 1556, he gave up his

Spanish crown, and by the end of the year, he no longer had the imperial one. The next year, Charles retired to the Monastery of Yuste in Extremadura, Spain. However, the old emperor didn't lead a monastic life. He brought around sixty servants with him, and he often enjoyed luxurious dinner parties. He continued to follow politics and advise his son Philip until his death in September of 1558.

Ferdinand I (1503–1564)

FERDINAND· D·G· ROMAN· IMP· SEMPER AVG·
GERMAN· VNGAR· BOHEMIÆ· DALM·CROAT·REX
ARCHID·AVSTRIÆ DVX BVRGVND·COM·TIROLIS·ZC
M·D·LXXV

Emperor Ferdinand I, a posthumous portrait from 1575
https://commons.wikimedia.org/wiki/File:Ferdinand_I_by_Martin_Rota.jpg

Ferdinand was born and raised in Spain, but he became the regent of his brother Charles in the hereditary lands of Austria. When he arrived in Austria in 1521, although he was a Habsburg, he wasn't immediately accepted. Just like his brother did in Spain, Ferdinand had to deal with the xenophobia of the natives, who regarded him as a foreigner who brought many Spaniards and Netherlanders to his new court. By the time he arrived in Vienna, both Lower and Upper Austria were in revolt. However, Ferdinand was very methodical, and he dealt with the uprising immediately. He brought its leaders to trial and had them executed. He then started learning the German language and the situation in the country so he could rule more effectively. But unlike Charles, Ferdinand wanted to get close to the people, and he learned not only German but also Polish and Hungarian, which would be the languages of the territories he would come to rule later in life.

Already in 1526, the Bohemians chose Ferdinand as their king since their own king, Louis II, died in battle against the Ottomans. This wasn't strange because Ferdinand was Louis's brother-in-law, and Louis chose to pass the inheritance to a Habsburg. However, the Hungarians were not so eager to give the crown to Ferdinand. The Hungarian nobles chose Transylvanian magnate John Szapolyai as their king. But Ferdinand's sister and Louis's widow, Mary, took it upon herself to win some of the Hungarian nobles for her brother. She was successful, but it wasn't enough, as Szapolyai was ready to defend his right with arms. The conflict around the Hungarian crown lasted for years, although Ferdinand managed to defeat him in 1527. The Transylvanians managed to escape and form an alliance with Francis I of France and with Ottoman Sultan Suleiman. By 1530, Ferdinand had been crowned king of Hungary, but in reality, he only controlled a small portion of its territories: Croatia, western Hungary, and Upper Hungary, which is today's territory of Slovakia. Transylvania was in the hands of Szapolyai, and the rest of the Hungarian kingdom was occupied by the Ottomans. In 1538, Ferdinand and Szapolyai made a deal by which the Habsburg monarch would inherit Transylvania after Szapolyai's death. But when John died in 1540, Ferdinand wasn't strong enough to claim his inheritance. Instead, Szapolyai's son became the new voivode of Transylvania, as he was backed by the sultan. Hungary remained divided into three parts until the 17th century.

Ferdinand managed to lay foundations for the Habsburg monarchy in the Danubian lands, and this monarchy greatly outlasted the Spanish claims. The development of this monarchy was shaped by how Bohemia and Hungary became part of the Habsburg territories, as they entered as two separate and independent kingdoms. But the main reason why the Bohemians and Hungarians wanted the Habsburgs to rule them was that they believed the family was strong enough to defend them from the Turkish invasion. However, this was the only common goal of the three kingdoms, as Austria, Bohemia, and Hungary had very little in common during the course of the 16th century. Both Hungary and Bohemia were composite kingdoms, which means they were made up of different provinces with various degrees of autonomy. Bohemia consisted of Bohemia proper as well as Moravia, which had Czech-speaking nobility, and Silesia and Lusatia with German-speaking nobility. The later provinces were decentralized and controlled by independent families, but as a whole, Bohemia had a well-developed and prosperous mining and textile industries. Hungary also consisted of different provinces: Hungary proper, Croatia, Slovakia, and Transylvania (today part of Romania). But Hungary was in a more difficult position because its parts were occupied by the Turks, while Transylvania acted as a Turkish vassal (though not all the time). Because of that, Hungary lagged behind in industrialization, and it heavily depended on agriculture.

Ferdinand had a difficult task in front of him: to rule a territory made up of three different kingdoms, which, in turn, were made of smaller provinces with a certain autonomy. He had to think of a way to govern this disparate conglomeration if he was to be an efficient ruler and especially if he was to protect them from the Ottomans, who took a step closer to Vienna with each passing year. In 1521, they took Belgrade (today's capital of Serbia), and in 1526, they defeated the Hungarians. Austria stood next in line. Ferdinand had to mount a defense, but he had very limited resources. His realms had around seven million people compared to the Ottomans, who numbered around twenty million. While the sultan had no difficulties mustering around 60,000 soldiers, Ferdinand had a very difficult time recruiting even 20,000. But luck was on Ferdinand's side because for the Ottomans of the 15th century, the conquest of Austria wasn't a priority. They fought their main battles in the east against Persia. Nevertheless, they still posed a threat to Europe, and Ferdinand had to be prepared to go on the defense. He couldn't rely on the help of the Holy Roman Empire because his brother, Emperor Charles V, was fighting his wars against France and cared little about what was going on in the east. Ferdinand thought that the best defense was a strong offense, and he started raising money for an army by implementing a "Turkish Tax" (Türken Steuer) in 1523, a tax that was paid by every single man, woman, boy, and girl down to the age of twelve. But the decentralized state of his kingdom made it very difficult for him to collect this tax, so he had to personally visit the capitals of each province in order to do so. Unfortunately, all these efforts failed, and he didn't succeed in gathering money from his kingdoms. He was forced to turn to borrow, and his main source became the wealthy German Fugger family.

Finally, in 1529, Ferdinand experienced the most dramatic moment of his conflict with the Ottomans when they came to besiege Vienna. Suleiman sent an army of nearly 100,000 men, and although Ferdinand asked Charles for help, he stood alone against the might of the Turks. The city almost fell, but the sultan decided to cut his losses and pull the army back south. A close call turned into a wake-up call, and in 1532, Charles gathered 100,000 of his soldiers and came to help Austria's battle against the Ottomans. The Ottomans warred for two months but kept avoiding meeting the majority of Charles's army, and by September that same year, they gave up on their advance north. Vienna would come under such a threat much later, in 1683. Although Ferdinand didn't have immediate enemies at his borders, he tried to retake Buda in 1541. He failed, and he even lost the Hungarian cities of

Pécs and Esztergom. By 1547, Ferdinand was so weakened he had no choice but to sign a truce with the sultan and pay him an annual tribute of 30,000 florins. But three years later, he resumed the wars by reclaiming Transylvania. This time, Ferdinand was more successful, and by 1556, he managed to reclaim some of the Hungarian cities, such as Eger and Szigetvar.

When Charles V abdicated in 1556, Ferdinand became the emperor, but he wasn't officially crowned until 1558. The Peace of Augsburg he negotiated for his brother brought him great prestige, even though Charles saw it as a defeat. Nevertheless, the treaty brought religious peace to the empire, at least for the next several decades. In the meantime, though, Austria, Hungary, and Bohemia became predominantly Protestant territories, with the majority of its princes, nobles, and citizens opting for Lutheranism or Calvinism. Only Croatia remained firmly Catholic, and together with some of the minorities in Austria and Bohemia, the Catholics represented only one-third of the overall citizens. Ferdinand had to be very careful about his family's stubbornness in practicing Catholicism, and he also had to decide how he would govern his empire, as a Catholic or as a Protestant. To avoid direct decision-making, Ferdinand allowed the imperial crown to lose some of its importance, as he loosened up the centralization of the empire. Each local ruler had the right to decide the religion of their territory; thus, Ferdinand avoided the continuation of the religious conflict. Unlike Charles, Ferdinand resented conflict in general, and he decided not to pursue the wars with France that had been started by his brother. He spent his years as emperor ensuring his son, Maximilian, would be granted the succession.

Chapter 4: Religious Divide and the Years of War

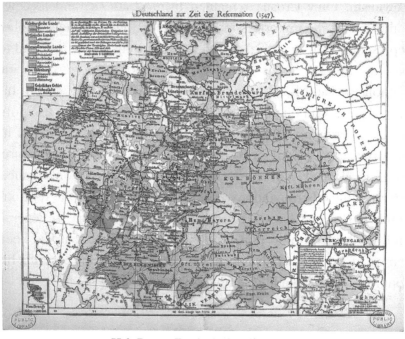

Holy Roman Empire in the 16th century
https://commons.wikimedia.org/wiki/File:Deutschland_im_XVI._Jahrhundert_(Putzger).jpg

The period between 1564 and 1619 saw Europe shaken to its core by the religious divide. This divide started earlier, during the reign of Charles V and Ferdinand I, but it was their successors who had to deal with mending the wounds that had been caused by the religious disagreements. Maximilian II, son of Ferdinand I, said, "I am neither a Catholic nor a Protestant—I am a Christian." However willing he was, Maximilian found it a difficult task to bridge the divide between Protestants and Catholics. In the end, the task proved impossible, as no politician of this period managed to achieve it. The rulers of the late 16th and early 17th centuries tried their best to stay neutral and not take sides, but they were under constant criticism from the conservative Catholics and extreme Lutherans. If the religious factions had something in common, it was the constant rejection of any kind of compromise. Maximilian II was an intelligent and conscientious king, but he failed to keep religious peace in his empire. His sons, Rudolf and Matthias, proved to be rulers who achieved very little. Rudolf was a black sheep in the family, more interested in the arts and the occult than in leading the country, and his brother, Matthias, had no other choice but to usurp the throne. Although these three Habsburgs are interesting to study as individuals, they failed as rulers.

Maximilian II (1527–1576)

Emperor Maximilian II and his family
https://commons.wikimedia.org/wiki/File:Giuseppe_Arcimboldi_003.jpg

Maximilian was always open to various interpretations when it came to religion, and his father, Ferdinand I, suspected he would leave the family's Catholicism behind if given a chance. That is why Ferdinand worried about making him a successor as early as the 1550s since Maximilian started voicing his opinions against the Jesuits and the pope's Catholicism. But the threats that he would disinherit Maximilian seemed to be working, so Ferdinand was content to see his son never officially convert to Protestantism. In truth, Maximilian got the pope's permission to receive communion in both Christian and Protestant ways. Maximilian's main problem with the Protestants was with the Calvinists and the Bohemian Brethren, whom he considered heretics. He was more sympathetic toward the Lutherans but restrained himself from actually converting to preserve the family's religious unity. He assumed the duties toward the Catholic Church once he became emperor, but he continued to criticize its hostility toward Protestants. Maximilian strongly believed that the religious divide of Europe could never be mended by the sword, and he greatly disapproved of the French St. Bartholomew's Day massacre of 1572 when thousands of Huguenots (French Protestants) were killed.

In 1548, Maximilian married his cousin, Maria of Spain, the daughter of Charles V, as a result of Charles's plan to keep the imperial crown in the Habsburg family and to alternate it between the Spanish and Austrian branches. By 1551, Maximilian had started scheming against Philip II of Spain to thwart his succession as the Holy Roman emperor. He befriended Protestant princes and presented himself as a defender of German interests. Maximilian succeeded in overtaking the imperial crown because Philip firmly believed in dogmatic Catholicism, while Maximilian was more willing to make compromises with the Protestants, who were a majority in the empire at the time, especially in Germany and the rest of the Danubian lands. In 1564, Maximilian received the imperial crown after his father died. Once he became emperor, Maximilian's attitude toward Spain mellowed, and he even sent his two sons to the court of his cousin, Philip II, to receive an education there. Religious duality was a reality in the Danubian lands, and the only thing that kept the Habsburgs sticking with Catholicism was the imperial role they had to play as the defenders of Christianity. However, throughout the empire, Catholicism was in decline, except in Tyrol. In Bohemia and Hungary, the decline was so steep that at one point, the monasteries started emptying, and the nobles acquired abandoned church estates. Still, Catholicism hung on, mainly because the imperial family belonged to that religious faction, and none of the Protestant princes ever came near being powerful enough to overthrow the Habsburgs.

Like most of the rulers of the 16th century, Maximilian regarded religious dualism as dangerous. He believed that the empire could remain united only if all the people shared one religion, as it would give them a sense of community and the greater good. Maximilian dreamed about reconnecting his subjects and placing them under one religion. Unfortunately, his dreams remained only that. The harsh reality of politics prevented him from actively pursuing the question of the Reformation and reconciling the differences between Catholics and Protestants. The local rulers took advantage of that, requesting official acknowledgment of religious freedoms in return for financial support. By 1568, Maximilian had granted religious freedoms to the majority of those living in the Austrian and Bohemian territories, who converted to Protestantism, but that doesn't mean Maximilian ignored Catholics completely. He made concessions to them too. For example, he promised the Archbishop of Olomouc that he could freely persecute Protestants in his territory of Moravia. Finally, during the 1570s, Maximilian realized he could never hope to mend the religious rift, and he concentrated on keeping his empire in peace.

But in 1574, Maximilian gave up on keeping the peace. He found the task impossible and admitted his failure. His own cousin, Philip II of Spain, started recruiting men from German soil to fight the rebels in the Netherlands. Philip claimed there was no religious unrest in the Netherlands, but his extreme Catholicism had created a revolt among the religious sects that managed to penetrate the territory. At first, Maximilian was against Philip's usage of arms to fight the religious war because he knew the Spanish king would deepen the internal problems of the empire by making Germans fight other Germans. But then he started worrying that the Dutch religious revolt would grow to become a revolt against the monarchy. Maximilian changed his opinion and started supporting Philip's recruitment in Germany, which only made the German Protestant princes turn against Maximilian. Defeated, the emperor gave up on governing the empire altogether. He was old, ill, and overpowered. His last act was in 1575 when he secured the title of the king of the Romans for his son Rudolf so he could be the official heir of the empire. The next year, Maximilian was on his deathbed, where he refused the Catholic last rites. He died as he lived, not as a Catholic nor as a Protestant. Maximilian's tragedy was that he found himself between competing religious sects when everybody in his realm expected him to choose one side or the other.

Rudolf II (1552-1612) and Matthias (1557-1619)

Emperor Rudolf II meets his brother, Archduke Matthias (1608)

Rudolf's religious attitudes were similar to his father's, though one might say he committed to Catholicism more than Maximilian ever did. However, Rudolf also refused the last rites. He hated the papacy and the conservative Catholicism of his Spanish relatives, but he also had no love for the various Protestant sects, which all claimed political rights. Because of this, Rudolf decided to avoid meddling in the religious conflict that was raging in Europe at the time. He was afraid that if he actively tried to resolve the conflict, he would undermine his power and integrity, making the empire more vulnerable to Turkish attacks. Rudolf resented the idea of conflict, but he hoped to achieve some kind of compromise that would appease both Catholics and Protestants. He wanted a realm united in faith, as only then could the empire be strong to resist outside threats. However, Rudolf had no concrete plan on how to deal with religious pluralism. He tried to maintain the peace by example, gathering Catholics, Lutherans, Calvinists, and other members of different sects to serve in his court. In the end, Rudolf took no action to solve the conflict, and he simply let the events unfold on their own.

During 1600, the religious conflict was becoming more intense, both in Germany and in the Danubian regions. A younger generation of princes took over, and they proved to be more ready to fight than to discuss a compromise. This readiness to fight led to the formation of the Evangelical Union, which consisted of nine Protestant princes and seventeen imperial cities. In response, the Catholic League was formed by the twenty Catholic princes, under the leadership of Bavaria. During these events, Rudolf remained passive, as he didn't want to be associated with either side. From Spain, Philip II encouraged the Catholics, who became more militant and tried to retake the Church land previously confiscated by the Protestants. They also persecuted the Protestants as heretics more vigorously and refused tolerance to any of the Christian sects. But the strongest supporter of the Catholic cause came from within Austria, specifically from Rudolf's brother Ernest and their cousins, Charles of Inner Austria and Ferdinand of Tyrol. Rudolf's inactivity on the religious front would soon result in a family conflict that would promulgate further divide.

Until the 1600s, Rudolf was an involved emperor who governed his lands personally. He was intelligent and cultured, although shy. His contemporaries praised his wisdom, but Rudolf proved to be a troubled man. Although history cannot claim he was mentally ill with certainty, he exhibited all the signs of clinical depression and even schizophrenia. After the 1600s, his dark characteristics became more prominent as he became victim to his psychological problems. He disengaged himself from the rule, and he refused to see his advisors. Nevertheless, he thought of himself as a grand authority. Rudolf's psychological instability created a leadership vacuum, and his younger brother Matthias stepped in, with Melchior Klesl at his side as a personal advisor. Klesl was the bishop of Vienna and Rudolf's advisor. He devoted his life to the Counter-Reformation, as well as to the conversion of the Protestants. Once Rudolf's political strength started waning, he turned to Matthias, who showed all the signs of great ambition but also a lack of political prowess. Matthias started meddling in imperial politics in 1577 by breaching dynastic etiquette and accepting the invitation of some nobles to mediate in their conflict. However, Matthias soon proved to be useless and was pushed aside by 1579. Once Rudolf started ignoring his imperial duties, Matthias became the focus of the dynasty's attempts to salvage their realm. When the middle of the three brothers, Ernest, died in 1595, Rudolf made Matthias his heir in Upper and Lower Austria. Under the influence of Melchior Klesl, he pushed Rudolf to make him his imperial heir as well since he lacked male children. But first, Matthias had to convince his youngest brother, Maximilian, and his cousin, Ferdinand of Styria, to elect him as the head of the house, which he succeeded in doing in 1606.

Rudolf considered this a personal betrayal, and he escalated the family split into an armed conflict. In 1608, Matthias convinced Austrian, Hungarian, and Moravian nobles to support him, and in return, he promised them considerable religious freedoms. That year, he was crowned as the king of Hungary, forcing Rudolf to cede the rule of Austria and Moravia too. In order to get the support of Bohemia, Lusatia, and Silesia, Rudolf had to issue a Letter of Majesty in 1609, by which he granted religious tolerance to both Catholics and Protestants of these territories. The conflict continued, but when Rudolf proved unable to pay his army, they plundered Bohemia. As a result, in 1611, Bohemia deposed Rudolf as their ruler. Matthias marched to Prague with his army, where he found Rudolf and imprisoned him. Matthias became the king of Bohemia, meaning he only lacked the imperial crown. However, the imperial titles remained with Rudolf until he died in 1612. Matthias was then elected emperor without any dispute, but he did nothing during his reign to improve the situation in which the Habsburg dynasty had found itself.

After Matthias acquired the imperial crown, he proved to be a lethargic ruler, just like his older brother. His ambitions ended once he was crowned, and he showed no interest in actually governing the empire. Matthias was strongly criticized by his contemporaries and completely forgotten by history. The only one who benefited from his passive rule was his advisor, Melchior Klesl, who assumed the head of the privy council. He was even mockingly called "vice-emperor" because he essentially ruled from the shadows. Under his influence, Matthias returned the capital to Vienna from Prague and banned the construction of Protestant churches. He even censored Protestant publications and forbade them the right to assembly, but these decisions didn't raise the power of the Catholics; instead, they only sharpened the religious conflict within the empire.

Matthias also failed to provide the empire with an heir, just like his brother Rudolf. This brought uncertainty to Europe and tense relations between the German princes, who realized that soon, they would have to elect a new ruler. But this time, it wasn't as simple as choosing the ruler who would best bring stability and protection from outside threats. The real problem was choosing between a Catholic or a Protestant ruler. The major contestants were

Friedrich (Frederick) V, the Elector Palatine who was a Calvinist, and Philip II of Spain, a Habsburg who claimed the right to the imperial crown because of his family ties. The German princes didn't want a Calvinist or a Spaniard as a ruler, so they wholeheartedly supported another Habsburg, Ferdinand of Styria.

Ferdinand II (1578-1637)

Ferdinand II and his second wife, Eleonora
https://commons.wikimedia.org/wiki/File:FerdinandII.Eleonora.JPG

Unlike his predecessors, Rudolf and Matthias, Ferdinand II was very much a Catholic, fanatically hating the Protestants. He started the branch of the Habsburgs that is well known for their pompous Catholic piety, which would define the dynasty. Ferdinand was already forty-one when he came to the throne, but he was a hard worker and very liked by the people. Unfortunately, he wasn't a politician, and his rule failed to bring any advances to the empire. As an incredibly pious Catholic, he spent several hours a day praying, and he distanced himself from women and any temptations, though he was married twice. Ferdinand had very strong moral convictions, which influenced his opinion on Catholic doctrine, which, in turn, influenced his rule. Ferdinand believed upholding the Catholic Church was his dynasty's mission on earth, and he refused to consider the broader implications. Instead of ruling pragmatically, he turned to dogma and ended up being a poor leader. Ferdinand's attitude toward the Protestants is largely due to his mother's influence. When he ruled the patrimonial lands of Styria before he became an imperial candidate, his mother pushed him to persecute the Protestants. In 1600, he expelled many Protestants from Inner Austria, trying to make the region purely Catholic. He saw the Counter-Reformation as the guiding light of his politics, and under his rule, the intense conversion of the Protestants began.

Once Ferdinand became emperor in 1619, he expanded the persecution of Protestants from his native Styria to the Danubian lands and Moravia. In 1620, he started burning books and enlisting the Jesuits to convert the Protestant nobles of Austria, Bohemia, and Hungary. However, the nobles of Hungary proved to be too strong for him, and thus, they managed to retain some religious freedoms. But whenever he could, Ferdinand opened Catholic schools and churches to promote the doctrine in which he believed. Soon, the Catholic Church had a monopoly on education, and with the rigorous censorship of books, the Church largely contributed to the intellectual isolation of Habsburg Austria from the rest of Europe. Religious unity was still considered essential for an orderly state, so Ferdinand only pursued the trends of his time. He was never completely despotic, as he allowed some of the Austrian nobles to continue practicing Protestantism since they gave him support during the elections.

The religious split followed the geopolitical trends, as two major opposing groups formed: the pro-Habsburg Catholics and the anti-Habsburg Protestants. However, the factions remained fluid to some extent, and some Protestants remained loyal to the emperor. The weak rules of Ferdinand's predecessors had distanced the emperor from his princes, so Ferdinand had very little authority over them. The main fear of the anti-Habsburgs was that the family (both the Austrian and the Spanish branches) would grasp too much power. Because of this, they often conspired with the French and later with the Swedes, attempting to bring balance to the European powers. All of these splits, both within the family and in regards to religion, resulted in the Thirty Years' War, which raged across Europe during the reigns of Ferdinand II and his son, Ferdinand III. The conflict began in the Habsburg lands, and it remained centered around the family and its position in Europe. Even though it was divided, the family showed a tendency to work closely during the war. For instance, Philip IV of Spain continuously sent troops to help his Austrian relatives fight in Germany and Bohemia. Austria and Hungary saw very little combat, but that doesn't mean the war didn't affect them. Austria, as the heartland of the Habsburgs, suffered the most economically. Famine and poverty brought about outbreaks of disease, which further decimated the population. The Thirty Years' War can generally be divided into four different phases: the start of the conflict in Bohemia and the Palatinate from 1618 to 1625, Danish involvement from 1625 to 1629, the Swedish invasion from 1630 to 1635, and the confrontation of the Habsburgs and the French from 1635 to 1648.

The war started during the last year of Matthias's reign, as the religious divide in Bohemia had reached its boiling point. By then, Ferdinand had already been crowned as the king of Bohemia, and he promised he would respect the religious freedoms promised to the Protestants in Rudolf's Letter of Majesty. But he started undermining the Protestants' rights to build churches and start assemblies, sparking anger in the majority of Bohemia's population. On May 23rd, 1618, a group of Protestant nobles burst into the government offices and threw the king's officials—two Catholics named Martinic and Slavata— through the window. This remains known in history as the famous Defenestration of Prague (throwing out of the window). This incident was the spark for the Bohemian revolt, which would soon grow into the Thirty Years' War. Defenestration wasn't uncommon for the period, as it is taken as a sign of serious protest. It has the elements of lynching and is often done by a mob, whether they were the commoners or the nobles.

Ferdinand refused to believe that Bohemia alone revolted against his authority, and he tried to blame the Palatinate, which remained Calvinist. As if to prove him right, the nobles refused him the Bohemian crown, and in his place, they chose Friedrich V of the Palatinate. He received support from some of the Austrian lords, as well as the support of the Transylvanian prince, Gabriel Bethlen, who tried to use the situation to grab Habsburg Hungary. The Bohemian nobles gathered an army, which they led to Vienna, where they hoped to meet Transylvanian military support. But Ferdinand refused to acknowledge the danger he was in, as he believed God would protect him. Instead of mounting a defense, he chose prayer. However, his salvation came in the form of a very earthly alliance he made with Maximilian of Bavaria, Philip III of Spain, and John George, the Elector of Saxony. The latter was Protestant, but he considered Friedrich a usurper, so he objected to his coronation. Friedrich remained in Vienna while his allies led the war to preserve his authority and prerogatives as the Holy Roman emperor.

Aside from the Protestants, Friedrich didn't have much support. England and France didn't want to meddle in the internal conflict of the Holy Roman Empire, and they especially didn't want to be associated with the throne usurper. Even the Protestants were reluctant to openly confront the emperor, and Friedrich didn't have the full support of the Evangelical Union of Protestants. In the end, when the conclusive clash was about to occur between Friedrich and Ferdinand, the rebels managed to raise only a small, untrained army. In November of 1620, at Prague, the decisive Battle of White Mountain took place, which lasted for only one hour. Friedrich and his amateur army were quickly forced to run. Thus, Friedrich became known as the "Winter King" in Bohemia because his rule lasted for only one winter. After the victory,

Ferdinand set about hunting the rebel leaders to end the revolt against his authority once and for all. The task was finished on June 27th, 1621, when the bodies of the rebel leaders were left to hang from Charles Bridge in Prague as a warning.

Bohemia was back in the empire's fold, but the full reintegration took several years since sporadic uprisings against the imperial authority continued to break out. But once the reintegration was complete, the imperial grasp over Bohemia was greater than ever before. Protestantism was completely outlawed, and those who refused to convert to Catholicism were exiled. Some 200,000 people left Bohemia over the next few decades. Rudolf's Letter of Majesty was torn up by Ferdinand, and the emperor confiscated the property of the Protestant nobles just so it could be awarded to the loyal Catholics. In 1627, Ferdinand gave a new constitution to the Kingdom of Bohemia, known as the *Verneuerte Landesordnung.* With this constitution, the Habsburgs became hereditary rulers of Bohemia, and they had complete authority over the civil servants in the country. It also moved the main government office of Bohemia from Prague to Vienna. The estates of the noble families retained some authority over the collection of the taxes, but their administrative freedoms were significantly reduced. In time and due to this new constitution, Bohemia became Habsburg's hereditary kingdom, and it became Habsburg to the point of fusing with the Austrian patrimony.

The Battle of White Mountain filled Ferdinand II with confidence, and he set out on a path of exterminating other resistance groups throughout the empire. At this point, it seemed as if Ferdinand would become the most powerful emperor of the Habsburg dynasty, but his control of Bohemia alarmed nearby states, and they intervened. Sweden was the first to meddle and bring the conflict to its next phase, also bringing down Ferdinand from the peak of his power. By 1623, the imperial army was occupying the Palatinate to apprehend Friedrich V, who continued to refuse Ferdinand's overlordship. But the imperial army was divided, as Ferdinand had to send a number of soldiers to help his cousin, Philip IV, against the Dutch rebels. Maximilian of Bavaria helped greatly in the Palatinate occupation, and as a reward, Ferdinand awarded him with the rule of this territory. Maximilian was resented in the Palatinate, as his takeover was seen as nothing else but a breach of imperial laws. The other princes of the empire were alarmed by the ease with which Ferdinand replaced them with those who were loyal to him.

King Christian IV of Denmark, encouraged by England and France, marched to protect Protestantism, and he invaded Saxony and Westphalia in 1625. This meant that Ferdinand had to fight both in western and northern Germany at the same time. But his eastern territories were not safe either because Gabriel Bethlen of Transylvania posed a serious threat to Habsburg Hungary. To mount a defense on all three fronts, Ferdinand needed a bigger army. He approached Albert von Wallenstein, a Bohemian noble and warlord, who repeatedly used his army to save Ferdinand's monarchy. For this, the emperor was extremely grateful, but he was also afraid of his new ally. Wallenstein was a powerful individual, and his contemporaries often described him as a true ruler in all but title. In 1625, Wallenstein and General Tilly, who won the Battle of White Mountain, joined forces and defeated the Danish king. In 1628, Ferdinand named the Bohemian aristocrat "General of the Oceans and the Baltic" because Wallenstein pushed his forces all the way to the north of Germany.

In 1629, Ferdinand made what had become regarded as the biggest mistake of his rule. He announced the Edict of Restitution without consulting the imperial council, the electoral princes, or even his own advisors. This brought him a complete series of new enemies because the edict declared around 500 secularized abbeys, two archbishoprics, and two bishoprics to be reversed to Catholic properties belonging to the Catholic Church. These properties had been appropriated by the Protestant German princes gradually since 1552 because they were abandoned when Catholicism lost its popularity. The Protestant princes who seized these lands were suddenly threatened, as they could lose their sources of income, but the Catholic princes were also antagonized because they thought the emperor overstepped his authority. On top of the unrest brewing in Germany because of the Edict of Restitution, the Habsburg presence in the Baltics threatened Swedish integrity, and in 1630, King Gustav Adolf of Sweden invaded Germany.

That year, all the gains Ferdinand made were taken away from him. Even some of his German allies abandoned him, instead allying with the Swedes and the Protestant coalition. The largest defeat for the Catholics occurred in September of 1631 at the Battle of Breitenfeld. The Saxon army overran Bohemia, while the Swedes took over the Rhineland. In 1632, during another clash with the Swedes, General Tilly suffered another defeat for the empire, and he was killed. Gustav Adolf moved to take over Bavaria and came to threaten Vienna with the proximity of his army. Ferdinand had disposed of Wallenstein by this point, as he believed the old Bohemian warlord was planning a coup, but he needed him now, so he recalled him. Wallenstein quickly mobilized an army, and he chased away the Saxons from Bohemia. In November of 1632, at the Battle of Lützen, he confronted the Swedes but suffered a defeat. Nevertheless, Gustav Adolf was killed in battle, and even though Swedish involvement in Germany continued, it lacked the force of a single-minded leader. During this period, Wallenstein became too powerful. Ferdinand even heard rumors of him conspiring with the French and Protestants. Ferdinand realized he had to remove the old warlord, as he was a threat to the Bohemian throne, and Ferdinand had him assassinated in February 1634.

Ferdinand named his son, Ferdinand III, as the supreme general who would lead the Habsburg army in the next decisive battle. In September 1634, the Battle of Nördlingen took place, and Ferdinand III managed to win because his Spanish cousin, Philip IV, sent his army to help. The Protestant princes were forced to negotiate peace, and in 1635, the Peace of Prague was signed by Ferdinand II. But the emperor made a compromise with the Protestants, and he retracted his Edict of Restitution to secure the peace. This wasn't enough, and the strife continued because the Swedes weren't satisfied. Threatened by the Habsburg victory, France also declared war on the empire. Unfortunately, Ferdinand II didn't have much longer to live, and he focused on preparing the empire for the succession of his son. In 1637, before his death, Ferdinand II had Ferdinand III elected as the king of the Romans, thus securing the title of the Holy Roman emperor for the Habsburg dynasty.

Ferdinand III (1608–1657)

Emperor Ferdinand III ratifies the Peace of Westphalia
https://commons.wikimedia.org/wiki/File:Westfaelischer_Friede_in_Muenster_(Gerard_Terborch_1648).jpg

When one compares the rules of Ferdinand III and his father, it seems that the son achieved very little, except for the conclusion of the Thirty Years' War. As a ruler, Ferdinand III wasn't really interesting, but as a man, he was a very enigmatic person. His politics were unremarkable because he tended to follow the trends laid down by his father, including the continuation of the Counter-Reformation throughout his realms. Ferdinand III managed not to be in the center of the events that marked his reign, such as the Swedish military threat and the close alliance with Philip IV of Spain. It was as if the emperor was a spectator who barely influenced the events that were happening all around him. But as a personality, Ferdinand stands out even today. He was deeply pious but rational and pragmatic. He didn't allow the dogmas of Christianity to cloud his view, and he showed great curiosity in science, arts, and military warfare. He conducted his own chemistry experiments, composed music, and displayed excellent competency in strategic military command.

Ferdinand III wanted peace, and as soon as he was crowned as emperor, he launched an effort to bring about a peaceful conclusion to the Thirty Years' War. However, the peace kept getting pushed back, as the emperor wanted to gain the battlefield advantage to sign a peace that would bring gains to Austria. Ferdinand's armies won some of the battles against the Swedes in 1636 and 1637, but the enemy closed the ranks because France gave them even bigger subsidies in order not to pursue a separate peace treaty. In 1639, the Swedes launched an attack and took large parts of Bohemia. Ferdinand's prospects were rapidly deteriorating, and in 1640, he even lost Spanish subsidies because Philip IV had troubles in Catalonia and Portugal. Over the next few years, Silesia and Moravia were occupied, and the Swedes posed a serious threat to Vienna.

In the east, Ferdinand had to deal with attacks too. Sweden allied with a Transylvanian prince, who invaded the Habsburg domain in 1643. Ferdinand managed to appease the situation by granting religious freedoms to these territories, but it was too late as Austria was already hurtling down a catastrophic slide. In 1645, the combined forces of Ferdinand and his Bavarian ally, Maximilian, lost the battle against Sweden in Bohemia. Bavaria had no other choice but to sign a separate peace. In 1648, the Swedish army sacked Prague, utterly humiliating Ferdinand. The emperor had no choice but to abandon his Spanish cousin and sue for a separate peace.

The Peace of Westphalia came about through a series of negotiations that had taken place sporadically since 1644. It was named such because it took place in Westphalia's cities of Münster and Osnabrück. In the modern era, this peace was the first major international congress, and it included Spain, France, Sweden, the Holy Roman Empire, and some individual German princes. During the negotiations, Ferdinand didn't shy from making difficult decisions. Probably the most difficult one was breaking the alliance with Spain so the empire could remain neutral during the conflict with France. But Ferdinand knew this would hurt the dynasty, and he hoped he could mend the wound as quickly as possible. The Peace of Westphalia gave much of the Alsace region to France, and this was a heavy blow to the dynasty, as it contained some of its oldest patrimonies. Ferdinand also had to undo his father's Edict of Restitution, and he had to increase the powers of the princes within the empire. Sweden, Bavaria, and Brandenburg gained territory with the conclusion of the peace.

For Austria, the Peace of Westphalia had very mixed results. The Habsburg powers were reduced, although the family retained some prerogatives as the hereditary emperors. They were able to appoint the bishops, even though their role was more symbolic. The family court in Vienna remained the most prestigious in the empire, and with the emperor at its head, it acted as the place of many diplomatic events. The Habsburg dream of restoring Catholicism throughout the Holy Roman Empire ended since the individual princes gained more power. A significant decentralization of the state occurred, and the Habsburgs started concentrating on strengthening their rule in Austria, Bohemia, and Hungary. In general, the dynasty started paying less attention to the empire from this point on, as their role was reduced to a symbolic one. Many future emperors would continue working in Austrian interests instead of those of the empire, as the hereditary Habsburg lands retained their powerbase. The last decades of Ferdinand III's rule were marked by efforts to recover from the consequences of the Thirty Years' War. Bohemia suffered major destruction during the war, and hundreds of thousands of people lost their lives. Ferdinand's administration started rebuilding Prague and repopulating the abandoned areas.

Ferdinand III died in April of 1657 at the age of forty-eight. He suffered gout throughout his life, and his body had been weakened by the many military campaigns he undertook personally. The Peace of Westphalia was his main contribution to the Holy Roman Empire and the Habsburg dynasty.

Chapter 5: The Dynasty and the War of the Spanish Succession

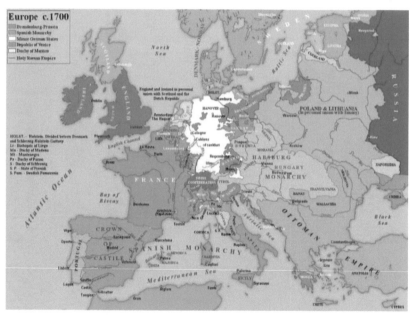

Europe at the beginning of the War of the Spanish Succession
Rebel Redcoat, CC BY-SA 3.0 <https://creativecommons.org/licenses/by-sa/3.0>, via Wikimedia Commons https://commons.wikimedia.org/wiki/File:Europe_1714.png

At the end of the 17th century, the events on the Austro-Turkish front took a different turn. Emperor Leopold I signed a treaty with the Ottomans and ended the conflict that had ravaged the eastern regions of the Habsburg Empire. With peace, the Habsburg dynasty was able to rise to its full potential, and the days of glory began. But in reality, the dynasty had been steadily rising since its beginning. The only change that occurred with the peace treaty was that the Holy Roman Empire and the Habsburgs became the ones who could guarantee the power balance of Europe. Up until this point in history, the rulers of England, France, and other European kingdoms had only seen them as a threat.

However, the peace also brought stagnation to the dynasty. After Leopold I, his sons reigned for short periods of time. They often squabbled, and Joseph I and Charles VI didn't achieve much. They were more concerned with the succession rights of the family than with the matters of the empire, and history remembers them only as throne seat warmers. They started reforms but had no energy or will to finish them, and they tried to influence the outcome of the Spanish succession war, but their actions were empty, so their reigns remained more or less uneventful.

Leopold I (1640–1705)

Emperor Leopold I in 1667
https://commons.wikimedia.org/wiki/File:Jan_Thomas_-
Leopold_I_as_Acis_in_the_play_%22La_Galatea%22.jpg

Leopold was the second son of Ferdinand III and Maria Anna of Spain, who was Ferdinand's first wife and first cousin. His older brother, Ferdinand IV, died in 1653, so Leopold became the heir apparent. Contemporaries describe Leopold as the ugliest Habsburg ever to rule, and modern historians think that the cause of his very intriguing physical attributes lies in the fact that his parents were close cousins. As a second child, Leopold was given an education fit for a career in the Church, and during his reign, he remained a reluctant statesman, preferring the company of books. Like so many Habsburgs, Leopold was extremely pious, to the point that even the papal diplomats criticized his constant visits to churches and monasteries. He prayed several times a day, which left him with little time to devote to the governance of the empire. It didn't help that Leopold was a very shy person, which, in turn, made him a passive leader. As he grew older, his reign became even more passive, as he was unable to make decisions. Leopold was never a visionary or an inspiring leader, but he managed to get the best he could out of the events that occurred during his reign.

Leopold I was never intended to take the throne, so his father failed to secure his succession before he died. This means that it was up to Leopold and his advisors to deal with the German electors and try to convince them to make him the emperor. He wasn't in a good position, as his Spanish cousin, Philip IV, had no male heir, which meant that Leopold might become the successor to the Spanish possessions. If Leopold gained both thrones, it would have posed a threat to the European power balance. The German electors told Leopold that if he was to become emperor, he could not marry the daughter of Philip IV, Maria Theresa, as he had planned. Eventually, she became the wife of King Louis XIV of France. Leopold also had to promise that he would stay neutral in the conflict between Spain and France. Leopold became emperor in 1658, and only two years later, he was at war. However, Leopold kept his promise about remaining neutral in the Franco-Spanish conflict. He sided with Denmark and Brandenburg against Sweden in the war over the Polish territories, but this war ended with a stalemate in 1660. For Leopold, it was an utter waste of time.

After the Thirty Years' War and the Peace of Westphalia, the German princes still held some resentment toward the emperor's authority, lowering his significance in the empire's governance. Leopold held some judicial powers and played an important role in foreign policy, but he was mostly a symbolic figurehead. He had no executive powers within Germany, but he was able to influence the princes and politicians, and he used this ability to persuade to rebuild the Habsburg reputation. Leopold formed effective alliances with the German princes and the administrative figureheads. He even managed to win the loyalty of the Catholic princes by appointing bishops in the churches that were under his authority. But the most important event that influenced Germany's opinion of the Habsburg dynasty was the French seizure of the Duchy of Lorraine in 1670. Previously, the German princes often allied with the French rulers to secure protection from their own emperors. But now, during the reign of Leopold I, it became obvious that France was more a threat than help. King Louis XIV led expansionist politics, and Leopold I decided to take a firm stand against him. This led to the German princes returning their loyalty to the Habsburg emperor and even openly supporting him and creating a feeling of patriotism. However, this patriotism came about not only because of France but also because of the Ottomans. Thus, the empire agreed to finance the efforts on its Turkish front.

When France attacked the empire by taking over Lorraine, Leopold was unable to act because he was dealing with the rebellion in Hungary. But when Louis XIV attacked the Netherlands in 1672, Leopold could not remain neutral. He joined the Protestant Dutch to defend the Spanish Netherlands, and surprisingly, the German princes supported him. Nevertheless, the efforts were fruitless, and Leopold even lost control of Freiburg in southwestern Germany. In 1683, Louis again invaded the Netherlands. At the time, Leopold's empire was being threatened on the eastern front by the Turks, so he had to quickly make peace with the French. By then, the Spanish Habsburgs had lost Luxembourg to Louis, which displeased many of the German princes. Luckily, Louis had a sense of Christian solidarity, and he refused to attack Germany while Vienna was under the Ottoman siege that same year.

Leopold took advantage of the peace with Louis, and he made a pact with William III of Orange (who would become the king of England in 1688), as the two shared an interest in countering France. Thus, Leopold secured Netherland support in claiming the Spanish succession. In 1686, the League of Augsburg, also known as the Grand Alliance, was formed. It included some of the German princes, the Netherlands, Brandenburg, Spain, and Sweden, and their goal was to stop French expansion. The war that ensued is remembered as the Nine Years' War, and it lasted from 1689 until 1697. The Ottomans saw an opportunity to attack Austria once more, thinking the duchy was weakened by the war with France, but the German military commander Charles of Lorraine proved to be able to mount a defense on both fronts, saving Austrian interests. The Nine Years' War ended with the Peace of Ryswick, which forced Louis XIV of France to return some of the territories he had conquered earlier, such as the territories on the right bank of the Rhine and Lorraine, but he kept Alsace and the Palatinate. But this peace was only a pause in the conflict, as the war would resume three years later as the War of the Spanish Succession.

The empire's trouble in the East wasn't only with the Ottomans. The Hungarians and Transylvanians were a thorn in Austria's side, as much of the duchy, together with Bohemia, reverted to Catholicism. In Hungary, the nobles remained Calvinist, refusing to admit the success of the Counter-Reformation. The minorities within the empire also refused Catholicism and continued to practice their original faith, such as the Orthodox Serbs and Uniate Ruthenians. The new generation of church officials would not tolerate the separation of religion within the empire, and they started the mass conversion of minorities and the persecution of Protestants. Those who refused to convert lost their properties, and those who were stubborn in their resistance were hanged for disloyalty to the crown. The court helped the church officials fight the Protestants, and all the court titles and offices were reserved for Catholics. Jews were also a target of the forced conversion, and the persistent ones were exiled from the cities. By the 1700s, the Austrian hereditary lands were predominantly Catholic, with only tiny pockets of Protestants. Hungary resisted, and the majority of nobles remained Calvinist in Transylvania. Nevertheless, with the majority of Austrians being Catholic, the empire saw a turnaround from 100 years earlier when most of the princes and their subjects were Protestant.

During Leopold's reign, the Austrian lands saw an economic rise, but the empire, as a whole, struggled to keep the economy on equal levels in all of its parts. The colonization of the New World brought new crops, such as potatoes and tobacco, but it was the noble families who grasped the opportunity to prosper from these crops. The crown tried to bring some justice for the peasants by limiting the forced labor requirements to only three days a week and forcing the magnates to pay money for the rest of the days a peasant would work on his property. But Leopold's executive power was very limited, and he was unable to enforce these new regulations. Bohemia, in particular, lagged economically beyond the western parts of the empire because of the depopulation that followed the Peace of Westphalia. Hungary also had a lot to catch up with because its territories had been the battlefields on which the Ottomans fought the Habsburgs. But the empire didn't lose any of its territories, and with the Treaty of Ryswick and the defeat of the Turkish army, which besieged Vienna, it even gained back previously lost regions. The Austrian Habsburgs held the largest territory in Europe, but its population numbered only nine million. France had twenty million, which meant the Habsburgs needed strong allies for their final battle against Louis XIV over the Spanish succession.

Charles II (1661–1700) and the War of the Spanish Succession

Charles II of Spain
https://commons.wikimedia.org/wiki/File;Juan_de_Miranda_Carreno_002.jpg

Charles II was the last ruler of the Spanish Habsburg line. Due to his many illnesses, he was more of a political pawn than an actual ruler. Charles was the only surviving son of Philip IV of Spain and his wife, Mariana of Austria. Since Mariana was Philip's niece, modern historians believe many of Charles's troubles are a result of inbreeding. However, there are no DNA remains that can be tested to provide further proof to this theory. Charles was so ill that his biggest achievement in life was the fact he lived for thirty-eight years. He had a typical Habsburg jaw, which was common for all the family members, but Charles's jaw was so deformed he had trouble speaking and eating. Nevertheless, this was the least of his problems. He suffered dreadful health ailments, such as convulsions, intestinal problems, edemas all over his body, and possibly even epilepsy and hydrocephalus. During life, he contracted deadly illnesses, including smallpox, rubella, and measles, but he managed to survive them all. Nevertheless, they left scars on his already disfigured body, and his contemporaries describe him as scary to look at. Aside from physical ailments, it is possible Charles suffered intellectual disabilities, but this is often disputed. It is noted that he didn't learn to walk or talk until the age of four, and he needed help with walking until the age of eight. However, those who met him later in life often said his mental abilities were intact. Still, Charles was left uneducated, though he did learn how to read and write much later in his life. It is now believed his mother demanded her son avoid schooling to avoid stressing his fragile body and mind. Later in life, Charles was nicknamed "El Hechizado," "The Bewitched," because the Spanish nuns decided his many problems were a result of an evil spell. After he died, an autopsy was done as well as exorcism.

Charles II was unable to produce an heir even though he was married twice. His first wife was Marie Louis d'Orléans, the daughter of the duke of Orléans. It is wrongfully believed that Marie didn't want to marry Charles because he was ugly, but the truth was she was already in love with one of her cousins. She was devastated by the news of her betrothal but ended up having a happy life with Charles, for she claimed as such in her private letters. Due to his many illnesses, Charles was probably infertile, though not impotent. Marie wrote to the French ambassador in Spain that she was not a virgin anymore but that she believed she would never have children. This proves Charles was able to be sexually active, but his infertility would only be proven after his death when the autopsy showed he had only one testicle that was atrophied. But during their life together, Marie was blamed for not having any children, and her French courtiers were blamed for plotting against the Spanish crown. Nevertheless, Charles was in love with his first wife and would remain so until his last days. Marie died suddenly after ten years of marriage, probably due to appendicitis.

Only a few weeks after Marie's death, Charles was forced to marry again. This time, the bride was chosen from the Neuburg family, which consisted of twenty-three children and was praised for its fertility. The Spanish hoped the new queen, Maria Anna of Neuburg, would be capable of bringing a Habsburg heir into the world. She married Charles in 1689 and stayed by his side until he died in 1700. Maria Anna became a very powerful political figure in Spain, as she was the promised mother of the future king. But as the years passed, it became obvious that this would not happen. Several times, Maria Anna claimed she was pregnant, with the joyful news ending in a miscarriage. However, these pregnancies were never confirmed, and it is now believed she fabricated them to prove that the fault was in Charles, not her. Thus, she would keep the power as the potential mother of an heir.

Spain was ruled by the powerful figures behind the sickly Charles. At first, it was his mother, Mariana. Charles was only four years old when his father died, and Mariana ruled as his regent for the first ten years of his reign. She had no experience in government and brought instability to Spain. Mariana ruled until 1676, when Charles's half-brother, the illegitimate son of Philip IV, Juan José, gained the support of the nobles and expelled Mariana from the court. She was shipped to Toledo, which diminished her influence over the Spanish crown. José took over the role of the Spanish prime minister for the next two years until his death at the age of fifty. Two prime ministers governed Spain before the power was passed to Maria Anna, Charles's second wife. She gathered Spanish and German nobles around her to help her exercise royal power, but her government brought the state to bankruptcy, as she approved Spanish involvement in the Nine Years' War.

Spain lacked strong leadership. Charles's regents and prime ministers were unable to provide for the country, resulting in famine, plague, and the massive migration of people. The death toll during Charles's reign was around 500,000. But the situation turned for the better during the last few years of the 1600s. Trade picked up in Catalonia, and the shipbuilding industry rebounded in the Basque Country. The population started growing too, and with it, agriculture started recovering. Still, the future looked bleak because there was no heir to the Spanish throne, and foreign leaders started meddling into the succession, hoping for personal gain. The first to put a claim on the Spanish crown was Louis XIV of France, and he was prepared to enter into open conflict to get it. However, he wasn't the only one with a claim. The Habsburg and the Bourbon dynasties also laid claim to the succession, and the conflict that ensued from these three parties led to a war that would entangle the whole world.

Charles II was Leopold I's nephew, and Leopold thought these family ties were enough for him to claim the succession. Leopold wanted the Spanish crown for his second son, Charles, since the central European territories would be ruled by his eldest, Joseph. Louis, on the other hand, wanted the Spanish crown for his grandson, claiming the right based on the fact that his grandmother, as well as the mother of his grandson, were of the Habsburg dynasty. Other claimants were also tied to the Habsburg family through marriage. Joseph Ferdinand of Bavaria was the son of Leopold's daughter, Maria Antonia. By this family relation, he was the great-grandson of Philip IV. The English and the Dutch favored this Bavarian claim. William III (who ruled both England and the Netherlands) saw Joseph Ferdinand as a ruler who could restore the balance between the European powers and prevent it from being concentrated in Habsburg and Bourbon hands.

The negotiations of the Spanish succession began during the reign of Charles II, as nobody believed he would be able to produce an heir. Unfortunately, an agreement was never reached, even though Leopold's advisors recommended that he simply give up because he would never be able to control both the Holy Roman Empire and Spain in case of a war. By the end of the 1690s, Louis wanted a peaceful solution for the Spanish succession because he wasn't able to finance yet another war due to the conflicts he had led with the Dutch and Germans. Diplomatic solutions were taking place, but all of them failed to take into account the interests of Spain. The Spanish nobility wanted to avoid the division of their kingdom's territories. They favored the Bourbon succession, as they considered Louis's grandson, Philip of Anjou, to be able to hold and defend the whole Spanish territory together with the overseas colonies. None of the Spanish nobles, including Charles II, believed the Habsburgs would work for Spanish interests. The Habsburgs were preoccupied with their hereditary territories in Austria and with the Holy Roman Empire. They couldn't afford to split their attention and serve all of their territories equally. Charles II personally favored the Bavarian candidates, but his will was easily subdued by the machinations of the Castilian nobility and his wife, Maria Anna. She was pushing for the Austrian succession. Perhaps it was his disdain for his second wife that caused Charles to refuse to help his own dynasty. In fact, during the last two years of his life, Charles wrote three different wills. In the first one, he named Joseph Ferdinand of Bavaria as his successor. In the second one, pressured by his wife and the Austrian supporters in his court, he named Charles, the son of Holy Roman Emperor Leopold I, as his heir. The last will was signed only days before his death, and in it, he named Philip of Anjou. By this time, Charles was very ill and probably unaware of how his nobility manipulated him.

Charles II died in November of 1700. A few days later, Philip of Anjou was proclaimed the king of Spain. The war was inevitable, and it started in 1701 when the Habsburgs stubbornly claimed the right to take the Spanish throne. The war might not have even happened if the third claimant, Joseph Ferdinand, hadn't died in

1699. Upon his death, Louis and Leopold both gave up on any possible diplomatic settlement and rejected any offered compromise. It didn't matter that the Spanish nobles had chosen Philip of Anjou. Instead of accepting the will, England, the Netherlands, and Austria united to fight the French and the Spanish. Germany (the Holy Roman Empire) split, with Hanover, the Palatinate, and Brandenburg standing by Emperor Leopold while Bavaria chose to side with France. Even Spain did not remain completely united behind the cause, as Catalonia rebelled and offered support to Archduke Charles VI of Austria. The war lasted until 1714, and it included many shifting alliances and temporary territorial gains for both sides. While Leopold was still alive, the Habsburgs held Italy but suffered losses in Germany. Even with their allies, the English and the Dutch, the Habsburg forces were often outnumbered by the French. Nevertheless, with the great leadership of the Duke of Marlborough and Prince Eugene of Savoy, the Habsburgs managed to defend their realms. The combined forces of Eugene and Marlborough won a stunning victory at the Battle of Blenheim in 1704. They defeated the French and forced Bavaria out of the war, saving Vienna from the invasion the enemy had planned.

In order to turn its fortune, France made a deal with a Hungarian noble named Ferenc II Rakoczi, paying him 10,000 ecus (crown; French coin) a month to start a rebellion and divide the Habsburgs' attention on two fronts, the western one with France and the eastern one with Transylvania. This rebellion harassed the Habsburgs until 1711. But as Leopold aged over the course of the war, he refused to take an active governmental role, leaving it to his advisors. They, too, were old men, who held the offices due to their loyalty, not skill. Leopold's son and successor, Joseph, was unsatisfied with the development of the war, and in 1703, he took over the government and pushed out some of the old officials, replacing them with young and ambitious men. Among them was Prince Eugene of Savoy. This young court started reforming the empire, and they urgently addressed the financial disaster that was about to break out. They started getting loans from England and the Netherlands to secure the empire's ability to remain in the war. Leopold died in 1705, and Joseph became the emperor.

Joseph I (1678-1711) and Charles VI (1685-1740)

Joseph ruled for only six years, and his whole rule was marked by the ongoing war with the Bourbons. He is remembered as an energetic ruler who wisely employed his advisors. He was also filled with patriotic feelings toward Germany, and he started but never finished the complete reformation of the monarchy. Joseph was, in fact, so patriotic that he insisted on marrying a German woman. He was a devout Catholic, but in matters of state, he advocated secularism. Because of this, he was generous toward religious minorities and even started employing Protestants as high servants. In many ways, Joseph was a modern ruler. He was a secular ruler who believed in his enterprises and worked devoutly on the monarchy he inherited. However, he remained a profligate aristocrat, and he was very vain and a womanizer. For this, he was often criticized during his reign.

Joseph based his rule on the military successes of his great commanders, Eugene of Savoy and Marlborough. Under their advice, he decided to make Italy a prime target of Habsburg military attacks, borrowing money from Queen Anne of England to finance the army. Under the leadership of Eugene, the Habsburg army won a major victory at Turin in 1706, forcing the French to abandon their efforts in northern Italy. The Habsburg army also took Naples, which seemed to satisfy Joseph, as he commanded Prince Eugene to move his army to the Low Countries in 1708. There, the alliance won a battle at Oudenaarde, opening the way to the Spanish Netherlands. But while the Habsburgs and their allies were successful in Italy and the Low Countries, France pushed into southern Germany. However, by

1709, France had lost so many battles that it was forced to go to the negotiating table.

Aside from the War of the Spanish Succession, Joseph had to deal with the revolt in Transylvania, which was led by Ferenc Rakoczi. The Hungarian nobleman declared the Habsburgs to no longer be the rulers of Transylvanian lands, but by the time Joseph took over the empire, the rebel leader had started losing his support. The defeats France suffered during the war made Louis XIV unable to continue financing the Transylvanian rebellion, so the nobles started siding with the Habsburgs. Once Joseph secured Italy, he was able to deploy his forces to Transylvania to end the revolt once and for all. At Trencin (now Slovakia), in 1708, the rebel army was defeated, even though it greatly outnumbered the Habsburg forces. It was an untrained army of peasants, and it posed no real threat to the professional Habsburg army. Rakoczi fled into exile, but Joseph had to deal with the remaining pockets of resistance carefully. His allies, the English and Dutch, were against using force on the Hungarian Protestants, and the final peace with the rebels was only signed after Joseph died in 1711.

Although Joseph I ruled for a short period of time, he continued the war his father had started to much success. However, he never finished it, and the task would fall on his successor, Charles VI. Joseph also failed to elevate the empire during the war. The Holy Roman Empire gained very little, but to Joseph, that didn't pose a problem because his goals were purely dynastical. His main effort was to display Habsburg superiority over the House of Bourbon and thus gain the Spanish crown. He subordinated the whole empire to his personal goals, which was not unusual for the period. Other German princes did the same, siding with whoever they saw as the leader who would bring them the most personal gain. Joseph's strategy seemed promising, and it might have even brought him a final victory if it wasn't for his sudden death. Joseph died on April 17th, 1711, of smallpox, the epidemic that had ravaged Europe that year. His only son died as an infant, and he left two daughters behind him. Thus, the crown passed to his younger brother, Charles.

When Charles II of Spain died in 1700, Charles proclaimed himself the king of Spain and was well received in Catalonia, spending six years there, from 1705 until his brother died in 1711. Charles's involvement in the War of the Spanish Succession displayed his political inadequacy, although he did have a few shining moments. His predecessors, both Leopold and Joseph, were aware that they could never gain all of Spain, and they never aimed to do so. But this was the goal that Charles pursued. His limited military capabilities were obvious as soon as he arrived on the Iberian Peninsula in 1705. Although he had the help of the English and Dutch, he didn't permanently take any territory; thus, he remained bunkered up in Barcelona. It was his brother who successfully led the war up until 1711, and after his death, the Habsburg allies started seeking peace with France on their own terms. But Charles was determined to keep fighting for the Spanish crown.

In 1713, England, Portugal, and the Netherlands started peace negotiations with France at the city of Utrecht. Charles continued his efforts against France, sending Prince Eugene of Savoy on one last campaign. However, the Habsburg army suffered from the plague, and without allies, Charles was unable to achieve anything. Finally, pressured by his advisors, the new emperor agreed to end the war in 1714 and join the peace negotiations in Utrecht. The negotiations stretched well into 1715 because Charles stubbornly refused to admit Philip of Anjou was the king of Spain. But the outcome of the peace treaty ended out being a well-balanced Europe without a single ruler accumulating too much power in his hands. Philip received the Spanish crown but only under the condition that he renounce his succession rights in France, which he accepted. Thus, the union of Spain and France was prevented. In return, the Habsburgs gained the Netherlands, which had been previously ruled by Spain. They also got to keep large parts of Italy along with Naples. France got to keep some of the territories it acquired during the war, such as Alsace and Strasbourg.

With the end of the War of the Spanish Succession, the Habsburg rule of Spain ended. They had Italy in their hands, but its territories, although rich, proved to be very difficult to defend, as the Habsburgs had no real naval military power. Charles also received Belgium, a country so far away from the dynastic powerbase that it proved very difficult to defend. The fact that Charles agreed to these terms shows how he let his imperial pride overpower his reason. He wanted to rule a large empire, and he did not care how efficient that would be. Like his medieval predecessors, Charles thought the Habsburgs would rule everywhere, and he did not care how much the dynasty would lose from acquiring territories that were impossible to defend.

For the rest of his reign, Charles obsessed over a document known as the Pragmatic Sanction, issued officially in 1713. He devised this document to be a code for the Habsburg succession, and it served as the legal foundation on which the empire's monarchy was based until its end in 1918. Previously, Charles had signed another document with his brother, Joseph. Because neither of them had a male heir, the Mutual Pact of Succession, which was signed in 1703, dictated that Joseph's daughter, Maria Josepha, would be the legitimate heir to the throne if Charles produced no male child. When Charles signed both the Mutual Pact of Succession and the Pragmatic Sanction, Charles had no children. All of his sons died in infancy, and his future heiress, Maria Theresa, would only be born in 1717. However, Charles had to think ahead, so he issued the Pragmatic Sanction to secure the Habsburg principle of primogeniture, which applied to both male and female children. The document demoted Maria Josepha to the second line of inheritance even though she was from the elder Habsburg line. Charles's motivation for this wasn't only the wish for his successors to inherit the lands but also to make the Habsburg territories indivisible. He didn't want another split in the dynasty, as that would result in the division of the empire. The document tied the Habsburg lands to law and not only dynastic principles.

The Pragmatic Sanction altered the dynasty's legal relations toward the different realms of the empire, such as Bohemia, Hungary, and even Austria. Because of this, Charles felt the document needed formal recognition. He spent the next twenty years lobbying to secure this recognition by other European powers. Austria and Bohemia ratified the document as early as 1721, but Hungary proved to be much harder to persuade. Before signing, the Hungarian nobles wanted Charles's promise that the Habsburgs would continue respecting all of their privileges they had gained after the War of the Spanish Succession, such as the tax exemptions the Hungarian nobles enjoyed, as well as complete religious freedom of the realm. In 1723, Hungary and Transylvania finally accepted the Pragmatic Sanction, followed by the Netherlands and Lombardy in 1725. In order to get Spanish approval, Charles had to promise he would marry his daughter, Maria Theresa, to one of Philip's sons. This meant the Austrian Habsburg branch would bind itself to the French Bourbon. And this was something of which the English and the Dutch would have none, and Charles was forced to end the pact with Philip of Spain. To further gain English and Dutch approval, Charles also had to promise he would close Austria's overseas trading company, which was just starting to be a serious competitor in the global trade market. By 1732, Charles had secured the ratification of the document by all of Germany's princes, but this also came with a price. He had to promise Maria Theresa would marry a German prince, he had to support Friedrich August of Saxony as the pretender on the Polish throne, and he had to acknowledge some territorial acquisitions Prussia had previously made.

Charles was a very cautious ruler, and after the War of the Spanish Succession, he led a very quiet life. However, he couldn't avoid entering several wars during his reign. The first one broke out in 1717 when Philip of Spain broke the Treaty of Utrecht by attacking Italy. However, the Habsburg monarch didn't have to defend his empire alone. The Netherlands, England, and France came to Charles's aid and stopped the Spanish. Even though Philip didn't achieve much with this attack, he finally got Charles to recognize him as the legitimate ruler of Spain.

After the death of Louis XIV, Habsburg's allies saw no danger in France anymore, and they stopped offering their support to Charles VI. However, with the upcoming Turkish invasion, Charles was very much in need of the alliance. Because of this, he turned his politics eastward to Russia. This new alliance meant the possibility to defeat the Ottomans, for which, in turn, Russia would officially recognize the Pragmatic Sanction. But Charles neglected the diplomacy with the western allies, allowing them to slip away. This proved disastrous during the 1730s when new wars started. The Habsburgs were dragged into the War of the Polish Succession (1733-1738) because they had promised they would give their support to Friedrich August of Saxony. They succeeded, and eventually, Friedrich became the king of Poland. Around the same time, though, Philip of Spain attacked Italy, taking Naples and Sicily and again dividing the Habsburgs' attention. France took the opportunity and invaded Lorraine, a territory ruled by Francis, Charles's son-in-law. The emperor offered Tuscany to Francis as compensation for Lorraine.

At the end of Charles's reign, in 1737, the Holy Roman Empire entered into a war with the Ottomans to support their new allies, the Russians. This was the second Ottoman war that Charles led during his reign. The first one occurred in 1716 when the Turkish army was defeated at Petrovaradin (located in today's Serbia), which legend states happened due to the miraculous snowfall in August. The Habsburgs gained the territories all the way to Belgrade. But in 1737, Charles had no miracle to help him, and even though his army won several battles, they lost the territorial gains that had been acquired in the previous war.

Charles died in 1740, leaving the empire in great debt. His contemporaries expected the Habsburg rule to end with his death, but due to his efforts to change the succession laws to include female children, they continued to rule. However, Charles's Pragmatic Sanction proved ineffective, as his daughter, Maria Theresa, had to resort to war to claim her rightful place on the throne.

Chapter 6: Habsburgs in the Age of Enlightenment

Holy Roman Empress Maria Theresa's coat of arms
Tom Lemmens (in collaboration with Heralder), CC BY-SA 3.0
<*https://creativecommons.org/licenses/by-sa/3.0*>, *via Wikimedia Commons*
https://commons.wikimedia.org/wiki/File:Middle_Coat_of_Arms_of_Maria_Theresa,_Holy_Roman_Empress.svg

After a series of emperors who achieved little to nothing, the Holy Roman Empire finally had a leader motivated by pragmatism and the will to compromise tradition to achieve concrete results for the empire, at least in the political sense. But this ruler, Maria Theresa, had to overcome the tradition of male rulers that was so deeply engraved in European minds. In the end, she couldn't even rule in her own name. Instead, she became empress by title only due to her marriage, but she was still a politician from the shadows. Maria Theresa pulled all the strings of the vast empire her husband officially ruled, and thus, she left a deep mark on the history of the world. But while Maria Theresa inspired the people to grant her esteem during her forty years of reign, her successor and son, Joseph II, received only hostility from the very same people.

Maria was not an enlightened ruler, but she surrounded herself with enlightened advisors and was able to grasp the wisdom of reform. Joseph II, on the other hand, was a true enlightened despot who sought to institute reason and the primacy of the state as the main government's principles. His reforms were very intelligent, but he was not very effective in implementing them. Emperor Leopold II found the middle ground between his mother's carefully led politics and his older brother's need for complete control. Unfortunately, his time as ruler was very short, and he only ruled long enough to clean up the mess Joseph II left behind.

Maria Theresa and her two sons were not revolutionaries. The Age of Enlightenment is not to be mistaken with the revolutions that would come later in the 19th century. The Enlightenment was a movement within intellectual circles and the ruling class, not the masses. Therefore, the Enlightenment mostly resided in the minds and as ideas, not in the hearts of the people. The movement evolved from late medieval Humanism and the Renaissance, and it was an epilogue to the Scientific Revolution of the early modern period. Even though the Enlightenment wasn't revolutionary by itself, it paved the way for the great revolutionary year of 1848, when almost all of Europe felt the rage of the people demanding an end to monarchical rule. The main philosophical ideas of the Enlightenment were reason, progress, tolerance, constitution, and secularism. In essence, the Enlightenment sought to undermine the authority of the ruler, but the movement reached only a small number of the uppermost social classes. It could not reach the common people because it was only the elite who had access to education and books.

In the Habsburg lands, the Enlightenment was state-centric, which means that before it could endanger the dynasty, its members acted quickly to pick up some of its principles to strengthen their own rule. While, in general, the movement called for the formation of a constitutional parliament, this would never happen in the Habsburg lands since it was seen as a move that would weaken the state, not strengthen it. But in the end, the Enlightenment allowed the Austro-Hungarian empire to emerge stronger than ever before, with a modernized economy and improved education and government systems. The relationship between the Habsburg rulers and their subjects greatly changed during this period, as the people's welfare became the prime focus.

Maria Theresa (1717–1780)

Empress Maria Theresa
https://commons.wikimedia.org/wiki/File:Kaiserin_Maria_Theresia_(HRR).jpg

Maria Theresa was twenty-three when she assumed the throne. However, it seems that Charles VI relied too much on trust that the surrounding states would honor his Pragmatic Sanction. Instead, the female succession was still frowned upon, but mainly because other claimants to the throne showed up very quickly. Furthermore, Charles's wars and failed diplomacy had left the state with a huge debt and a poor army. In addition, Maria only had a council of old men to help her, and they were unable to deal with modern problems. Maria also had no experience in government, a problem the surrounding powers took advantage of. Charles Albert of Bavaria, who was married to one of Emperor Joseph I's daughters, claimed the right to succeed the Holy Roman empire's throne, and France openly supported him. Friedrich August of Saxony, the king of Poland, also claimed the empire for himself, as he was also married to one of Joseph's daughters. Maria Theresa had no experience and no support. King Frederick II of Prussia (also known as Frederick the Great) seized the opportunity and attacked Silesia in 1740, starting the War of the Austrian Succession.

Charles VI was the last of the Habsburgs to rule the Holy Roman Empire without interruptions since 1438. The war that followed his death was of enormous proportions, as it involved all of Europe. Everyone wanted to exploit the inexperience of Charles's successor, and everyone wanted a piece of the empire's territory. In 1741, Bavaria invaded Bohemia, while France and Spain joined their armies to attack the Austrian Netherlands and Lombardy. As if these vultures weren't enough, Maria Theresa also had her own people abandoning her and joining the cause of Charles Albert. The very next year, the German electors abandoned the Habsburg dynasty completely and chose the Bavarian prince as the new Holy Roman emperor. He ruled as Charles VII, and although he didn't carry the Habsburg name, he was related to the dynasty by blood and by marriage.

At this time, nobody thought of Maria Theresa as a threat to their goals, but the young queen of Austria and Bohemia thought differently. In 1741, she went to Hungary, where she gathered the nobles and held her famous speech in which she pleaded to their feelings of chivalry to defend the young mother. Dressed in the Hungarian style, with infant Joseph in her arms, Maria reminded the nobles of their oaths of loyalty to the dynasty. Over 100,000 men gathered to form an army that was loyal to their new queen, pledging to protect her and her family from the empire's enemies. In November, Maria Theresa was crowned as the queen of Hungary in a ceremony where she pledged to protect the realm from its enemies. But this moment was only a culmination of months of negotiations in which Maria had to promise several privileges for Hungary. The people remained exempted from imperial taxes and kept their religious freedoms, but more importantly, Hungary got to maintain separate institutions from the empire and have its own constitution. All these would later help this kingdom in avoiding much of the reforms Maria and her son, Joseph II, tried to implement. Hungary's support to the young queen came at the right moment, and Maria was able to fight her enemies with her own army. She took Prague in 1743 and was crowned as the queen of Bohemia in May that year. England, always aware of France's growing power, saw an opportunity in Maria Theresa and started investing money in Austria's cause. Thus, the young queen received English naval assistance and money grants, which she used to conquer the rest of Bohemia and to drive back the French Army from Germany.

In 1745, Charles VII died, having ruled for not even three full years. His son, Maximilian III Joseph, made peace with Austria and promised he would help Maria's husband, Francis, to get elected as the next Holy Roman emperor. In return, Austria finally recognized Charles's election, though posthumously, and returned Bavaria to Maximilian. Francis I became emperor, and Maria Theresa finally succeeded her father's crown, though it was through her husband. She was the sole queen of the Habsburg lands, which included Austria, Hungary, Transylvania, Croatia, the Austrian Netherlands, Galicia, Mantua, Milan, Lodomeria, and Parma. But she is mostly remembered as the empress of the Holy Roman Empire; even though her husband was the official ruler, she pulled all the strings.

Maria's armies didn't have as much luck in Italy, as the battles she fought there were inconclusive. However, her attention was always drawn to Prussia, where Frederick II ruled, a man she always considered to be evil and ruthless. He was a man capable of reorganizing his army and making it the most efficient in Europe. With great effort, Maria expelled him from Bohemia, but she couldn't do the same in Silesia, and she was forced to sign a peace in 1748. The terms of this peace were, in some ways, a triumph for the Austrian queen because they were the proof of her survival. She also showed that she was capable of fighting Prussia, the greatest military power at the time, to a standstill. Silesia remained her only major loss since this territory was well developed economically. With it, she lost around 20 percent of the government's income. The loss of Silesia wasn't only an economic loss. Habsburg's position also diminished, as the Prussian dynasty, the Hohenzollerns, rose to power.

Understanding her weakened position, Maria Theresa worked with what she had, and to improve her standing within the empire, she reformed her territories. She did embrace some of the ideas of the Enlightenment, but only the ones that suited her cause. The institutions had to be reorganized in such a way to meet the demands of the people while at the same time remaining completely obedient to the ruler's authority. Maria wanted to build a state that would be strong, as this strength would mirror her regal authority. The most immediate problems that had to be dealt with were the military and financial weaknesses of the Habsburg domains. To deal with both, Maria employed Count Friedrich Wilhelm von Haugwitz, who initiated the centralization of both foreign and military politics. The military power was divided between administrative bodies that had greater autonomy and effectiveness. When Haugwitz reformed the institutions, he started thinking about the taxes. Instead of having the different regions— Bohemia, Austria, and Moravia—approve the taxation policies once a year, they had to do it once a decade. Noblemen were no longer exempt from taxes, which meant they had less control. The central government now had more power in administering tax collection, not the separate estates.

These initial reforms were focused on the immediate survival of the Habsburg state, but the subsequent ones concentrated on changing all of the aspects of Maria Theresa's rule. The government became even more centralized with the creation of the

Directory of Administration and Finance and the joint Austrian-Bohemian Chancellery in 1749. All bureaucratic organs were reorganized, and the new Supreme Court was founded with the intention of reducing the nobles' and towns' powers. In 1766, the *Codex Theresianus* was completed, which was a unitary law codex of the hereditary Habsburg territories. But besides all these governmental reforms, Maria made sure that measures were taken to improve the lives of her subjects. However, she did not do this out of altruistic motives. She only implemented those reforms that would improve the people's education, religious affairs, and economic standing while also strengthen the state as a whole. The education ordinances were implemented, with primary education becoming obligatory, in Austria (1774) and Hungary (1777). Maria Theresa's empire had the most exemplary education system in Europe of the time. The people's access to education was expanded so anyone could send their children to schools. The curriculum was also modernized, placing great emphasis on the German language, mathematics, science, and engineering. With such a modern education system, the influence of the Church started diminishing. However, this was all part of the government's plan to weaken the Church institutions and put them under state supervision. Thus, the secular courts were able to try priests in non-ecclesiastical matters, and the state was able to take control of some of the Church's revenues. But most importantly, the government appointed the high Church offices, and the clergy was no longer exempt from taxes, allowing the Church to serve the state more efficiently.

All of these reforms were territorially limited. For example, the Italian and the Flemish territories hardly experienced these reforms, and while Hungary was affected, the deal it had made with Maria Theresa at the beginning of her rule protected it. Hungary remained administratively and financially independent from the rest of the state. Maria always respected her promise to the Hungarian nobles, and she summoned the Hungarian Diet only three times during her forty-year rule. The overall reforms Maria implemented brought much good to the state, but they proved not enough to finance the military ventures of the Habsburg monarchy. Silesia remained a thorn in the monarchy's side, and Maria was determined to get it back. To achieve this, she had to end the long alliance with Britain since it demanded Austria must give up on Silesia and turn Bavaria over to Prussia. Maria was forced to turn to France for help, and although reluctant, France agreed on an alliance in 1756 after it entered a conflict with Britain. The formation of the defensive alliance between the Habsburg monarchy and France marked the start of the Seven Years' War.

The war was yet another conflict that involved all of the major powers of Europe. Frederick of Prussia initiated the conflict by invading Saxony in 1756, which caused Austria to unite with France, Russia, Poland, and even Sweden against Prussia. To persuade France to join the alliance, Maria Theresa gave up some of the territories in Flanders and Italy, but even backed by its allies, Austria was unable to bring forth a decisive victory. There were several battles between the Prussian and Austrian armies, but they were all inconclusive. The proxy battles fought between France and Britain in India and North America brought grave losses to France, and it could no longer give subsidies to Austria. After Empress Elizabeth of Russia (r. 1741–1762) died, Russia withdrew from the war. Her successor admired Prussia, and he decided Russia had no place in the conflict. When Britain and France ended their roles in the conflict, Austria was forced to sign a peace with Prussia at Hubertusburg in 1763. Maria had failed to achieve any of her goals, and Prussia ended up the victor, confirming its position among the great European powers. But there was a consolation prize, as Frederick of Prussia promised he would vote for Maria's son Joseph to become the king of the Romans and the heir to the imperial throne. Maria had to make peace with the permanent loss of Silesia.

In 1765, Maria's husband, Francis I, died, and the empress formed an unofficial triumvirate with her son Joseph and one of her main councilors and chancellor, Prince Wenzel Anton of Kaunitz-Rietberg. However, Maria made sure she held the most power while the two acted as junior partners, although Joseph was officially crowned the Holy Roman emperor. Maria and Joseph often clashed, as Joseph supported the Enlightenment reforms Kaunitz supported, while Maria remained stubbornly conservative. Slowly over time, Maria allowed her son to take matters into his own hands, primarily the affairs of the empire, the military, and finance. In turn, Joseph spent all of his time outside of Vienna, traveling around his empire and visiting his immediate neighbors to build diplomatic relations. This kept him away from Maria, and the two managed to lead a productive partnership that benefited Austria and the greater Habsburg Empire.

During the last fifteen years of her reign, Maria was less active in governing, leaving the matters to her son Joseph, who she proclaimed her co-regent. Therefore, Joseph dealt with the War of the Bavarian Succession and the first partition of Poland. To keep Empress Catherine the Great of Russia from prying apart Habsburg territories, Joseph made a deal with Prussia and Russia to divide Poland between these three powers. The first of the three partitions of Poland occurred in 1772, and it brought Galicia and most of southern Poland under Habsburg rule. In 1774, Joseph wisely maneuvered the politics and acquired Bukovina from the Ottomans, adding it to Transylvania and Galicia. However, the new lands were very poor and didn't bring much to the dynasty. Maria was personally against the division of Poland, as it was a sovereign state, but she was too pragmatic to miss the opportunity and add more territory to her realm. However, with these territories, the ethnic makeup of the empire diversified, which meant more trouble. The new addition of Poles, Ruthenians, and Jews meant more political maneuvering was required to satisfy the needs and demands of all the nations that made up the Habsburg Empire.

Maria Theresa died of a common cold in November of 1780 when she was sixty-three. By the end of her life, her body was very fragile, which was due, as she claimed, to her many pregnancies that made her age prematurely. She gave birth to sixteen children, with ten surviving to adulthood. One of them was the famous French queen Marie Antoinette. When hearing of the death of Maria Theresa, her greatest enemy, Frederick of Prussia said she was an honor to the empire and her sex. He further claimed he had never considered her his enemy, even though he fought her in three different wars. Maria Theresa was the last ruler of the House of Habsburg, and the dynasty died out after her. However, it was replaced with the House of Habsburg-Lorraine, which was started by her son, Joseph II. Through this new dynasty, the Habsburg name continued to live along with the family's influence on the politics of the world.

Joseph II (1741–1790)

Emperor Joseph plowing the field in 1769
https://commons.wikimedia.org/wiki/File:Joseph2pflug_1799.jpg

Maria Theresa is remembered as one of the most accomplished Habsburg rulers, but her son, Joseph II, was probably the most ambitious one. Although he ruled less than ten years, he issued over 6,000 edicts, trying to enforce reforms that brought about many modern ideas. However, Joseph lacked political skills, and some of his reforms were quickly annulled. Nevertheless, he managed to strengthen the dynasty's grasp. Because of this, many historians praise him for his ability to think in the modern sense, but he is harshly criticized for his authoritarianism. Even so, Joseph believed in the equality of the people. He saw himself as the chief servant of the state, which was the only reason he thought he should have the utmost power. To him, nobility was meaningless, and everyone should work in the service of the state. Therefore, everyone should obey his will and listen to his reasoning without resistance.

As an autocrat, Joseph believed he had the best insight into the monarchy's needs, and he saw no reason for a diplomatic approach to internal matters. He even issued military disciplinary orders, forbidding the cadets to masturbate. He also set the exact hour for the lighting of the street lamps and at what hour they should be extinguished. His behavior was despotic, but Joseph firmly believed he was working for the empire's welfare. He often overturned the privileges of the nobility and clergy when he thought they stood in the way of the common good. However, the emperor didn't trust that the people understood what the ultimate good was. He was an arrogant ruler, and his arrogant style on which he based his monarchy explains some of the mistakes he made.

Just like his mother, Joseph believed in the implementation of the ideas of the Enlightenment so long as they served the purpose of strengthening the state. But while Maria Theresa often hesitated on the reforms out of her sense of traditionalism, Joseph believed the changes were too slow. Once he became the emperor, Joseph jumped on the opportunity to transform the economic, administrative, and social affairs. His most effective reforms were of an administrative nature, as Joseph strived to create a strong centralized control over the whole empire. He created more professionalized and unitary institutions, making German the common language of the administration throughout his realm. This was done to standardize bureaucracy and governance. He filled many positions of the bureaucracy and judiciary with commoners because he wanted to promote the equality of the people. He wanted to make sure that the people knew birth did not necessarily mean distinction. Because of the excellent education reforms, Joseph was also able to employ more professional judges and lawyers into his new, modernized judicial system.

In 1787, a new legal code was promulgated. With it, Joseph tried to modernize his mother's old code and expel some of the archaic laws, such as capital punishment and the persecution of sorcery. But the main goal of the new code was to emphasize the equality of the people, with all social classes being equal in the eyes of justice. Joseph also reformed the healthcare of the empire by opening a general hospital in Vienna in 1784 and by making it obligatory for all communities to have a registered doctor and a nurse. He sent many German doctors abroad to learn the most modern medical practices and bring them home. On the economic and social sides, Joseph worked hard on boosting manufacturing, trade, and small industries. He also relied on agriculture, and to promote it, he made drastic improvements in the living conditions in the countryside. In 1780, serfdom was abolished in the majority of the empire. Peasants no longer had to obey their landlord's will, and they gained the freedom to marry and to choose their profession. However, the nobility strongly resisted these reforms, so Joseph was unable to equally implement them throughout the whole empire. The peasants in the western parts of the empire lived better lives and had more freedoms than those in the east.

Joseph's reforms finally met resistance in 1784 when a revolt broke out in Transylvania. The peasants thought the reforms were not going far enough. They went against their landlords, who still collected taxes on their own terms and paid lower wages for the obligatory labor. Joseph was sympathetic toward the peasants, but he had the obligation, as the emperor, to preserve the power dynamic. Therefore, he had to suppress the revolt. But instead of slowing down with the reforms, the emperor pressed on, ignoring the warnings of possible resistance. The new changes only managed to stir up the nobility and the bourgeois, especially when Joseph proposed that the taxes collected from the peasants should be shared between the state and the nobles. Joseph was warned by his advisors that this measure would further instigate the nobility because their incomes would be significantly reduced, but the emperor ignored them. In 1787, some of the estates accused Joseph of violating their legal rights, and they refused to pay taxes. Nobles across the Habsburg Empire resisted, but they were uncoordinated and without leadership, so the resistance was doomed to fail. However, it paints a picture of Joseph's political failures.

Joseph often neglected the overall empire, as he was more concerned with implementing his reforms in the Danubian realms. This is because he considered these lands his powerbase. The German princes were all aware the emperor favored Austrian interests above those of the empire, so they allowed Frederick II of Prussia to assert his influence. Frederick portrayed himself as being more loyal to German interests than Joseph, and he formed a league of princes in 1785 known as the *Fürstenbund*. This league excluded Joseph because its main goal was to thwart the emperor's intentions to trade the Austrian Netherlands for Bavaria, which would expand the Habsburg domain. However, the emperor's plans never came about.

The last years of Joseph's rule threatened to ruin all he had achieved. The domestic troubles, as well as the war with the Ottomans, pushed the Holy Roman Empire into a crisis in 1789. Belgium exploded in revolt, and Brussels was taken over by the rebels. They declared independence the next year; meanwhile, Hungary also rebelled. Tyrol saw some troubles, mainly about the obligatory military service. Prussia started financing the rebels, and when it allied with Turkey, it seemed as if it was preparing to directly attack the Habsburg monarchy. Joseph had no other choice but to appease the rebels by rolling back some of his reforms. Up until then, he had stubbornly refused the coronation in Hungary, as this move would have solidified Hungary as a separate administrative unit. Finally, he agreed to the coronation, and he even restored the Croatian Diet that he had previously disassembled. Joseph knew he had to resort to diplomacy due to the issues with Prussia, but he was aware that he lacked this skill, so he called on Britain to act as a mediator. In February 1790, Joseph died of an illness at the age of forty-eight.

Leopold II (1747–1792)

Emperor Leopold II

After the death of Joseph II, his younger brother, Leopold, became the head of the family. As the grand duke of Tuscany, Leopold had twenty-five years of experience in governing, which more resembled his mother's style than his brother's. He was also a visionary and reformist, but he did not favor Joseph's absolutism, which is why he had more success in implementing reforms in his domain. When Emperor Joseph II died in 1790, Leopold inherited all of his brother's titles and started his rule, which took place in the middle of the rebellions that raged all over the empire. Hungary, Belgium, and Bohemia were the most troublesome, but Leopold didn't even have the Habsburg army to call for help, as it was fighting the Ottomans in the Balkans. He had to use his sharp political instincts to deal with the rebels, and he was successful, mainly because of his constitutional tendencies. Back during Joseph's rule, in 1784, he even drew up a proposal for a constitution in Tuscany but was stopped by Joseph. Leopold was an educated, intelligent man, and there is no doubt his reign would have been incredibly successful if it didn't last for only two years.

Once Leopold took the imperial throne in 1790, he undid some of Joseph's policies, especially those that had the tendency to inflame the people, both peasants and nobles. He revoked new taxes that had been implemented by his predecessor, and he returned the tax collection power to the estates. Leopold also ended the military conscription in Tyrol, pacifying the people. The agricultural reforms that had antagonized the landlords evaporated too, but Leopold kept the protections for peasants in order to avoid another rebellion. To decentralize the government, he allowed local diets to run local affairs, even allowing them to do it in their native languages. In Hungary, he had to promise to respect the previous promises made to the nobles, respect the traditional Hungarian constitution, and had to be crowned as their king. He did the same in Bohemia. By doing all this, Leopold managed to quell major uprisings in Hungary, Belgium, and Bohemia by the end of 1790.

Leopold was very careful when it came to foreign policy. New negotiations with Prussia and Turkey ended the wars in the Balkans, freeing the Habsburg army. Leopold agreed to give up the most recent territorial gains in the war with the Ottomans, and in turn, Prussia promised it would not finance rebellions against the monarchy. Leopold successfully pacified the monarchy's outside threats, but he still had to keep a close eye on France, where a revolution was brewing. He wanted the Habsburg realms to remain neutral in France's internal conflicts, but he had to be cautious not to allow revolutionary ideas to spill over the border. He wasn't particularly concerned because some of the changes the revolutionists were proposing in France were already implemented throughout the empire. In the early stages of the French Revolution, Leopold even made positive comments about it, saying it was a good model of communication between the sovereign and the populace. However, his sister, Marie Antoinette, Queen of France, was a liability. Leopold advised her to convince her husband, Louis XVI, to accept the proposed constitution, but the king of France refused and fled Paris in 1791. Out of solidarity with his sister, Leopold had to modify his position, and in 1791, together with Frederick William II of Prussia, he issued the Declaration of Pillnitz. In it, they called for Louis to return to Paris and assume his rule as king.

Leopold died suddenly in March 1792. It is not known how he died; although it was most likely from natural causes, some suspect he was poisoned. His son, Francis II, would halt his father's and uncle's reformative politics, changing the course of Habsburg history.

Chapter 7: The Revolution and the Dissolution of the Empire

The Austrian Empire in the 1850s
https://commons.wikimedia.org/wiki/File:Austrian_Empire_(Johnston,_1861).jpg

In 1793, Louis XVI, King of France, was executed. Later that year, the same fate happened to his wife, Marie Antoinette. The European rulers were shocked to see how far the people were willing to go to achieve their goals of a constitutional republic.

Suddenly, no ruler felt safe, and the Habsburgs perhaps felt that fear most of all, as they were closely related to the French queen. Perhaps this was the reason why the new Holy Roman emperor, Francis II, ardently defended traditionalism, autocracy, and conservatism. He refused the new ideas of progress and demanded obedience as the ruler of the largest European empire. Until the very end of his life, he resisted change, and he became the symbol of the Habsburgs' hostility toward revolutionary ideas, even though his predecessors ruled with a more progressive mindset. After the traditionalist Francis, his feeble-minded son, Ferdinand I, ruled passively, leaving Austria in the hands of his advisors. But even with his good character and good intentions, Ferdinand failed to stop the revolution from consuming his realm.

Francis's rule saw the dissolution of the Holy Roman Empire and the creation of the German Confederation, but even so, the Habsburgs continued ruling their hereditary lands, proclaiming Austria to be their empire. Their well-deserved prestige allowed a Habsburg to become the first president of the German Confederation, and they continued ruling as the kings of Hungary, Croatia, and Bohemia. However, the Holy Roman Empire's failure was a prelude to the downfall of the dynasty and the revolutions of 1848, which engulfed all of Europe.

Francis II (1768-1835)

Francis I of Austria

Francis ruled as Emperor Francis II of the Holy Roman Empire, but he also ruled as Emperor Francis I of Austria. He was notable for his ability to grasp the royal power and successfully fight both revolutionary and Napoleonic France. Francis lost all of the battles against Napoleon Bonaparte, but his sheer will to fight eventually brought him a triumph. He outlasted Napoleon, but compared to him, Francis was unworthy of the role that was given to him. He was, by no means, unintelligent, but he was narrow-minded. Francis received the enlightened education that was so popular in his youth, but he remained unmoved by it. However, he managed to rule without being a despot. He firmly believed in the rule of law, and he even implemented some legal reforms in 1803 and 1811 to better the legal system. But the attitude of his government was one of centralization, and he did demand obedience, ignoring the innovative ideas of his advisors. But even though he was not a politically brilliant leader, he somehow managed to get his subjects to love him. Francis always knew how to relate with the common people. Perhaps it had something to do with his establishment of the "open door" court, where everyone could come and tell him what troubled them. Also, during the cholera epidemic in 1831, Francis visited hospitals and greeted the ill personally. He was known for loving the modest way of life while being generous toward those who were in need.

Francis's shrewdness in politics may be explained by his inexperience. He was only twenty-three years old when he succeeded the imperial throne and the conflict in France broke out. The revolution posed a serious threat to the established monarchical rule in Austria, but due to a lack of experience, Francis reacted with open hostility. Once he saw what happened to Louis XVI and his aunt, Marie Antoinette, he feared a similar fate would happen to him if he allowed the revolution to spread across the borders. That is why his only goal was to explicitly suppress the revolution. Under his rule, Austria became a symbol of resistance, embracing the old aristocratic order rather than the new republican ideas.

Ever since the Declaration of Pillnitz, France anticipated an attack on its territories, as Prussia and Austria wanted to reinstall the monarchy in France. In order to prevent the Austro-Prussian army from attacking, France launched its own attack, starting what would be known as the French Revolutionary Wars (1792–1802). In the first stage of the conflict, known as the First Coalition War, Great Britain, the Holy Roman Empire, and Russia joined the conflict, each with different motives. While some wanted to stop the spread of the revolution, others saw a personal territorial gain in attacking France. But for most of the conflict, France was the one winning, and it took Belgium and some parts of the Rhineland by 1795. Prussia signed a separate peace, and Austria had to plan its battles without Prussian assistance. Although the Habsburg military commander Archduke Charles (Francis's younger brother) won some of the significant battles against France, he was unable to thwart the rapid rise of Napoleon Bonaparte after 1796. The Corsican military genius won impressive battles against Austria in Italy, pushing the Habsburgs out of Lombardy. In 1797, Austria was forced to sign the Treaty of Campo Formio, in which Francis surrendered Belgium and some parts of Italy. Most notably, Francis II gained Venice and the territories of Istria and Dalmatia. But this treaty wasn't a defining peace. Francis used it to buy time and plan the next attack. An opportunity showed itself in 1799 when Napoleon led his disappointing mission into Egypt. This was when the second stage of the French Revolutionary Wars began, known as the Second Coalition War, but for Austria, it was no more successful than the first one. In 1800, the Austrian forces were defeated at Marengo and Hohenlinden. The Treaty of Lunéville was signed in 1801, and Francis had to acknowledge French gains in Italy and its acquisition of the Rhineland.

Francis was determined to fight the revolution abroad, and he was just as determined to quickly end any stirrings in his empire. He began strict police surveillance and a censorship campaign in the efforts to suppress intellectual and political life. Newspapers and intellectual groups were shut down, and even the mason's lodges were closed, as Francis personally didn't trust them. Still, the emperor knew he had to be careful not to use too much power and instigate people into revolting. That is why he refrained from taking political prisoners, and those who ended up in jails were treated well. There were no executions, and the monarchy, in general, maintained its anti-revolutionary sentiment. Even the most liberal nobles in Austria believed the French Revolution was too extreme. This is why it was not difficult for Francis to suppress any early signs of resentment toward the monarchical rule.

However, the Holy Roman Empire had a high price to pay for its war with France, as the German unity was a casualty nobody could foresee. Around 1800, there was a spike in German patriotism, which the Habsburgs used to their advantage, but they failed to use it to unite the political goals of the various German princes. In the war against France, Germany was not united because each territorial leader had his own goals. Bavaria and Württemberg, for example, turned to the French orbit of influence, seeking the protection of Napoleon, whose reputation was on the rise. When Habsburg suffered many losses against France, it was a clear sign that the dynasty was no longer able to protect German interests. After all, the Habsburgs paid little attention to the Holy Roman Empire as a whole, concentrating their efforts on Austria. Napoleon and his foreign ministers became as influential in Germany as any other Germanic dynasty.

Several more events inspired the dissolution of the Holy Roman Empire. In 1804, Napoleon declared himself the emperor of France, and Francis took that as an offense. He couldn't allow a commoner like Napoleon to put himself on a pedestal with equal prestige as the ancient Habsburg dynasty. But there was a real danger in Napoleon, and Francis was right to fear that the Corsican would attempt to take the Holy Roman Empire for himself or destroy it. Due to these fears, Francis established the Austrian Empire in August of 1804. This new empire gave him a new title, but it in no way changed the makeup of the Holy Roman Empire or the Habsburg lands. Francis made sure to explicitly say in his proclamation that he ruled several states and that he promised he would not change any of their constitutions. It was a very questionable proclamation from a legal aspect, but it was supported by the realm's subjects, even in Hungary. By proclaiming Austria an empire, Francis made sure the Habsburg dynasty would keep the imperial titles no matter what Napoleon managed to do with the Holy Roman Empire.

In 1805, Napoleon proved the weakness of the new Austrian Empire when he marched his armies all the way to Vienna and occupied it. This occupation was part of the Third Coalition War, which also involved Russia and Great Britain. The Habsburgs fled the city, but Archduke Charles mounted a counterattack by rerouting the Habsburg army from Italy. They met the Russian army, and the Battle at Austerlitz ensued that December. However, this battle proved to be one of the worst defeats for Austria because the new empire was forced to sign the Peace of Pressburg, in which Bavaria and Württemberg became separate kingdoms. These new kingdoms also received several Habsburg territories, such as Tyrol and Vorarlberg. Austria also lost the Adriatic territories and Venice, which it had acquired in 1797. With Vienna occupied and the signing of this horrible peace treaty, the Habsburg dynasty suffered an enormous humiliation. By July 1806, sixteen German princes had organized a new confederation under Napoleon's protection, known as the Confederation of the Rhine. Napoleon demanded that the crown of the Holy Roman Empire be brought to him, but Francis wouldn't allow it. He was also aware that he was in no shape to defend the empire, so he decided he would rather end the Holy Roman Empire than let Napoleon seize the imperial title. On August 6th, 1806, Francis announced the death of the Holy Roman Empire, an empire that existed for 1,006 years without interruption. Francis moved all the imperial regalia, along with the crown, to Vienna, as he needed the Habsburgs to keep the symbolism from the former empire.

In 1808, the hostilities with France were renewed when Napoleon attacked the Iberian Peninsula. Russia and Prussia declined to join the war, so Austria had to fight alone, though it was financed by Great Britain. Austria was defeated, and Archduke Charles made peace with Napoleon without Francis's approval. Francis used this opportunity to blame the defeat on his brother, whom he dismissed from the imperial service. Vienna was again occupied by French troops, and the Habsburgs had to sign yet another humiliating peace, in which they surrendered parts of Upper Austria and Salzburg, as well as parts of Galicia and the Duchy of Warsaw, to Bavaria (Napoleon's ally). To France, Austria had to give parts of Carinthia, Carniola, and all of Dalmatia. With this, Austria lost its access to the sea and became a French satellite state, which limited its army to only 150,000 members. But perhaps the worst humiliation for Francis was the fact he had to marry his daughter, Marie Louise, to Napoleon to seal the peace treaty.

The next forty years of Habsburg history were marked by the leadership of its foreign minister, Klemens von Metternich. He was a skilled diplomat, a reactionist, and an extraordinary political puppet master. Metternich was strictly against revolution and equality because he believed they were the reason for the collapse of the existing social structure and monarchy. He didn't believe in despotism either because he strongly believed a monarch should act by the laws. Metternich never really replaced Francis II as the ruler of Austria, but he was very stubborn and usually got what he wanted. However, Metternich was often unable to change his stance or adapt to new situations, and those faults would ultimately decide Austria's fate. In 1809, Metternich pursued peace so the Habsburg monarchy could recuperate and later renew the conflict with France.

Metternich persuaded Francis to follow in his ways of dealing with France, and the two built a remarkably good working relationship, but Francis proved to be smart and did not allow his foreign minister to take full control. Both Metternich and Francis deeply believed in conservatism and the central role of the monarch. Thus, they limited free speech, kept control of the secret police, and created new central ministers, who were tied to different realms of the empire, such as Hungary and Bohemia. On the international level, Metternich worked hard to tie Austria to foreign powers to create alliances against Napoleon. But when Metternich announced Austria was ready to return to combat in 1809, Francis was against another war. The two disagreed, and Metternich managed to change Francis's opinion by turning him against his anti-war wife, Maria Ludovika of Modena. Metternich devised a whole plan on how to rearrange the postwar world order and make Habsburg Austria the central European power that would hold the balance of the continent in its hands.

However, in the Battle of Wagram, which took place in July 1809, Austria was defeated and forced to sign a peace with Napoleon. Once again, it became the satellite state of France. But this renewed hostility was very costly for France. Napoleon didn't want to force Austria into conflict with Russia during his attack in 1812. However, Austria sent around 30,000 soldiers to help with Napoleon's disastrous campaign. In 1813, the new Coalition was formed, which included Russia, Prussia, Britain, Spain, Portugal, and Sweden against France. Austria was bound to Napoleon until Metternich found the right time to abandon this forced alliance and join the confederation. Austria's foreign minister was so good at scheming that when Austria joined the war against France in 1813, it found itself in a leading role. In October 1813, in the Battle of the Nations, Napoleon was finally defeated. The Coalition forces marched to Paris and managed to take it in March of 1814. The very next month, Napoleon abdicated. Metternich's plan came true, and Austria became not only the leader of the Coalition but also the host for the famous congress in which all of Europe would be rearranged.

In the Congress of Vienna (1814–1815), Metternich managed to get most of the things he wanted. The only problem was that not all of it was good for Austria in the long term. France's goal was to restore Europe to what it had been before the French Revolution. Pre-revolutionary leaders had to be put back in their respective places, and they had to promise they would keep to the boundaries of their realms. The idea was to finely calibrate the balance of power in Europe. The new German Confederation was created, with Austria at its head; thus, the Prussian ambitions in Germany were confined. A new Polish state was also created, but it was a Russian satellite. The Habsburgs gave up on Belgium, but they won back Venice and its former territory on the Adriatic Sea. Neither Francis nor Metternich wanted to press for more territorial gains because the monarchy needed to be seen as neutral—not too powerful but not too weak either.

Metternich might have gained most of what he desired, but it proved to be less of an achievement in hindsight. The new position Austria gained in Italy made it less involved in Germany. The rise of Italian nationalism created a series of problems for the Habsburgs, and this was only the tip of the iceberg. Francis and his foreign minister returned Europe to its pre-1790s condition, but they neglected to take into consideration the flow of revolutionary ideas and the rise of nationalism and liberalism the revolution had started. The main mistake the Habsburgs made was to suppress the modern political and social changes instead of harnessing them to serve their personal goals. Thus, the government system created by Metternich after 1815 couldn't last for long. But in the years it existed, its prime goals were to suppress nationalism and revolutionary feelings in German-speaking countries and even wider. Metternich and Francis both feared nationalism because it tended to claim popular sovereignty, making it a true enemy of the monarchy. Austria, Prussia, and Russia made an alliance in which they were supposed to help each other fight revolutions, and they did so in the early 1820s in Naples and Piedmont.

Domestically, Austria entered a period known as the Austrian Biedermeier, which was a very peaceful period. Because of this compliance in Austria, the monarchy stagnated. The governmental system was purely conservative, giving the monarch completely centralized power. During the last twenty years of his rule, Francis implemented some reforms, such as the formation of the Austrian National Bank in 1816 and the expansion of education, which now included young girls. But in other areas, such as the military, there was no interest for improvement. The army was chronically underfunded, and Austria constantly lacked soldiers, which were necessary for defense. This undermined Austria's claims of being a European superpower. Although the Habsburg dynasty continued to resist the changes that were happening all over Europe, the monarchy was stable, as its subjects respected Francis.

Because of its conservative stubbornness, Austria lagged behind other Western powers in the area of industrialization and the economy. Austria proper and Bohemia saw industrial improvements, but Hungary remained primarily agricultural. Individual regions, such as Lombardy and Bohemia, had vibrant developments, but other parts of the empire weren't so lucky. Steam engines were widely used throughout the empire by 1830, but only Bohemia managed to completely industrialize its textile production. Mining was on the rise everywhere, but again, Bohemia's industrial development allowed this region to account for 50 percent of the total coal production of the Austrian Empire. Because of it, the first railway in the monarchy was opened between Linz and České Budějovice in 1832. Bohemia needed to be connected with foreign markets, and canals that connected Danube and Vltava to the Elbe were dug. These transportation improvements served Hungary as well, as it gained access to these markets for its agricultural production. Francis took a personal interest in these industrial developments and sought to encourage road and rail expansions.

Industrial developments led to an increased population, and the monarchy suddenly had to deal with the new social changes. By 1848, the monarchy had 34 million inhabitants, with Vienna having over 360,000 and Prague over 115,000 people. The Austrian Empire remained a patchwork of different nationalities and was the most diverse country of Europe. Only in Vienna could one could meet Austrians, Croats, Serbs, Moldavians, Wallachians, Polish, Turks, and Greeks, to name but a few. But during the time of social reforms, this wasn't necessarily a good thing. Every minority demanded rights; however, most of them, at least for the time being, remained loyal to the monarchy. They created a new layer of society, a growing bourgeois, and they were unified by the German language as a common means of communication. Some of them were rich capitalists, while others were middle-class functionaries. Under this new layer of the middle class was a small but steadily growing working class, who lived and worked under harsh conditions. They had to spend up to fourteen hours a day in factories, and even children had to work. However, in 1839, some efforts to improve their conditions were made. Child labor was abolished, and the work hours were shortened to twelve per day. But this wasn't nearly enough, and worker revolts started occurring. In 1840, in Prague, a large workers' demonstration was held during which the people attacked and dismantled factory machinery.

Aside from the shifting social structure of the monarchy, international events also undermined the conservative government system set up by Metternich. Several international congresses took place in Aachen (1818), Troppau (1819), Ljubljana (1820), and Verona (1821), but they all failed to change Europe's political vision. At the Ljubljana congress, it was decided that Austria should intervene in Naples's popular revolt, but this action only made liberals throughout Europe hate the monarchy and Emperor Francis I. When the Congress of Verona decided that France should suppress the revolt in Spain, Great Britain retreated, making Russia's influence in European matters too strong. The balance of power was lost. The new revolutions in France, Belgium, and Poland started causing new problems for Metternich and Francis. They tried to seal off the Habsburg parts of Poland to prevent the revolutionary ideas from seeping into the empire.

Francis remained popular in the German Confederation, and many even regarded him as an emperor of a renewed Holy Roman Empire. However, the Prussian influence was steadily growing, and Metternich's politics did little to help the situation. Also, Francis remained uninterested in the affairs of the German Confederation, and he concentrated his efforts on his hereditary lands and the Habsburg powerbase of Austria. In 1830, new rumors started of a possible war with France, and the people realized that Austria had very little to offer because it completely neglected its army. Prussia, on the other hand, was able to muster a huge force and mount a proper defense. Suddenly, Prussia was regarded as the main defender of the German Confederation, and its influence skyrocketed. Austria started being excluded from the economic integrations of various German states, which was now led by Prussia. Metternich finally realized his previous politics was now failing, as Prussia had become a superpower.

The renewed revolutionary stirrings in Italy and Hungary were an interlude to the explosion of 1848, the year of the revolutions. Nationalism and liberalism were continuously on the rise, despite Austria's efforts to suppress them. The elite started gathering the population around themselves, calling for national autonomy. Francis and Metternich feared Hungary's autonomist sentiments, and they feared that liberals would push for the complete independence of their state. To prevent that from happening, they installed central control over the Hungarian government, increased censorship, and used the secret police to suppress the liberal activists. But Hungary had internal problems too. While the Hungarians demanded national freedom concerning the empire, the Croats and other nationalities within Hungary demanded their constitutional freedoms. All these tensions led to Francis becoming paranoid during his last years. Both he and Metternich knew that Francis's oldest son, Ferdinand, wasn't capable of ruling. However, the paranoia of a possible revolution made them push for the principle of primogeniture. In the late 1820s, they started including Ferdinand in the imperial councils, hoping to prepare him for the succession. In 1830, he was crowned as the king of Hungary, which meant he was the legal successor of his father on the imperial throne of Austria. When Francis was on his deathbed in 1835, he left a series of instructions for Ferdinand, in which he urged him to change nothing in the state and to keep to the conservative principles of the monarchical rule. Francis also told his son to trust Metternich and rely on his advice. On March 2nd, 1835, after forty-two years of ruling, Francis II died. The last Holy Roman emperor and the first emperor of Austria was loved by his people, who continuously visited his coffin for three days after his death. Although highly regarded by his contemporaries, history remembers him as a stubborn monarch who was unable to adjust to the changes of the period.

Ferdinand I of Austria (1793–1875)

Ferdinand I, former Emperor of Austria, in the 1870s
https://commons.wikimedia.org/wiki/File:Ferdinando_I_d%27Austria.jpg

As the eldest son of Francis II and his wife, Maria Theresa of Sicily and Naples, Ferdinand was the successor of the imperial throne of Austria. However, due to his many illnesses and possible intellectual disabilities, he was unfit to rule. Francis and his wife were cousins, and it is possible that due to their genetic closeness, Ferdinand was born with epilepsy and encephalitis. Modern historians suspect his mental capabilities were intact because he had a very precise and well-written journal, spoke five languages, played piano excellently, and studied botany. Still, Ferdinand suffered around twenty seizures per day, which was enough to make him unable to rule effectively. Therefore, his father wrote a will before his death, urging Ferdinand to take his uncle, Archduke Louis of Austria, Foreign Minister Metternich, and Minister of Domestic Affairs Count Francis Anton von Kolowrat as advisors. But the three men never really liked each other, and they couldn't work together, which was why the Austrian Empire was kept in stasis until the events of 1848.

One can see that Ferdinand had mental capabilities in some of his actions, such as when he decided not to follow Metternich's advice. The emperor realized his advisor favored conservatism, and he thought there was no room for it in modern times. Ferdinand made the liberal Count Kolowrat his main advisor, and he allowed his uncle and brother, Archduke Ludwig and Franz Karl, to help influence his decisions. But Metternich was still in power, and his ideas of progress were very different from those of Count Kolowrat. The two often complained about each other and were unable to make any progress.

However, Austria continued to develop as more railroads were built and new factories were raised. The Austrian Academy of Sciences was founded in 1847, and the state implemented very strict laws about child labor. But the emperor's authority started declining within the empire, as well as outside of it. Metternich continued to interfere with Austria's foreign policy as he strove to preserve the European balance of power and the monarchy. However, the minister of foreign affairs continued his hostile attitude toward the more liberal and nationalist countries, which made his system of diplomacy out of touch. Britain, under the leadership of Prime Minister Lord Palmerston, called for all European monarchies to adopt the constitutional rule. Even Prussia and Russia loosened their grip on power by introducing some liberal reforms, but in Austria, little changed. Because of this, Austria was mostly ignored in European politics. Domestically, Austria's population started resenting the monarchy because their economic conditions deteriorated quickly after the harvest failures in 1845. Aside from hunger, there was a lack of job openings across the empire, and the monarchy decided at that point to raise taxes. The people were outraged.

These economic failures almost led to the country proclaiming bankruptcy in 1847, as 30 percent of its budget was swallowed by debt services. The nobles across Bohemia, Moravia, and Lower Austria called for access to the state budget, as well as for the end of censorship. The conservative nobles wanted to stop the liberal reforms pushed by Kolowrat, while the liberal ones demanded a constitutional rule. The growing bourgeois called for the end of autocratic rule, but there was little to no wish to completely overthrow the monarchy. Most people remained loyal to the emperor and the dynasty, even though they desired political changes.

Another factor that unsettled the Austrian monarchy was the growing nationalism in the empire. The main problem was Hungary, which had several factions, mostly consisting of the nobility. While the moderates only wanted a looser relationship with Vienna, as well as Hungarian cultural development based on the language, the radicals demanded complete independence from Austria. But, as mentioned above, Hungary had minorities who each demanded similar things. Therefore, the Hungarian nobles had to be careful in their machinations, as they did not want to disturb the many ethnicities that lived within the state. The radicals were very vocal, and they demanded the right to rule over all the minorities within their kingdom, while moderates wanted slower changes and the institution of the Hungarian language, separate administration, and education. Unlike the radicals, they were willing to allow Austria to continue administering the minorities of the Hungarian kingdom. The Croats were Hungary's biggest problem because the Croatian nobles insisted Croatia was a historic state that deserved equal rights of administering itself, just as Hungary. The Czechs in Bohemia also engaged in nationalism, but this nationalism evolved from a cultural movement to a political one. The Czech nationalists were very anti-German, but in the early stages, they, too, refrained from criticizing the Habsburg rule. But perhaps the most separatist region of the empire was Italy. There, the radicals were the majority, and they called for immediate independence, though radical political activism was confined to secret societies. Nevertheless, the Italians were the loudest complainers of the autocratic rule and the elevated taxes.

In the years before 1848, these nationalist sentiments were just emerging. They were not yet regarded as the basis of political communities, but that would soon change. The Habsburgs' problem was that their empire was made out of scattered ethnic groups that were only weakly connected by a common European culture and Viennese institutions. There was only a fragile sense of unity between the Germans, Italians, Poles, Hungarians, Czechs, Croats, Serbs, Romanians, etc. The Habsburg dynasty was the strongest connection they shared because they were all ruled by the same emperor. However, beyond that, there was almost nothing to hold these peoples together. This was why the nationalist movements claimed the right to self-administration, but the Habsburgs also claimed their historic right to rule them all.

This clash between the monarchy and the people eventually led to the revolutions of 1848. But in the case of Austria, it is hardly viable to speak about revolutions, as the people rose against the dynasty in only Hungary and Italy. The other realms of the empire remained pro-Habsburg. They merely demanded political changes that would lead to the formation of a constitutional monarchy rather than an autocratic one. The other problem with the "revolutions" in the Austrian Empire was the lack of unity among the different nationalist groups. Each one of them had separate demands, and they worked separately on achieving their goals, even if they were very similar.

The main spark for the revolutions of 1848, which engulfed the whole of Europe, came from Paris. In Vienna, there was some unrest at the beginning of March, but it escalated quickly. On March 13th, a large mass of people moved toward the chancellery. To prevent the masses from storming the imperial offices, the soldiers fired at them, but the protests continued. The inner circle of the Habsburgs decided that the liberals had to be appeased, and for that purpose, Metternich had to go. He escaped the city the next day, but the masses continued, escalating the revolution. In several cities, people took control of the police and started implementing justice on their own. But the majority of the people who protested pushed for a constitution. In Hungary, around 20,000 people marched on Buda Castle, a symbol of the imperial rule over their kingdom. In Bohemia, the liberals demanded a separate administration, similar to what Hungary enjoyed. Poland mostly saw the rise of the liberal intellectuals in Lviv and Krakow, who demanded a constitution and political changes. But some of the demands were the same for all groups, such as the freedom for political prisoners, trials by jury, the end of censorship, the freedom of speech, the abolition of serfdom and of the tax exemptions for the nobility based on the Hungarian model, and the creation of legislative assemblies that would represent national groups' interests.

To answer some of these demands, the imperial representatives tried to draft a constitution for the Habsburg hereditary lands, but they failed to take into account suffrage and the creation of a parliament. The constitution draft was rejected by the people. Even fiercer riots erupted in Vienna during May, and the royal family was forced to flee to Innsbruck. The following day, the dynasty proposed a parliament, and in June, the first elections were held. This first assembly is known as the Kremsier Parliament, named so by the German name for the city in Moravia. The parliament was a multi-national and cross-class assembly, but it was not really effective.

By this point, the royal court was held in the nearby city of Olomouc, and Archduke John was proclaimed the official viceroy of the Austrian Empire. But the governance was in the hands of various members of the dynasty, including Archduchess Sophie, the wife of the emperor's brother Franz Karl. Sophie wanted her son to take the throne, and she convinced her husband to give up his rights. When her son, Franz Joseph, later took the throne, Sophie assisted him in state affairs.

The Hungarian government was separated from Austria with the introduction of the April Laws, which declared a constitutional monarchy. This significantly diminished the monarchical powers of the dynasty within Hungary, but the bigger danger was when Bohemia demanded similar laws. Suddenly, the dynasty was in danger of losing its imperial grasp over several realms. Soon, the Croats, Serbs, and Romanians demanded their autonomy, not only from the Austrian Empire but also from the Kingdom of Hungary. In Bohemia, the revolution was marked by the split between the Czechs and the Germans, but the majority of the people were pro-Habsburg, as the emperor was a symbol of unity, no matter what ethnicity or social class they were. The leader of the Czech moderates and the Czech national revival, Frantisek Palacky, made a famous comment that if Austria didn't exist, it should have been invented. He was talking about the Habsburgs' ability to hold all the nations together in unity. The Czechs aspired to federalize the empire and put Bohemia on an equal footing with the monarchies of Austria and Hungary, but the dynasty wouldn't allow it. By June, the uprising in Bohemia was crushed by the Habsburg army.

Italy was pushing to overthrow the Austrian Empire. The Italian aristocracy felt that Austria excluded it from politics, and they were the leaders of the uprisings in Milan and Venice. The Austrian army was pushed farther north by the rioters, and Charles Albert, the king of Piedmont-Sardinia, launched an attack. His goal was to unify the whole Italian Peninsula under his rule. But by July 1848, the Piedmontese Army was defeated at Custoza and again at Novara later that year. With that, the Italian uprising ended. The Habsburg dynasty also tried to bring an end to the Hungarian revolution and bring it under centralized imperial rule at the end of 1848, but this conflict saw many indecisive battles until the succession of Franz Joseph I.

Ferdinand did not influence the events of the 1848 revolutions. He was merely a spectator, and the government was led by his advisors, regents, and cousins. But during the early days of 1848, the emperor was willing to make great liberal concessions, to which the dynasty strongly objected. This may have been the real reason behind his removal from Vienna. In Innsbruck, Ferdinand was in no position to cause trouble for his more ambitious family members. In November of 1848, Habsburg decided on a new governmental cabinet that would lead the empire into the future. But to reestablish control across the realms, Austria needed a new emperor. In December, Ferdinand was persuaded to abdicate in favor of his nephew, Franz Joseph. The old emperor and his wife decided to retire in their beloved Bohemia, where they spent the next twenty years living a quiet but happy life. But Ferdinand's abdication didn't influence the ongoing revolution as his successor hoped it would. Franz Joseph spent his first years on the throne trying to reassert absolutism throughout the empire, but the revolutionists continued to challenge him.

Chapter 8: The Great War and
the End of the Dynasty

French Propaganda Poster from 1917
https://commons.wikimedia.org/wiki/File:Maurice_Neumont,_War_is_the_National_Ind
ustry_of_Prussia,_1917,_Cornell_CUL_PJM_1185_01.jpg

The revolution in Austria brought some changes, but it was mainly a setback for the conservative dynastic rule of Franz Joseph I. The new emperor was constantly challenged and had to fight for his imperial prerogative over his nearly sixty-eight-year-long rule. The late 19th-century monarch had to adapt as modern political thought consumed Europe. And Franz did adapt, though he never truly stopped dreaming of the absolute power his predecessors held. The last seven decades of Habsburg power was a period of modernization but also a period of resistance to modernization. The society, culture, economy, and industry were experiencing rapid changes, but the monarchs, who were set in their old ways, were unable to follow these changes. The middle and lower social classes started asserting themselves in politics, and the dynasty was slow to react to it. The rising nationalism also continued to fragment the empire, and there was nothing the sovereigns could do but watch as the power shifted from their hands to the hands of the people. The last effort of the Habsburg dynasty to assert their monarchic power over their realms resulted in the outbreak of the Great War, which included all of the major powers of the world. This war was also known as the First World War, and it was the last one the dynasty would see, as it was the war that brought down the Habsburgs.

Franz Joseph I (1830–1916)

Emperor Franz Joseph
https://commons.wikimedia.org/wiki/File:Emperor_Francis_Joseph.jpg

Franz Joseph I had a very strong sense of duty, propriety, and legitimacy of his dynasty. Throughout his long rule, he continuously tried to assert his imperial power. This conservatism is mirrored in his behavior, as the emperor refused to install a modern bathroom in his quarters or even sleep in a proper bed. Instead, he slept on an old iron military-issued bed his whole life. He refused to acknowledge modernization in his private life and in his politics. Franz was not an intellectual, but his sense of duty pushed him forward, and he worked every day on many imperial issues. It is believed he dealt with as many as 4,000 official papers in a year. Archduke Franz's education was influenced by his mother, Archduchess Sophie, who was politically active even before he became emperor. She was a traditionalist and was firmly against the federalization of the empire. Another person who supervised Franz's education was Metternich, who was known for his conservatism. In contrast to other Habsburgs, Franz never learned to appreciate art and music. Instead, he preferred the military life and simple domesticity.

The abdication of Ferdinand I and the succession of Franz Joseph were orchestrated by Archduchess Sophie and the new chief minister, Felix Schwarzenberg, with the goal of ending the revolutions that engulfed the Austrian Empire. Franz was only eighteen then, and his advisors thought that a fresh, young face on the imperial throne would convince the people of the dynasty's modern intentions. However, due to the emperor's youth, Sophie and Schwarzenberg remained the main influence on Austrian politics. Upon his succession, Franz had to deal with the suppression of the remaining revolutions. While those in Vienna and Prague had already been dealt with in October of 1848, Hungary and Italy remained problematic. By March of 1849, the Habsburgs were restored to power in Italy, but the Hungarian nobles refused to recognize Franz Joseph's authority because he was not crowned as the king of Hungary. In March, a new constitution was announced, and its intention was to replace the earlier Kremsier Constitution. But it was never fully implemented by the emperor because he didn't like the fact he would be forced to work together with the parliament. In April, Hungary officially declared it was independent and overthrew the Habsburg dynasty. This was a drastic move, and the European powers frowned upon such disposal of a monarch. Russia was the first to start threatening an intervention, as it was ruled by the very conservative Tsar Nicholas I.

In June 1849, Russian troops invaded Germany, and Franz felt humiliated that he needed outside help to reclaim one of his realms. The Hungarian army avoided confronting the Russians in an open battle, but the ultimate defeat eventually came because Hungary was simply weaker than Austria and Russia. It never attracted an international ally, and its industry wasn't large enough to supply the whole army by itself. In August, the Hungarian forces surrendered, and Austria retaliated for the rebellion. It implemented a military state, and it captured and executed all the ringleaders of the rebellion. Austria was so ruthless that it condemned the leaders of the rebellion who managed to escape to death, hanging them in absentia. Even the moderate leaders were executed without a chance for a trial. The Habsburgs finally managed to end the revolutions, and the Italian and Hungarian dreams of independence were crushed. But some goals of the revolutionaries were achieved. For example, serfdom was abolished; the peasants, students, and workers were politicized; and the elected representative assembly shared power with the monarch. In the long term, these changes brought absolute victory to the revolutionaries. The Habsburgs thought they had won, but ultimately, these changes only inspired constitutionalism and nationalism in their subjects.

For the next decade, Franz Joseph embarked on a mission to strengthen his absolutist monarchical power. On December 31st, 1851, Franz issued a royal patent known as the "Silvester Patent" (the name comes from the German word for New Year's Eve), and its role was to replace the constitution. The patent centralized the authority in Franz Joseph's hands by restricting trials by jury, instead joining the judicial system with the imperial administration. The emperor gained the right to appoint all of his ministers and most of the officials throughout his realm. Previously, this role was assigned to regional authorities. German again became the primary language of the administration, and it also became the official language of education, even in Hungary, where it replaced Magyar. Franz also censored the press, limited the freedom of speech, and organized trials out of the populace's sight. All of these measures were designed to restore the old order in the empire and to set the stage for strengthening the monarchy even further, both domestically and internationally. Franz Joseph ruled as a modern dictator, and his absolutist regime lasted until 1860. It should be noted that this regime did not embrace how Austria was prior to 1848. Franz didn't dare reestablish the old model of serfdom. Modernization couldn't be stopped, and industry continued to develop. Franz invested in repairing the empire's economy and continued investing in education and healthcare. His model of the rule was similar to Maria Theresa's—a rule for the people but not by the people. However, Franz Joseph was an inexperienced politician, and he made several crucial mistakes that led to the dissolution of his authority.

In 1853, the weakened Ottoman empire started the Crimean War (1853-1856). When the Ottomans left the Balkan territory, Russia became interested in it. Franz was alarmed by Russian influence in the Balkans, which was close to his empire. Franz made a secret pact with Prussia to attack Russia, and he even approached Britain and France to persuade them to fight against Russia, which intended to seize the Ottoman territories. Britain and France had different goals in mind, though, and while they saw Austria as a good ally, for the time being, they never really intended for the alliance to last. France wanted Austria's territory in Italy, and Britain simply saw Franz as too authoritative and restrictive. Austria found itself in the middle, right between France, Britain, and Russia, and it became quite clear that Austria was no longer essential for the maintenance of the European power balance. When the Crimean War started, Austria officially supported the Franco-British alliance, but it was completely ignored. France and Britain allied with the Ottoman Empire in an effort to stop Russia from seizing Ottoman territory, and although they were successful, the ultimate end of the Ottoman Empire could not be stopped, with it dissolving in 1922.

In Italy, Austrian control was unpopular with the people, and ultimately, this unpopularity cost the Habsburgs their possessions in Lombardy. When the Habsburgs defeated the revolutionaries in 1849, their reputation only worsened. When Franz Joseph made a state visit to Venice in 1856, the nobility dared to openly decline the court's invitation. He was hated as a ruler, and he did little to nothing to change the people's minds about his dynasty. This hate for the Habsburgs was noted by neighboring rulers, and the prime minister of Sardinia-Piedmont, Camillo Benso, Count of Cavour, made a deal with Napoleon III of France to support the war against Austria. Benso had a dream of a unified Italy, and he proposed the negotiations to Franz before launching an attack. The Habsburgs were supported by Britain and Prussia, but this support dissipated once Franz refused to negotiate. He opted for war because he believed that backing down from Italy would mean a great loss of honor for his family. When the war broke out in 1859, Austria realized it had no allies. The Habsburg army struck quickly to knock Sardinia-Piedmont out of the war before the French could come to help them, but Franz Joseph's military commanders turned out to be so incompetent that, even though they had superior numbers, they were unable to defeat the Piedmontese Army at Magenta. Franz came to personally command his army at the Battle of Solferino in June 1859. Napoleon III was also there, and this battle was the last one in Europe where monarchs faced each other as the commanders of their armies. Austria was defeated, and the Treaty of Zürich followed. Under the treaty, the Habsburgs had to give up Lombardy, Modena, and Tuscany. Everyone in Austria was outraged at their monarch's incompetence. Nobles, politicians, and even bankers demanded that Franz Joseph abandon his dream of an absolutist reign and implement a constitutional rule.

In 1860, the Austrian Empire's government started moving in the direction of a constitution, even though it wasn't quite ready to implement it. An edict known as the October Diploma was issued to appease the aristocracy. In Hungary, the Austrian government returned the people's traditional rights, such as the existence of a national diet. It also created an empire-wide assembly that would deal with economic matters, such as tax collection, customs, and currency. This body was named the Reichsrat. The government tried to build a conservative federalized empire, but they failed to please their subjects. For Hungarians, the October Diploma didn't go far enough in granting them autonomy, and for the Czechs and Croats, it failed to give them equal status as Hungarians. The bourgeois was divided into two main factions: the liberals, who thought that the Reichsrat didn't have enough power, and the conservatives, who believed the Reichsrat took too much power from the monarch. To please the people, in 1861, Franz Joseph issued the February Patent. This patent increased the power of the Reichsrat to be above the regional diets. This satisfied the conservatives because the power of the diets was lowered, but the Hungarians and Czechs were outraged. The next several years were peaceful because the monarchy was on the path to a constitution, but the aristocracy, the national groups, and the bourgeois had to explore how the new government would work in practice.

In Germany, the Habsburg authority had been quickly deteriorating since the 1850s. A unification campaign began in the 1860s, and there were two main options on how it would go. The first one was *Kleindeutsch* ("small German solution") that would exclude Austria but would be dominated by Prussia. The second solution was *Großdeutsch* ("greater German solution"), and it was the opposite of *Kleindeutsch*. It would include Austria, and the Habsburgs would become the dominant power within this unified

Germany. Bavaria, Württemberg, and Saxony supported the second option because they feared Prussian dominion. However, the Habsburgs failed to push for their case in Germany, mainly because of the domestic affairs they were struggling with at the time. Franz Joseph's centralization policies were discredited in 1859, and this doomed their dominion in Germany. The Hungarians, Czechs, Croats, and other minorities prevented Austria from connecting with the rest of Germany. While Austrian influence, not only in Germany but the whole of Europe, was sinking, Prussia was on the rise. With Prussia's new minister president Otto von Bismarck, who was elected in 1862, Germany started sympathizing with Prussia and slowly forgot about the Habsburg dynasty. Some of Franz Joseph's advisors told him to attack Prussia and prevent it from becoming a European superpower. He listened, but it was an unwise move, as, at the time, Austria was dealing with many domestic problems, such as failed harvests and uprisings in Hungary and Galicia. But Franz believed that the people would rally around him, as the possibility of winning the war against Prussia and Italy would bring large indemnity payments that would be used to elevate Austria above the threatening economic crash.

The Austro-Prussian War started in 1866, and Austria once again found itself without any allies. French neutrality was bought first by Prussia and then again by Franz, who promised he would cede Venetia even if he defeated his enemies. Britain wanted no part in this power play, and Russia had been estranged from Europe since the Crimean War. At the time, Italy was a young kingdom, and even though it was backed by Prussia, its main role was to keep Austria occupied on the second front. However, the Habsburg army had no difficulties defeating the young kingdom's army at Veneto and on the Adriatic Sea. But in Germany, Prussia overpowered Austria. The main battle took place in Bohemia, near the town of Sadová. This battle is known as the Battle of

Königgrätz, which the Prussians won, crushing Austria.

The Austrian army faced many problems, one of which was that it had failed to modernize. During the reign of Franz Joseph, the military never received necessary funding, and the soldiers had to rely on old bayonets while the Prussians wielded modern artillery. There were also many nationalities in the Austrian army, which led to many languages and uncoordinated commands. Some Hungarian and Czech soldiers even deserted during the battle.

Bismarck was satisfied with the quick war, and during the negotiations, he didn't pursue harsh punishment for Austria. His main goal was to drive it out of the German Confederation, which he was successful in accomplishing. The Habsburgs had ruled for four centuries as the most influential and richest German family, and now, it was all over. It was a major blow for the dynasty's prestige, but ultimately, it was Franz Joseph's insistence that their honor must be defended that brought this fate down on the family. Franz dreamed of revenge, but his monarchy was in no financial state to launch another attack on Prussia.

Abandoned by all the European powers, Austria could no longer claim its German heritage. The Habsburg Empire had to admit its hybrid nature, as it consisted of so many nationalities. Austria was expelled from Italy and abandoned by Germany. The only place where it could still insert its influence was the Balkans. Unfortunately, the Balkans would end not only the monarchy but also the dynasty's power. But first, Franz Joseph had to deal with the domestic consequences of his defeat against Prussia. Back home, he lost reputation, and the defeat empowered the Hungarians and the liberals all over the empire, giving them the leverage to demand autonomy and a constitution. In 1867, Franz Joseph reached the so-called *Ausgleich* ("Compromise"), by which the empire transformed to reflect its dualistic nature. The Austrian Empire became known as the Austro-Hungarian Empire, and it would exist until 1918. Hungary was given all the powers of an autonomous kingdom, but it was still united with Austria through the same ruler. The Hungarians, who were afraid Russia would strive to take over Hungary if it was completely autonomous, were satisfied with the union with Austria. Franz Joseph retained power over the foreign and military policies for both Austria and Hungary, but aside from that, the two governments had very little in common. They also had a joint financial ministry, but the details, such as Austria's or Hungary's share of the budget, remained open for negotiations every decade. Nearly everything else was separate, from the legislative and judicial systems to education, healthcare, and industry. There was still the problem of the Czechs and Croats, though, who were still dominated by the Austrians and Hungarians, respectively. Even though Franz Joseph was aware of this, he chose to ignore it.

The creation of Austria-Hungary was an admission of the Austrian nobility that the Hungarians were their equals. The duality of the state had its benefits, such as the ease of administration and government, the promulgation of religious freedoms, and the freedom of speech and the press. The empire was slowly but steadily becoming a truly democratic society. However, there were often more troubles than benefits. The unified economy meant that the two sides had to work together on overcoming the problems of modern trade and industry. The Austrians and Hungarians had a hard time with this, as they were often at each other's throats. As a result, the economic progress of the empire was slow. It was also a landlocked empire, and access to some of the major trade routes depended on the canals and rivers that crossed both Austria and Hungary. The regulation of the traffic was one more problem the Austrians and Hungarians sought to deal with in different ways, and it created yet another rift between the two parts of the empire. However, the biggest rift remained in their societies. The many nations living under the rule of the Austro-

Hungarians sought their own freedoms, but neither half of the empire worked on giving them. There were some attempts around 1871 to elevate the Czechs on an equal level with the Austrians and Hungarians, but the project was soon abandoned. Croats gained some autonomous freedoms with their *Nagodba* ("Agreement") they reached with Hungary in 1868, but they were not nearly enough to satisfy the nation. Nevertheless, society flourished. Vienna was transformed into an educational and cultural center for all the peoples who lived within the empire, and many prominent Czechs, Hungarians, Poles, Serbs, and Romanians worked and lived in Austria's capital. The growth of education among the people led to an increased number of liberals, and by the 1880s, Franz Joseph had to admit he had become a constitutional monarch. He resented the idea, but he was true to his ideals, and he ruled according to the law.

The Austro-Hungarian Empire entered a period of peace, and Franz Joseph, who had now ruled for over forty years, started slowly retreating from politics. He was still the head of the state, and his decisions were final, but he left more and more work to his ministers. However, his personal life wasn't so peaceful, as Franz had to deal with family tragedies. Franz Joseph was married to Elisabeth Wittelsbach; to her family, she was simply known as Sisi. She was a self-absorbed, energetic, emotionally unstable, and very intelligent woman who refused the unconditional love her husband offered her. Franz was very dissatisfied with the marriage, but his love for Sisi is evident from their intimate correspondence. He was always gentle toward her, and his stoic demeanor was always broken in front of her. He was devastated when his empress was stabbed to death in Italy by an anarchist activist in 1898. But Sisi's violent death wasn't the first such loss for Franz Joseph. His younger brother, Maximilian, became emperor of Mexico in 1864. He never managed to defeat the republican strife of the nation, and in 1867, he was captured and executed by his political enemies.

But the worst of the family tragedies Franz had to endure came in 1889 when his only son and heir committed suicide. The final blow, although not as personal as his son's death, was enough to bring Franz Joseph's empire down. This was, of course, the assassination of his nephew and heir presumptive Franz Ferdinand on June 28th, 1914.

The Austro-Hungarian Empire strived to be a colonial power, which was its motivation for acquiring the Balkans. They also thought acquiring this territory would be compensation for the loss of the Italian possessions. However, the Balkans were populated by many Orthodox Slavs, and Russia strived to assert its own interest in the region. At the Berlin Conference of 1878, it was decided that Austria-Hungary would occupy the former Ottoman territories of Bosnia and Herzegovina. However, the region was so poor that there were practically no benefits in acquiring this territory. In addition, Austria-Hungary had even worse relations with Russia and eventually Serbia. Franz Joseph's decision to get Bosnia-Herzegovina only shows how his imperial intentions clouded his judgment.

In domestic affairs, the acquisition of the Balkan territory made the Austrians and Hungarians suspicious since it helped add to the Slavic nation already present within the empire. Another problem was that the Hungarians didn't want the new territory to fall fully under Austrian jurisdiction, as that would once more diminish their importance in the dualist empire. A compromise was reached, in which Bosnia-Herzegovina was administered through joint ministry. During the early 1900s, Austria worked with Russia to define the borders of their spheres of influence. Serbia was satisfied with being an Austro-Hungarian satellite state, at least until 1903. But the Serbian Karadjordjevic dynasty changed all that, as it pursued a more nationalistic and Russophile course in politics. Franz Joseph was afraid of the unification of the South Slavs, as that would pose an open threat to Austria-Hungary. This was why Austria annexed Bosnia outright in 1908, but it failed to prepare the diplomatic acceptance by other European powers. Franz Ferdinand, on the other hand, had slightly different plans than his uncle. He wanted to unify the South Slavs within the Austro-Hungarian Empire and create a national identity that would be able to counter Hungarian prevalence in the dual empire.

The Serbians realized the annexation of Bosnia was an Austro-Hungarian attempt to unify the South Slavs without including Serbia. Russia supported Serbia's view on annexation, and it was soon followed by Britain and the Ottoman Empire. Austria-Hungary's reaction was unexpected. Instead of answering with conciliation, it sent an ultimatum to Serbia to back down. It became clear that Austria wanted a war, which it hoped to win, as it would return Austria to its former position of a European superpower. Even before these events, the power was shifting in Europe. Russia started demanding former Ottoman territories, while at the same time, Germany started ascending to power. Britain and France made an alliance to counter Russian and German aspirations, but Austria backed Germany. The situation in the Balkans was just an excuse for a war that would reshape the European balance of power. When Austria-Hungary worked against Serbian interests during the Balkan Wars (1912–1913), many Slavs who lived within the empire wanted to break out and achieve independence. In Serbia, radicalism started rising.

Before 1914, Austria-Hungary was in a difficult position, both domestically and internationally. Many nations within the empire loudly demanded the restoration of the states that they had before the Ottomans came to the Balkans. Historic kingdoms, such as Croatia, Transylvania, Wallachia, and Serbia, strived to separate themselves from the empire, but the government wouldn't allow it. To strengthen its grip on domestic politics, the monarchy pressed down on human rights, such as the freedom of the press and speech. The Bohemian and Croat diets were shut down, as was the Reichsrat. Franz Joseph once again attempted to rule as an autocrat. However, modern society would not have any of it. Even the foreign monarchs complained about Austria reverting to old habits, especially when compared with modern states, such as Great Britain or Germany.

The last spark that ignited the war was the assassination of the Austrian heir presumptive, Franz Ferdinand. He was on a formal visit to Sarajevo on June 28th, 1914, when a young Bosnian-Serb extremist named Gavrilo Princip shot him. Austria wanted to crush Serbia immediately and deal with the Balkan problem once and for all, but they had no legal cause to start a war since the Serbian government had nothing to do with the assassination. The Habsburgs found themselves in a very difficult position. If they didn't respond to the murder aggressively, they would surely lose their reputation as a European power. They needed this war in order to put Austria back on the political scene of Europe, even though the war meant conflict with Russia and probably other European countries. Germany, for its own reasons, also wanted the war, and its emperor, Wilhelm II, assured Franz Joseph that their two empires would be unstoppable. Austria-Hungary drew up another ultimatum for Serbia, this time designed in such a way that Serbia had to reject it. However, Serbia showed it was willing to keep the peace, accepting all the terms except for one. This term demanded Austrian authorities had the right to investigate the murder of Franz Ferdinand within the borders of Serbia. This meant that Serbia had to give up its sovereignty, a term no country would accept. Even though it was clear the Austro-Hungarian government was looking for conflict, the Serbian government proposed negotiations. This time around, Austria was the party that declined, and it declared war on July 28th, 1914, starting World War I. Austria had no finances to sustain a long war, so the state leadership hoped for a quick victory before Russia got involved. However, Franz Joseph was right when he predicted that the war would be long, bloody, and end in defeat and revolution.

The initial plan was for Austria-Hungary to quickly defeat Serbia and halt the progress of the Russian army while Germany dealt with France. But the empire's army was in such a poor state that the Serbians managed to defeat it. Some of this was the direct fault of Franz Joseph, as his government never raised funds for the army. He also personally opposed its modernization. Franz was worried modern guns and armored vehicles would scare the horses, rendering the soldiers useless. By the end of 1914, Austria had lost half of its army, and Germany wasn't faring much better against France. It became apparent the chance for a quick end to the conflict was missed, as Austria found itself fighting the war on two fronts: against the Serbs in the Balkans and against the Russians in Poland. In 1915, Italy joined the war against Austria-Hungary, starting another front. The empire was no longer fighting for its place among the European powers; instead, it was fighting for its very survival, as a defeat would mean its territorial dissolution.

In 1915, the Austro-Hungarian Army completely depended on Germany. It barely had any troops left, and it had no supplies or money. Germany delivered everything and even turned the course of the war, as Russia was defeated on the eastern front and Serbia was overrun. But Britain and France put the Central Powers (an alliance of Germany, Austria, Bulgaria, and the Ottoman Empire) under an economic blockade. Food shortages began, and although the war had public support within the Austro-Hungarian Empire at the beginning, that support started dissipating. People were dissatisfied with the costly war, the lack of food, and extreme censorship. Aside from that, the empire still struggled to appease all the nationalities it contained, as little had been done to meet their political needs and demands. When Franz Joseph died of pneumonia on November 21ˢᵗ, 1916, the outcome of the war was not yet certain.

Charles I (1887-1922)

Emperor Charles I of Austria
https://commons.wikimedia.org/wiki/File:Emperor_karl_of_austria-hungary_1917.png

After the assassination of Franz Ferdinand, the Austro-Hungarian succession fell on Charles, the son of Otto Franz and the grandnephew of Franz Joseph. Charles never received the proper education for a governing position, as nobody could have predicted the events that led to Charles becoming an emperor. However, Charles ended up being a modern ruler who sought peace, even though he was not a politician, and many considered him unfit to wear the imperial crown. Charles served during the war on both the Italian and Polish fronts. He had seen battle up close, and he wanted peace. He also wanted to use the peace to reform his empire so he could answer the demands of the Czechs, Slovaks, and South Slavs within the monarchy. But the truth is Charles was a weak ruler whose inexperience made him indecisive, which caused him to damage the monarchy.

Charles was crowned as the king of Hungary in the last days of 1916, but by accepting this crown, he accepted the provisions of the *Ausgleich*, the agreement that had established the dual monarchy of Austria and Hungary. This means he was in no position to effectively pursue his plans for reforms, which upset many nationalities in the empire. But no matter how inexperienced Charles was, he could do little to stop all the problems the monarchy was dealing with at the time. The population was angered by the ever-present censorship, hunger was looming due to the economic blockade, and industries were suffering due to coal, iron, wool, cotton, and people shortages. The government printed currency to cover its massive losses, but this only made inflation rapidly rise. By 1918, the cost of living in Austria rose more than tenfold in just four years. Bread rations were introduced for both the army and the civilians, and the overall consumption of meat dropped to half of what it was before the war. The empire's subjects were holding the regime responsible for the situation, and although Charles had just ascended the throne, he was the regime's representative. Major uprisings started in Austria in 1917. The following year, they spread throughout the empire. One of the most tragic events was the demonstration of Budapest railroad workers in November of 1918, as police shot at them. This incident caused workers all over the empire to go on strikes and protest the regime. The workers' uprising lasted for nine days before it was suppressed.

During Charles's first year on the throne, Russia left the war after the Bolshevik Revolution and the Peace of Brest-Litovsk. Although this was good news for Charles, as it signaled the end of the war, the United States of America joined in the fray, making it impossible for Charles to persuade Wilhelm II of Germany to negotiate peace. Wilhelm wanted ultimate victory, and nothing would stop him from his goal. Charles reached out to Britain and France, and in his pursuit of peace, he offered Alsace-Lorraine to France. However, this region was Germany's possession, and it wasn't his to give out. This diplomatic failure of Charles is known as the Sixtus affair, as his main intermediary was his own brother-in-law, Prince Sixtus of Bourbon-Parma. Soon, it became publicly known that Charles supported the French claim on Alsace-Lorraine, and the emperor suffered a heart attack due to the stress. But the damage was far greater than just his personal health, as his and the dynasty's reputations were ruined. Germany even abandoned the alliance for a brief moment. Charles had to surrender most of his foreign policies and the whole Austro-Hungarian economy to Germany to reform the alliance. But what was worse was that Charles lost all his diplomatic credibility, and the European powers started regarding Austria as Germany's satellite state. Britain and France even started proposing the dissolution of the monarchy.

During the summer of 1918, it became clear that the Central Powers were losing the war. The American troops were pushing Germany eastward, while Romania joined the Allied Forces. The British Army landed in Italy and pressed forward from the south. In the Balkans, the Allied forces marched toward Hungary. Non-German soldiers of the monarchy started deserting in great numbers, and with the riots back home, the days of the Austro-Hungarian Empire were numbered. Charles tried to appease the national minorities by reopening the Reichsrat, in which everyone had their own representative. However, this assembly became a place where the people angrily called for more riots and the empire's dissolution. The Slavs, who until then only wanted autonomy, started calling for independence. Both the Austrian and Hungarian leadership refused to even think about giving autonomy to the national groups. In the summer of 1918, the empire became known as the "prison of nations." American President Woodrow Wilson envisioned the future of the monarchy as a federation. However, the nationalistic cries for liberty and democracy within the empire convinced him that the independence of the Czechs and South Slavs was imminent.

The final days of World War I came in October of 1918, and with it came the final days of the Austro-Hungarian Empire. There was nothing Charles could do to stop it. He proposed a federation on October 16th, but by then, his efforts and his crown had become irrelevant. At this time, the different nationalist groups of the empire called the shots. The Romanians within Hungary demanded Transylvania be united with the Kingdom of Romania. The Germans of Austria declared their right to self-rule. The Czechs declared independence, and by October 28th, they had formed Czechoslovakia. The next day, Croatia cut all ties with Austria and declared it would join the newly founded Yugoslavia. The Ruthenians in Galicia announced their succession on October 3rd. Only eleven days later, Galicia joined the Republic of Poland. To top it all off, the Hungarians announced the end of the dualist monarchy on November 1st. Charles was still officially the head of the monarchy, but he had been completely abandoned, as only a few loyal servants remained to tend to his needs. On November 11th, 1918, the emperor announced he was giving up his powers temporarily. He never formally abdicated, and he even tried to retake the Hungarian crown in 1921, but he was unsuccessful. He spent his last days in exile in the autonomous Portuguese province of Madeira.

Conclusion

Modern historians often ask themselves if the Habsburg monarchy could have been preserved. It was, after all, one of the two oldest and influential dynasties of Europe (the second one being the French Capetian dynasty). The prestige it enjoyed in Europe was enormous, and its members proved to be capable rulers throughout the centuries. But in 1914, their empire was doomed to end. The members of the dynasty certainly played a big role in it, but they were not the only ones to blame. The state had many problems. Ever since the dissolution of the Holy Roman Empire, Austria had suffered financial troubles. The empire consisted of various nationalities, and although it was landlocked, it had strong colonial ambitions. In the end, the Habsburgs were unable to forge a path in the ever-changing modern world. The dynasty's fault might be its traditionalism, its stubbornness, and its unwillingness to understand the direction other European kingdoms were taking. Even the enlightened rulers, such as Maria Theresa and her successor Joseph II, were willing to implement modernization only if it suited the dynasty's needs. The rulers of the last decades of the 19th century and those of the 20th were much like their predecessors. Franz Joseph, with his conservatism and worries about the family's prestige, started a war that was impossible to win.

He might have even thought that preserving the family's honor was more important than preserving the monarchy. His successor, Charles, although full of good intentions, failed to ensure the peace. His inexperience as a diplomat and a statesman cost the Habsburgs their empire.

But if we look at the beginnings of the Habsburg dynasty and their extraordinary ability to rule many nations and even keep them loyal to the united monarchy, we can easily conclude that the Habsburgs were needed. It was due to their house that the modern idea of a united Europe was born. Although they had imperialistic ideals of ruling over everyone else, they provided many nations with political, economic, and cultural unity. This is mirrored in the fact that before 1914, when nationalism was on the rise in France, Spain, Britain, and Russia, the many nationalist groups within Austria-Hungarian never had the intention of breaking from the empire. They demanded their national rights, recognition, and representation in the constitutional parliament, but there were no mentions of independence. The Hungarians, Czechs, Slovaks, Croats, Romanians, Serbs, and Poles all wanted a national assembly that would lead them forward while keeping them united under the same monarch. But the conservative Habsburgs were not ready to give up their absolutist power, even when criticism by their international peers.

When the Habsburg monarchy ended, the dynasty lost its prestige and was humiliated into exile. However, the family continued to exist. Charles's son, Otto von Habsburg, renounced any claims of the rule over Austria and Hungary on May 31st, 1961, and was allowed to return to his fatherland. Before that, he had worked actively on restoring the dynasty to its rightful rule. However, during World War II, he resented Nazism and what his home country had become. He was a leader of the Austrian resistance against Hitler, and he gained many supporters. Otto strongly believed in European integration, and he even served as vice president and president of the International Paneuropean

Union from 1957 until 2004. Once he became a member of the European Union Parliament, he advocated for the inclusion of the Eastern European countries. Today, Otto's son, Karl von Habsburg, is the head of the house. He is an Austrian politician, and he follows in the footsteps of his father as a pro-European advocate. Karl has one son, Ferdinand Zvonimir. Ferdinand, who was born in 1997, is a racecar driver. Ferdinand is the heir apparent of the House of Habsburg, and it seems the future of the family will likely fall into his hands one day.

Here's another book by Captivating History that you might like

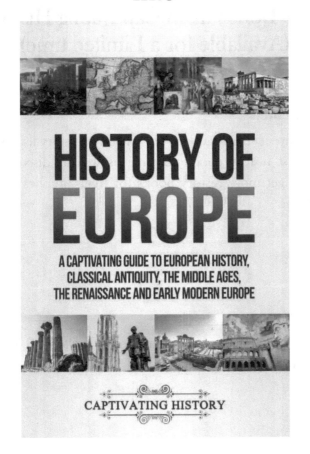

Free Bonus from Captivating History (Available for a Limited time)

Hi History Lovers!

Now you have a chance to join our exclusive history list so you can get your first history ebook for free as well as discounts and a potential to get more history books for free! Simply visit the link below to join.

Captivatinghistory.com/ebook

Also, make sure to follow us on Facebook, Twitter and Youtube by searching for Captivating History.

References

Churchill, W. (2005). *The Second World War*. London: Penguin.

Herwig, H. H. (2014). *The First World War: Germany and Austria-Hungary 1914-1918*. London, UK: Bloomsbury.

Judson, P. M. (2018). *The Habsburg Empire: A New history*. Cambridge, MA: The Belknap Press of Harvard University Press.

Kann, R. A., Király, B. K., & Fichtner, P. S. (1977). *The Habsburg Empire in World War I: Essays on the Intellectual, Military, Political, and Economic Aspects of the Habsburg War Effort*. Boulder: East European Quarterly.

Macartney, C. A. (2014). *The Habsburg Empire: 1790-1918*. London: Faber and Faber.

May, A. J. (1966). *The Passing of the Hapsburg Monarchy, 1914-1918*. Philadelphia: University of Pennsylvania Press.

Okey, R. (2002). *The Habsburg Monarchy: From Enlightenment to Eclipse*. New York, NY: Palgrave Macmillan.

Pelling, N. (1996). *The Habsburg Empire 1815 - 1918*. London: Hodder and Stoughton.

Rady, M. (2017). *The Habsburg Empire*. Oxford: Oxford University Press.

Taylor, A. J. (1996). *The Hapsburg Monarchy, 1809-1918: A history of the Austrian empire and Austria-Hungary.* Place of publication not identified: Penguin.

Tucker, S., & Roberts, P. M. (2005). *World War I: Encyclopedia.* Santa Barbara, CA: ABC-CLIO.

Williamson, S. R. (2007). *Austria-Hungary and the Origins of the First World War.* Houndmills: Macmillan.

Bérenger, Jean. (1994). *A History of the Habsburg Empire 1273-1918.* New York: Longman. 247.

Fichtner, P. S. (2003). *The Habsburg Monarchy, 1490-1848: Attributes of Empire.* New York: Palgrave Macmillan.

Fichtner, P. S. (2014). *The Habsburg Monarchy Dynasty, Culture and Politics.* London: Reaktion Books.

Ingrao, C. W. (2005). *The Habsburg Monarchy: 1618-1815.* Cambridge: Cambridge University Press.

Mamatey, V. S. (1995). *Rise of the Habsburg Empire, 1526-1815.* Malabar, FL: Krieger Pub.

Rady, M. C. (2017). *The Habsburg Empire.* (2017). Oxford University Press.

Schubert, F. N. (2011). *Hungarian Borderlands: From the Habsburg Empire to the Axis Alliance, the Warsaw Pact and European Union.* London: Continuum.

Sked, A. (2001). *The Decline and Fall of the Habsburg Empire 1815-1918.* Harlow: Longman.

Taylor, A. (1990). *The Habsburg Monarchy 1809-1918: A History of the Austrian Empire and Austria-Hungary.* London: Penguin Books.